NEW JOURNALISMS

In this current period of uncertainty and introspection in the media, *New Journalisms* not only focuses on new challenges facing journalism, but also seeks to capture a wide range of new practices that are being employed across a diversity of media.

This edited collection explores how these new practices can lead to a reimagining of journalism in terms of practice, theory, and pedagogy, bringing together high-profile academics, emerging researchers, and well-known journalism practitioners. The book's opening chapters assess the challenges of loss of trust and connectivity, shifting professional identity, and the demise of local journalism. A section on new practices evaluates algorithms, online participatory news websites, and verification. Finally, the collection explores whether new pedagogies offer potential routes to new journalisms.

Representing a timely intervention in the debate and providing sustainable impact through its forward-looking focus, *New Journalisms* is essential reading for students of journalism and media studies.

Dr Karen Fowler-Watt is a senior principal academic at Bournemouth University where she is research theme lead for journalism education in the Centre for Excellence in Media Practice. As a BBC journalist and editor for Radio 4 News and Current Affairs, she worked in Moscow, the Middle East, Northern Ireland, and the United States. Her research focuses on questions of empathy and voice with specific interest in reimagining journalism education, trauma awareness, and conflict reporting. She works with the Salzburg Academy on Media and Global Change and is engaged in a pedagogy project with Global Voices.

Stephen Jukes is Professor of Journalism in the Faculty of Media & Communication at Bournemouth University. He worked in Europe, the Middle East, and the Americas as a foreign correspondent and editor for Reuters before moving into the academic world in 2005. His research focuses on areas of objectivity and emotion in news with an emphasis on affect, trauma, and conflict journalism. He works with the Salzburg Academy on Media and Global Change, chairs the Dart Centre for Journalism and Trauma in Europe, and is a trustee of the Institute for War and Peace Reporting.

Routledge Research in Media Literacy and Education

Series Editors: Pete Bennett and Julian McDougall

Media literacy is now established by UNESCO as a human right, and the field of media literacy education is both growing and diverse. The series speaks to two recurring concerns in this field: What difference does media make to literacy and how should education respond to this? Research and practice have aimed to protect against negative media messages and deconstruct ideology through critical thinking, developing media literacy through creative production and a social participatory approach which focuses on developing active citizens to play a constructive role in media democracy.

This series is dedicated to a more extensive exploration of the known territories of media literacy and education, while also seeking out "other" cartographies. As such, it encompasses a diverse, international range of contexts that share a conceptual framework at the intersection of Cultural Studies/Critical Theories, (New) Social Literacies and Critical Pedagogy. The series is especially interested in how media literacy and education relate to feminism, critical race theory, social class, post-colonial, and intersectional approaches and how these perspectives, political objectives, and international contexts can "decenter" the field of media literacy education.

New Journalisms
Rethinking Practice, Theory and Pedagogy
Edited by Karen Fowler-Watt and Stephen Jukes

For more information about this series, please visit: www.routledge.com/
Routledge-Research-in-Media-Literacy-and-Education/book-series/RRMLE

NEW JOURNALISMS

Rethinking Practice, Theory
and Pedagogy

*Edited by Karen Fowler-Watt
and Stephen Jukes*

Routledge
Taylor & Francis Group

LONDON AND NEW YORK

First published 2020
by Routledge
2 Park Square, Milton Park, Abingdon, Oxon OX14 4RN

and by Routledge
52 Vanderbilt Avenue, New York, NY 10017

Routledge is an imprint of the Taylor & Francis Group, an informa business

British Library Cataloguing-in-Publication Data
A catalogue record for this book is available from the British Library

Library of Congress Cataloging-in-Publication Data
Names: Fowler-Watt, Karen, editor. | Jukes, Stephen, editor.
Title: New journalisms : rethinking practice, theory and pedagogy / edited by Karen Fowler-Watt and Stephen Jukes.
Description: London ; New York : Routledge, 2020. | Series: Routledge research in media literacy and education | Includes bibliographical references and index.
Identifiers: LCCN 2019013681 (print) | LCCN 2019021747 (ebook) | ISBN 9780429487477 (ebook) | ISBN 9781138596740 (hardback : alk. paper) | ISBN 9781138596757 (pbk. : alk. paper)
Subjects: LCSH: Journalism—Methodology. | Journalism--Social aspects. | Journalism—Philosophy. | Journalism—Technological innovations. | Journalism—Study and teaching (Higher)
Classification: LCC PN4731 (ebook) | LCC PN4731 .N457 2020 (print) | DDC 070.4—dc23
LC record available at https://lccn.loc.gov/2019013681

ISBN: 978-1-138-59674-0 (hbk)
ISBN: 978-1-138-59675-7 (pbk)
ISBN: 978-0-429-48747-7 (ebk)

Typeset in Bembo
by Apex CoVantage, LLC

CONTENTS

CONTRIBUTORS

Nicole Blanchett Neheli is a professor for the Journalism programme at Sheridan College in Toronto, Canada. Her current area of research and study is participatory journalism, research that is showcased on her blog *Redefining Journalism*. Her master's thesis of the same name was published in 2011, nominated for a Governor General's Gold Medal Award, and won the Diana Beeson Memorial Award for a thesis demonstrating excellence of scholarship. She is currently investigating the use of analytics in newsrooms through a series of ethnographic studies in North America and Europe. Her research has been presented at conferences in Canada, Denmark, the United Kingdom, and Italy. She is also a section editor and regular contributor for The Canadian Journalism Project: J-Source and has acted as a jury member for the Gemini and Atlantic Journalism Awards. Before joining the academic world, she worked at Citytv in Toronto as a news writer and show producer.

Megan Fromm spent 11 years teaching in higher education before returning recently to secondary education. She is currently a high school journalism teacher in Grand Junction, CO, where she advises the award-winning Orange & Black student newsmagazine. She is also the educational initiatives director for the Journalism Education Association and the curriculum lead for the Salzburg Academy on Media & Global Change. Fromm earned her PhD from the Philip Merrill College of Journalism at the University of Maryland, College Park. Her co-authored textbook, *Student Journalism and Media Literacy*, was published by Rosen Press in 2014. Fromm regularly writes for both scholarly and journalistic publications on the role of media literacy and scholastic journalism in secondary education.

Roman Gerodimos is associate professor in Global Current Affairs at the Faculty of Media and Communication, at Bournemouth University. His research projects focus on the role of digital literacy in fostering civic responsibility and global citizenship; the relationship between digital media, urban public space, and the civic culture; youth engagement with global current affairs; and populism, extremism, and terrorism in Greece. In 2015, he wrote, directed, and produced two short films, *At the Edge of the Present* and *A Certain Type of Freedom*, based on his research on public space, young people, digital media, and the civic culture, including visual ethnography in many cities. As well as having received a number of awards, the films have been screened at international events in Salzburg, Budapest, and Boston, as well as at the 9th Thin Line Film Fest – one of the biggest documentary festivals in America. He is the co-editor of *The Media, Political Participation and Empowerment* (Routledge, 2013) and *The Politics of Extreme Austerity: Greece in the Eurozone Crisis* (Palgrave Macmillan, 2015).

Pablo Martínez-Zárate is an artist and professor of documentary film and photography in the Communications Department at Iberoamericana University, Mexico, where he coordinates the photography and the digital convergence labs. His work bridges memory, territory, and identity through film, photography, multimedia, and writing. His films have been showcased in over ten countries and received prizes in festivals in India, the United States, and Brazil. His multimedia work includes pieces such as the web-documentary *Santos Diableros*, the interactive poem and installation *Poema Panorama*, the interactive doc *Momento MX*, as well as other media art pieces and exhibits. He has published a novel, poetry, and essays, and writes for magazines and websites in Mexico and abroad. In 2016, as professor at Ibero University, he founded and now leads the Laboratorio Iberoamericano de Documental (Iberoamerican Documentary Lab).

Jad Melki is associate professor of Journalism and Media Studies and chairperson of the Department of Communication Arts at the Lebanese American University (LAU) and the director of the Institute of Media Research and Training. He is also a visiting faculty at the Salzburg Academy and an affiliated researcher at the International Center on Media and the Public Agenda (ICMPA) at the University of Maryland, College Park. His research is at the intersection of digital media literacy, media and war, and gender studies, and focuses on Arab media and journalism education. Previously, Melki was founding director of Media Studies at the American University of Beirut (AUB) and has taught at the University of Maryland, Johns Hopkins University, Towson University, and the Jordan Media Institute. As a former broadcast and digital journalist, Melki was part of the team that won a Webby Award and a National Press Club Award for covering the 2006 Lebanon-Israel war. In 2015, he won the UNESCO-UNAoC International Media and Information Literacy Award for advancing media literacy education in the Arab region through founding the Media and Digital Literacy Academy of Beirut (MDLAB), which he chairs.

Paul Mihailidis is associate professor at Emerson College in Boston. His research explores the nexus of media literacy, young people, and engagement in civic life. He is the director of the Salzburg Academy on Media & Global Change and has written extensively on published widely on media literacy, civic, and digital citizenship. His most recent books, *Civic Media: Technology, Design, Practice* (with Eric Gordon, MIT Press, 2016) and *Media Literacy and the Emerging Citizen: Youth, Engagement and Participation in Digital Culture* (Peter Lang 2014), explore the ways in which citizens use media to meaningful participate in civic life in the digital age. Mihailidis is the co-director of the Engagement Lab at Emerson College and the graduate program director of the newly launched master's of arts degree in Civic Media: Art & Practice.

Susan D. Moeller is the director of the International Center for Media and the Public Agenda (ICMPA), an academic centre that forms a bridge between the College of Journalism and the School of Public Policy at the University of Maryland, College Park. She is professor of Media and International Affairs in the Philip Merrill College of Journalism at the University of Maryland and an affiliated faculty member at the School of Public Policy. Her book *Packaging Terrorism: Co-opting the News for Politics and Profit* was published in 2009. She is also author of *Compassion Fatigue: How the Media Sell Disease, Famine, War and Death* and *Shooting War: Photography and the American Experience of Combat*. In 2007, Moeller's centre launched a three-week-long summer academy together with the Salzburg Global Seminar, an independent, non-governmental organisation based in Austria. Over a dozen faculty and 60 students from five continents gather each year in Salzburg to consider how media literacy can nurture good governance, corporate accountability, and economic development – and to create online lessons that allow them to bring their insights back to students at their home institutions.

Stephen Reese has been on the University of Texas at Austin faculty since 1982, where he is now the Jesse H. Jones Professor of Journalism. His research focuses on questions relating to press performance, including the sociology of news, media framing of public issues, and the globalisation of journalism. Along with some 50 articles and book chapters, Reese is co-author with Pamela Shoemaker of *Mediating the Message in the 21st Century: A Media Sociology Perspective* (Routledge, 2014), a follow-up volume to its predecessor, named by *Journalism & Mass Communication Quarterly* as one of the "significant journalism and communication books" of the 20th century. His edited volume, *Framing Public Life: Perspectives on Media and our Understanding of the Social World* (Erlbaum, 2001), has been widely cited. He is on the faculty of the Salzburg Academy on Media & Global Change and has lectured at universities around the world, including as Kurt Baschwitz Visiting Professor at the University of Amsterdam.

Ivan Sigal is executive director of Global Voices, a largely volunteer community of more than 1,400 writers, analysts, online media experts, and translators aiming to verify and curate stories that might not be seen elsewhere. Before working with Global Voices, he spent ten years in media development in the former

Soviet Union and Asia, supporting and training journalists and working on media co-productions. He is also a photographer and has worked and travelled in 80 countries. In 2012, he published *White Road*, a chronicle of travel in Central Asia. From 2013–2017 he was a fellow and affiliate at Harvard University's Berkman Klein Center for Internet & Society, furthering research in digital storytelling and networked publics. His creative work explores the boundaries of documentary, art, and literary expression.

Jon Snow has presented Channel 4 News since 1989. He joined ITN in 1976 and became Washington correspondent in 1984. Since then, he has travelled the world to cover the news – from the fall of the Berlin Wall and the release of Nelson Mandela, to Barack Obama's inauguration and the earthquake in Haiti. His many awards include the Richard Dimbleby Bafta award for Best Factual Contribution to Television (2005) and Royal Television Society awards for Journalist of the Year (2006) and Presenter of the Year (2009). He delivered the James MacTaggart Memorial Lecture at the Edinburgh TV Festival in 2017.

INTRODUCTION

The idea for a book that explores "new journalisms" came to us in the summer of 2017, as we were both presenting at media conferences from Segovia to Salzburg to Cyprus. Regular fare in the academic world, but in 2017, wherever we went, the atmosphere for debate was particularly high octane. Everyone was trying to make sense of the new media landscape: changed dramatically by political events and the election in the US of a president who openly derided and rejected the media. Changed permanently by the divisive Brexit vote in the UK. Challenged consistently by global terror attacks, extremist threats, and migration. A landscape distorted by disengagement, distrust, and disaffection. At the start of that summer in 2017, on June 14, the horrific fire broke out in the Grenfell Tower block in London, in which 72 people died. It was to mark a seminal moment in media history. A few days later, we flew back into London over the grim silhouette of the burnt-out tower block that would rapidly come to signify failed journalism, deficient politics, and voiceless, marginalised people.

As journalists, we had, between us, covered most of the big global news events of the last three decades, but the mood music in 2017 felt different. Journalists were now perceived to be the problem, attacked on all sides in this disruptive age. Words like "re-imagining" and "re-thinking" entered into our discussions about the future shape of journalism; we contemplated "new" practices, rather than seeking "best" practice. Somehow, the notion of plural journalisms seemed to offer a better fit in this shifting landscape – had the time come to jettison the monolithic view of journalism, to take a wider view?

So, the plural – new journalisms – is important in that this edited collection focuses on not only new challenges facing journalism (in the singular) but also seeks to capture a range of new practices that are being employed across a diversity of media. We aim to explore how these new practices can lead to a reimagining of journalism in terms of practice, theory, and pedagogy through a series of key themes:

- New challenges: towards a definition of "new journalisms," those challenges presented by a crisis of professional identity, changing patterns of consumption, and engagement with news and issues arising from public disaffection with elites, journalism, and the media.
- New practices: ways of connecting publics through listening to marginalised voices, the increased potential of alternative journalisms, the impact of analytics, and considering how journalists handle and verify images.
- Reimagining: how journalism education can lead to new journalisms, how to engage people in an age of distrust, pedagogies to enhance an understanding of narratives of genocide and threats to human rights, and teaching new ways of telling human stories.

The book strives to adopt an innovative approach in its aim to challenge the normative discourse about practice, theory, and pedagogy through encouraging contributors from industry and the academy to reimagine journalism in all its forms. It brings together high-profile academics, emerging researchers, and well-known journalism practitioners. These include some leading figures in the field. Many of them come together each year at the Salzburg Academy on Media & Global Change.[1] This global alliance of activist scholars, media makers, and experimental educators shares values reflecting a school of thought – now captured in the mission statement of the Salzburg Media School[2] – that advocates transformative pedagogies and practices, which also support civic impact. Given the current period of uncertainty and introspection in the media, we hope that the book represents a timely intervention in the debate about journalism but also aims to have a sustainable impact due to its forward-looking nature.

The spirit of Salzburg

The Salzburg Academy on Media & Global Change "builds digital literacies and engagement around critical challenges for society." Each summer, it runs a three-week programme to connect faculty, practitioners, and students from over 30 countries to critique media systems and create civic media for social change. Since its inception in 2007, more than 1,000 students and 300 faculty and guest scholars from a wide range of social and cultural backgrounds have participated in the academy, with each summer's cohort comprising around 75 undergraduate and graduate participants from a range of media disciplines. Students and faculty who have taken part in the academy often say it has been a life-changing experience, an epiphanic moment in their personal and professional development and thinking. The project engages with concepts of media, news literacy, and transmedia storytelling,[3] to tackle an intractable problem each year and to seek routes through: recent topics have included extremism, populism, migration, and terrorism. These enable the participants to explore how media influence and are influenced by social and civic infrastructures. The academy places a high value on human connections and collaboration in its quest for innovative media initiatives. These range from **prototypes** for media innovation, **global case studies** to explore media's role in the world, **global media literacy models** to engage communities, and **networks** and "**digital vignettes**" that illustrate media's impact on the world.

In 2017, the Salzburg Media School (SMS) was born out of a desire to capture the ethos and energy of the faculty and media practitioners who had been supporting the academy for over a decade. Its aim: "To bring together leading thinkers, teachers and activists to reimagine how media pedagogy, practice and research can embrace our current moment and define a new approach to social change through civic media literacies." The Salzburg School has these missions:

- To build capacity for pedagogy that lies at the intersection of skills and theory and that approaches learning from a point of critical consciousness
- To approach research not through the production of knowledge cut off from the world but applied and situated in the communities it studies
- To think of media practice as intervention into traditional models of storytelling that desperately need to be reimagined for the present day
- To reimagine narratives that push back against harmful extremist rhetoric and post-fact cultures

With four specific objectives:

- Critical experimental pedagogy
- Intervention-based practice
- Cross-border/cross-cultural applied research
- Media literacy and civic capacity

The evolution of the Salzburg Media School and its mission statement coincided with our book concept and, serendipitously, provided a framework for us to shape our ideas as we started to commission contributions. It felt as though there was a lot of positive energy flowing our way – people had things that they wanted to say.

New directions

Countless words have been written, academically and from the perspective of professional journalists, about how the digital environment and social media have disrupted the normative values and practices of journalism, along with its traditional business model. Much of this work has involved deconstructing and analysing the current media landscape, frequently lamenting a bygone era and pointing out risks to the profession of journalism and its role in society. This edited collection aims to go beyond that now familiar narrative, setting out instead new directions in terms of both practice and theory.

The chapters therefore seek to capture the exciting new practices that are evolving and explore how they might be contributing to a re-conceptualisation of what we understand by the term journalism. Crucially, we asked the authors to address whether it is time to jettison a mono-cultural view of the profession and to consider the plurality of journalisms which is emerging.

The contributors for this volume have been carefully selected to represent a mix of top academic names and emerging young researchers, plus well-known names from the field of journalism who have developed a voice that challenges the status quo. We have deliberately chosen some of the leading thinkers when it comes to addressing potential new directions for journalism – many of them connected to the Salzburg Academy.

Each is asked to challenge normative practice and thinking, to avoid material that is limited to explaining the current state of their field, and to imagine where new trends might lead. We asked them to consider a number of key questions:

- How are journalists reimagining their roles and what it means to be a journalist?
- How are journalists shaping a new relationship with their audiences, and are they succeeding in engaging them?
- What does journalism need to do to reconnect with local communities?
- What new practices are emerging as a result of the social media landscape, changes in distribution of news, and the emergence of detailed algorithms on usage?
- How do forms of participatory media fit in a new conceptual framework of journalisms, and how do such innovations maintain their identity?
- Can new forms of storytelling give voice to the marginalised in society, and what roles can empathy, compassion, and emotion play in new forms of journalism?

The book is divided into three sections, to look at new challenges, new practices, and new pedagogies:

Part I: new challenges

In Chapter 1, "New journalisms, new challenges" as co-editors, we aim to set the scene for the rest of the book. Today's journalism is full of paradoxes. In the recent past we have seen extraordinary scoops uncovering fraud and corruption; brave reporting from the cruellest of conflicts; and the exposure of sexual abuse, human rights violations, and people trafficking. On the face of it, news journalism is excelling in its duty to shine a light in the darkest corners and uncover the truth. But, at the same time journalism itself is mired in scandal, legacy and digital first news organisations are fighting for survival and trust levels have plummeted as journalists are vilified as "enemies of the people." This chapter sets out five key challenges, which we suggest must be addressed if trust is to be re-established and journalism is to emerge fighting fit from this turbulent period.

Jon Snow, journalist, author, and long-time anchor of the respected Channel 4 evening news bulletin in the UK, set off a period of introspection in the media with his frank assessment that journalists had become too comfortable with the elite and that today's media had lost touch with local communities. In Chapter 2, "Connected or disconnected?" he presents his personal perspective on what journalism must do to re-engage with people and regain trust. Arguing that social media has not fulfilled its promises of reconnecting communities, he maintains that media can no longer remain ignorant of the lives of others, that the news industry must widen its intake of new recruits to reflect better the people it reports on and open its doors to the unconventional, the different, and the diverse.

A key challenge is one faced by journalists themselves, as they grapple with their own identity in an age in which they are viewed with distrust. In Chapter 3, "Journalists in search of identity," Stephen Jukes charts how the recent period of social media disruption has fragmented journalism's monolithic culture as the prevailing objectivity paradigm that captured many of journalism's core values has been subjected to increasingly robust and virulent challenges. The result: growing antagonism between many professional journalists fighting a rearguard action to protect their boundaries and the "citizen journalists," bloggers, and purveyors of social media who maintain that traditional journalism is failing the public. This chapter explores how journalists today are searching for their identity in the face of these crosswinds.

Part II: new practices

This section of the book looks at new practices, with a focus on technology, participatory news, and the verification of visual images.

New technologies and audience data are transforming local, legacy newsrooms. In Chapter 4, Nicole Blanchett Neheli asks: "Can analytics help save local newspapers?" Focusing on observational study of, and interviews conducted in, two newsrooms, one in Canada and one in the UK, this chapter furthers understanding of the effects of digital production on journalistic values, identifies how a growing reliance on metrics and analytics is impacting editorial decision-making in local news operations, and posits how effective use of audience data might help such newsrooms survive.

Much of the world now lives in networked societies. In Chapter 5, "Connecting publics through Global Voices," Ivan Sigal, executive director of the participatory news website and Dutch non-profit Global Voices, looks at new practices arising from the Internet and considers routes towards greater connectivity through the Global Voices project. It is an international community of writers, bloggers, and digital activists that aims to translate and report on what is being said in citizen media worldwide via an entirely virtual newsroom. Societal and technological change has created shifts in the landscape for participatory news and, in 2018, the organisation declared that it had "reached a crossroads." The outcomes of the GV community's major deliberative project are shared here.

The practices of photojournalists are evaluated in Chapter 6, "Images: reported, remembered, invented, contested," by Susan D. Moeller, who as a practitioner and an academic, shares her latest thinking on how photography reports the news. She examines why political partisans challenge the veracity of news images and documents how bad actors misrepresent news images to manipulate audiences for political and economic ends. The chapter considers how free expression and journalism's core principles are being undermined by the roles that photographs have come to play in today's media environment and offers a call to action: media and the public need to reinvest in fair and accurate reporting and insist on transparency when publishing images in a news ecosystem awash in social media.

Part III: new pedagogies

The third section of the book turns to focus on journalism education and asks whether reimagining journalism pedagogies offers a potential – if partial – route to new journalism practices.

Hence, Chapter 7's title, "New journalisms, new pedagogies": Karen Fowler-Watt suggests that if journalistic storytelling is to have a meaningful, positive impact on society, in a disruptive age it needs to become more intuitive, more aligned. In seeking routes towards a more inclusive, more thoughtful, investigative, and globally aware journalism, this chapter asks: In a disruptive age, how can journalists' faith in their own ability to have impact be restored? Is a focus on emotional literacy the route to "new journalisms"? Embracing the psychosocial notion that journalists who are emotionally literate and self-aware are more likely to produce journalism that is inclusive, immersive, and connected, transformative pedagogies are presented as a starting point to inspire new journalistic practices.

The transformative potential of education is taken into the civic realm in Chapter 8, "Civic intentionality and the transformative potential of journalism pedagogies." In this chapter a trio of colleagues working out of the Salzburg Academy on Media & Global Change, Paul Mihailidis, Roman Gerodimos, and Megan Fromm, engage with debates in news and media literacy to ask whether, rather than focusing on concerns and looking for solutions, it is time to consider journalism education's civic mission. They argue for journalism education to embrace "civic intentionality": through prioritising meaningful engagement that emerges from the intersection of the personal and the public, the critical and the creative, the concept and the application. Through describing the Salzburg Academy model, this chapter highlights the processes and practices that place civic intentionality and transformation at the centre of a journalism education process.

In a world subsumed in crises of all kinds, in Chapter 9, "Emergent narratives for times of crisis – ideas on documentary art and critical pedagogy," documentarian and artist Pablo Martínez-Zárate proposes an experimental take on journalism education based on what he terms "documentary art." Documentary art should be understood as a methodological stance rather than a genre, one that demands journalists to explore alternative techniques for representing difficult situations and the building of bridges between journalism and art. Drawing on his own filmmaking practice, Martínez-Zárate presents a methodological standpoint – strongly rooted in Latin American radical filmmaking and critical pedagogy – and offers an alternative, global-south-inspired approach to address challenges faced by journalism in our contemporary turbulent world.

Challenging pedagogies provide a focus for Chapter 10, "Genocide and the mediation of human rights: pedagogies for difficult stories." In this chapter, Stephen Reese and Jad Melki explore ways in which media literacy approaches to journalism pedagogy can lead to more responsible reporting of human rights abuses across national and cultural divides. Journalism means bearing witness. This increasingly requires a "global outlook" in dealing with issues transcending specific communities and greater empathy across national and tribal affiliations. These challenges are explored here as encountered in teaching the Holocaust to a multi-national group of students at a media literacy academy. It is hoped that the lessons learned can be applied to preparing future professionals and media literate global citizens for other difficult stories that require cultural and historical sensitivity.

We would like to thank our colleagues at the Salzburg Academy on Media & Global Change for their support and interest in this project and for the many wonderful conversations that we have had over the past decade, as we tussle with the challenges presented to us by the seismic change within our industry and the wider socio-political context. The emergence of the collective now framed as the Salzburg Media School helped us give this book a shape and purpose, and we hope that this group and its mission will enable the conversations to continue as fruitfully as ever!

We appreciate hugely the time, care, and work that each contributor has put into the individual chapters and for the positive energy that they have brought to this project – making it fun and intellectually stimulating for us! Our thanks to Megan Fromm, Roman Gerodimos, Jad Melki, Paul Mihailidis, Susan D. Moeller, Nicole Blanchet Neheli, Stephen Reese, Ivan Sigal, Jon Snow, Pablo Martínez-Zárate, and to Stephen Salyer, president and chief executive of the Salzburg Global Seminar. We would also like to thank Bournemouth University and its Centre for Excellence in Media Practice. At Routledge our thanks go to Margaret Farrelly and Jennifer Vennall.

Finally, we hope that you enjoy reading this book as much as we have enjoyed producing it and that it starts many interesting conversations!

Karen Fowler-Watt and Stephen Jukes

Notes

1 Read more about the Salzburg Academy on Media & Global Change here. Available at: www.salzburgglobal.org/multi-year-series/media-academy.
2 More on the Salzburg Media School can be found here. Available at: www.salzburgglobal.org/multi-year-series/media-academy.html?pageId=8252.
3 See, Henry Jenkins. (2010). Transmedia storytelling and entertainment: An annotated syllabus. *Continuum*, 24(6), pp. 943–958; Carlos Alberto Scolari. (2009). Transmedia

storytelling: Implicit consumers, narrative worlds, and branding in contemporary media production. *International Journal of Communication*, 3, p. 21; Renira Rampazzo Gambarato and Lorena Peret Teixeira Tárcia. (2017). Transmedia strategies in journalism: An analytical model for the news coverage of planned events. *Journalism Studies*, 18(11), pp. 1381–1399.

PART I

New challenges

1

NEW JOURNALISMS, NEW CHALLENGES

Stephen Jukes and Karen Fowler-Watt

This chapter sets out five key challenges for journalism if it is to survive and flourish in today's post-truth world.

> *The liberating democratization of information made possible by the Internet not only spurred breathtaking innovation and entrepreneurship; it also led to a cascade of misinformation and relativism, as evidenced by today's fake news epidemic.*
> *— Michiko Kakutani*

Introduction

How is it that today's journalism can expose corruption around the world, uncover human rights abuses and chalk up significant "scoops" and yet at the same time be mired in scandal and be vilified as "fake news," its journalists disparaged as "enemies of the people"?[1] It is the very paradox that the former *New York Times* book critic Michiko Kakutani captures in her critique of our social media culture and her observations of "today's fake news epidemic" in *The Death of Truth* (2018). For on the one hand, we are witnessing some extraordinary examples of good journalism, fulfilling the classic definition of shining a light in dark places and exposing the truth. On the other hand, business crises at so-called "legacy" news organisations have led to layoffs, local newspapers have been decimated and even journalists at "pure play" Internet organisations such as BuzzFeed, Vice, and the HuffPost have experienced the cold reality of redundancy. There is a whiff of crisis hanging over the profession and a sense that the old anchors have become dislodged, leaving journalism adrift in turbulent seas.

Over the past 15 years, journalists have harnessed the power of the Internet, drawing on user-generated content to integrate material into their reporting that we would otherwise never have seen. It started with shaky video from holidaymakers who captured the Asian tsunami in 2004 and has graduated to what have been harrowing scenes of casualties from the Syrian civil war. We saw the wave of terror attacks during 2015–17 (Charlie Hebdo, Westminster Bridge, London Bridge, Manchester Arena, Barcelona, Berlin, Nice . . .) unfold in near real time through images and video uploaded by those caught up in the incidents. We now take it for granted that news organisations can capture breaking stories in distant places without the presence of foreign correspondents. As publics, we are infinitely better informed. Social media platforms and particularly Twitter have become normalised as a newsroom tool, an essential mechanism for the distribution of news and as a means of soliciting ideas, sources, and facts (Hermida, 2010, p. 299). And a new wave of investigative journalism, drawing on powerful collaborative alliances (Sambrook, 2018), has been able to handle massive data leaks that brought us the Panama and Paradise papers, exposing tax fraud and dubious offshore investments by the rich and powerful.[2] These examples only scratch the surface of what has been an extraordinarily successful period for journalism, embracing the potential of the Internet to break important news stories. There have even been encouraging signs that people are prepared to pay for fact-based journalism, with organisations such as *The New York Times* seeing a surge in subscriptions in what has been dubbed a "Trump bump."[3]

But that is only one half of the story. In Britain, newspapers have just emerged from a debilitating phone hacking scandal that engulfed tabloid journalism, led to the closure of the Sunday newspaper *News of the World* in 2011 and to cries of outrage that were given voice through a public inquiry[4] into the behaviour of the press. In 2017, the Grenfell Tower tragedy and failings of local newspaper journalism led to a further period of introspection and accusations that the media had lost touch with the people. The Channel 4 News anchor Jon Snow sets out in Chapter 2 of this volume the damage wrought by the collapse of a local press. American and British media are widely seen to have failed to report the news critically during the key US election and EU referendum campaigns (Zelizer, 2018). US reporting appeared to be in thrall to Trump, the lure of ratings, and advertising revenues, whilst UK reporting adopted a slavish approach to "stopwatch" balance that gave equal weight to campaign messages that were sometimes open to challenge. Social media platforms have given voice to such outspoken views that it is hard to know what is the truth and what is fiction. When the nature of facts is called into question and journalists are singled out as purveyors of false news, the very foundations of journalism and society are being attacked. As Kakutani concludes (2018, p. 172):

> Without commonly agreed-upon facts – not Republican facts and Democratic facts; not the alternative facts of today's silo-world – there can be no rational debate over policies, no substantive means of evaluating candidates for political office, and no way to hold elected officials accountable to the people. Without truth, democracy is hobbled.

While journalists have clearly fought back over Trump's bullying behaviour in America, the rhetoric undermining journalists has arguably given free rein to countries such as Turkey, Hungary, China, and Burma to crack down further on freedom of expression. At the least, such rhetoric has seriously undermined the credibility of established media and spawned distrust. According to Reporters Without Borders 2018 was the worst year on record for violence against journalists.

This chapter first attempts to chart how such a paradoxical turn of events came about, how audiences have changed their behaviour and expectations, and how, in turn, journalism's traditional role as a gatekeeper has shifted in our social media environment. It then poses five key challenges which, it is suggested, must be addressed if trust is to be re-established and if journalism is to emerge fighting fit from this turbulent period. Those challenges start with the need for a better understanding of audiences, audience behaviour, and their expectations which, in turn, leads to the need to connect more effectively with publics and marginalised voices. Further challenges focus on tackling fake news and the role of social media platforms in spreading it, recognising the increasingly diverse and fluid nature of today's labour market for journalists and, finally, evolving an innovative pedagogy to inspire the new generation of journalists about to enter the profession.

How the media world became destabilised

The obvious question is how on earth did we get into this mess?

In one sense, we have been here before, in fact in various guises and at regular intervals throughout the last 150 years since the onset of mass printing and industrialised news journalism. This is not the first time, nor the last, that technological change will bring what is euphemistically referred to as "disruption" to journalism. Today's Internet players such as, for example, BuzzFeed pride themselves rightly on taking the online environment seriously as a cultural force and basing their journalism on that from the bottom up, from a story's structure to the headlines. But as Ryan Broderick, one of BuzzFeed's senior reporters who has worked out of London and New York, explained in an interview for this book, this is a tried and tested method that can be traced back at least to the birth of the big news agencies like Reuters and the Associated Press in the middle of the 19th century. The founder of Reuters, Paul Julius von Reuter, began his news business transmitting stock prices by using homing pigeons but swiftly switched to the modern technology of his day, the telegraph – faster than pigeons or ships that plied the Channel between continental Europe and Britain. Throughout the history of news, one new technological medium has chased and disrupted the next, whether it be radio, television, satellite channels. . . . And, as McLuhan presciently observed (1964): "A new medium is never an addition to an old one, nor does it leave the old one in peace. It never ceases to oppress the older media until it finds new shapes and positions for them."

But it is also hard to escape the conclusion that journalism today is facing unprecedented challenges that have destabilised a culture of normative practice and values that has held firm for more than a century. It is, according to the conclusions of the review into British journalism by Dame Frances Cairncross, challenging the very future of news provision (2019). Such a challenge requires a radical new approach, and that goes beyond addressing issues of technology and form. The concept of a perfect storm may be overworked, but there is clearly a confluence of factors that has led us into one of the most uncertain environments in the modern history of journalism. The technological revolution that is the Internet and that gave birth to social media has, of course, destroyed the traditional business model of news, led to the collapse of some "old" media players and forced change on the survivors; it has launched a wave of Internet-only organisations such as the HuffPost, Vice, and BuzzFeed (all of which have been encountering their own difficulties in search of a viable business model). But over and above these technology-driven factors, we are witnessing wider cultural and societal changes that go hand in hand with the personalisation and subjectivity that is the hallmark of social media – the rise of the therapy culture (Furedi, 2003); the "affective turn" of the 1990s; and an auto/biographical postmodern society where personal, "life stories" are now omnipresent (Plummer, 2001). In this environment, a surge of populism through swathes of the United States and Europe, the ability to sew disinformation effortlessly through social media, and a growing distrust of "experts" has led to dire predictions from some that the very notion of "truth" is threatened. Kakutani, for example, laments how the term "truth decay" has now entered the post-truth lexicon that already includes phrases such as "fake news" and "alternative facts" (2018).

Audience behaviour and expectations have changed

It is now more than ten years since Jay Rosen made his observations about the shifts in news consumption brought about by the Internet, and his coining of the term "the people formerly known as the audience" (2006). In the meantime, they have drawn their own conclusions and taken matters into their own hands. As Deuze observes (2012, p. 261), people nowadays know that everything they do in life could be recorded, archived, edited, redacted, and publicised on a continuous basis – it is a world that lives in the moment of recording itself.

As a result of primarily technological changes and the instant connectivity afforded by smart phones, media organisations have clearly lost their monopoly on the news, both in terms of gathering information and distributing it. The 2018 survey of news consumption, taking in 74,000 people across 34 markets, by the Reuters Institute for the Study of Journalism shows that 65% of those questioned preferred to access news through a "side door" (2018, p. 13) rather than going directly to a news organisation's own website or app. Over 53% use search engines, social media platforms such as Facebook, or news aggregators, interfaces that rely on ranking algorithms to select stories rather than interfaces where news selection is by humans (such as on a news home page) (ibid). This trend appears to have stabilised over the past two years, but at the same time news is now migrating to closed and encrypted messaging apps (such as WhatsApp), especially in countries with authoritarian regimes such as Turkey where citizens are seeking a safe place for free expression. Not surprisingly, these patterns of news consumption have had serious consequences for the business of news, not least obscuring the brand of the provider. How often have we heard people say: "I read it on Facebook" rather than referring to the actual, underlying source of the news. It is one of the major headaches suffered by news providers and will be addressed in detail later in this chapter. But as Rosen observed, the relationship between the journalist and audience has also changed media flows fundamentally, with the direction of travel no longer one way. In the meantime, scholars have sought to define and characterise the participatory and interactive nature of today's relationship, something that Hermida, for example, has called "ambient journalism" (2010). Hermida suggests that this constitutes an "awareness system" that provides ways to collect, communicate, share, and display news and information from both professionals and non- professionals. The audience is thus a receiver and a sender (ibid).

This new interactive landscape has led some to question the traditional journalistic role of gatekeeping by which, in the one-way model of communication, journalists filtered information, decided what the public needed to know, then organised and packaged it for distribution. Bruns has suggested that this model has evolved into something he calls "gate watching" in which there is collaboration between journalists and non-professionals providing information (2003, 2011). The result is what he has termed "produsage" or user-led creation and distribution of content. But while the relationship has undoubtedly changed beyond recognition, it is clear that legacy news organisations have been fighting a rearguard action to maintain their grip on production and have a say in what user-generated content is incorporated into their reporting. The BBC's social media "hub,"[5] set up after the July 7 bombings in London in 2005, is a case in point – it is still the journalist who decides what user-generated content is used or not, and it is still the journalist whose job it is to verify whether such content is genuine or not. Indeed, a 2019 analysis by the Reuters Institute concludes that media companies may have lost control of distribution to social media companies and their platforms but they are still setting the news agenda. It stated (2019, p. 9):

> Far from the death of gatekeepers, we have seen the move to two sets of gatekeepers, where news media organisations still create the news agenda, but platform companies increasingly control access to audiences.

Searching for answers – five challenges for the new journalisms

So where does this leave the practice of journalism? In the following section we set out five key challenges that we feel must be tackled if journalism is to rebuild trust and emerge stronger from the current period of disruption. To couch this in terms of a manifesto may be overstating the case, but it is no coincidence that when we asked the contributors to this volume for their ideas, much of what is set out below emerged as critical themes. In fact, they run as a red thread throughout this volume. In this respect, the chapter sets the tone for many of the contributions to come and helps us construct an emerging picture of what we have called "new journalisms."

Understanding audiences

The first key challenge for responsible journalism is to understand audience behaviours and expectations better so that news can be shaped to engage readers and viewers without reducing output solely to a feed of fluffy cat videos that can be recycled on Facebook or "click bait." Entertainment journalism and celebrity news clearly have their place in the canon of what is news, and there is no intention in this chapter of slighting tabloid newspapers which have in the United Kingdom, for example, played a significant role in shaping political life (Chadwick, Vaccari and O'Loughlin, 2018, p. 4259). But today's journalism needs to avoid the trap of using audience data to justify dumbing down the news agenda and pandering to the lowest common denominator in the hope of boosting online advertising revenues.

While a wealth of audience data is now available, and we know the big trends, it is by no means clear how to translate the detail into journalism practice, and several common assumptions may well be false. As illustrated in the previous section of this chapter, comprehensive metrics on news consumption are now available at a top level from large-scale surveys such as that by the Reuters Institute or in finest detail from the widespread use of real-time analytics in newsrooms.[6] But it cannot be taken for granted that page clicks or automated categories such as "most read" accurately reflect audience preferences (Schrøder, 2019). This is not least because the way in which non-transparent algorithms employed by social media platforms can push news to the top of an agenda and create an artificial self-fuelled momentum. Nor, as another author in this volume Ivan Sigal points out, does the algorithmic sorting and personalisation of news mean we can be sure that we are all seeing the same information.[7] In short, despite the proliferation of audience data, journalists producing the day-to-day news are often in the dark, not knowing if audiences have a common basis of understanding to discuss and debate public interests. And as Sigal says, when trying to write stories based on people's interests, the journalist often has to wade through a mass of distracting content to find the ideas that matter.

Some of the digital first news organisations have tried to address the challenge of understanding audiences by using the opportunity of starting from scratch to build their news file from the bottom up (rather than adjusting existing output to shifting audience trends). BuzzFeed's Broderick argues that everything the news organisation has done since it was founded in 2006 has been based on user testing, from developing its app with school children to asking open questions about how the consumers of BuzzFeed's news want a story written.[8]

But we can see from other organisations that there are also dangers in relying solely on audience feedback and following prevailing trends. Several scholars have noted how online audiences are increasingly gravitating towards entertainment or sensational news. That development goes to the heart of the question "What is news?" and whether classic definitions may be changing in our digital age. Concerns that tabloid and social media outlets are combining to "dumb down" public discourse have been voiced, with Chadwick, Vaccari, and O'Louglin arguing that tabloid news coverage is providing a fertile context for misinformation or fake news (2018, p. 4270). Phillips has observed how the *MailOnline*[9] has become such a successful website by observing exactly what people share on Facebook and ensuring that its coverage is tailored to be shared in this way (2012). Thus "shareability" is a new factor that appears to be taking on increasing importance in determining what news people choose (Harcup and O'Neill, 2017, p. 1482), raising the risk that "soft" news will become increasingly prevalent. In this environment, it is hardly surprising that the Cairncross Review into securing a sustainable future for British journalism concluded that the public appetite for local news, given the constrained finances of newspapers, rarely justifies the cost of sending a reporter to cover the story (2019, p. 6).

There are, however, more optimistic models that could point the way to how journalists navigate their way through this difficult period and avoid falling into the shareability trap. Schrøder, for example, has also argued that news consumption is being driven by personal relevance. That certainly includes the desire to share material with friends or family on social media. But critically he suggests this is not always limited to the amusing, trivial, or weird (2019, p. 5); it can instead be of local, national, or international import. News must be relevant to the individual, the individual's family, workplace, leisure activities, or their local community. But just how that relevance plays out and the choice of what news is consumed depends on the interests of the individual. Schrøder proposes a model based on four main profiles: those interested in political and civic news; in social/ humanitarian issues; in cultural news; and finally in in-depth political analysis (ibid). The failure to make news relevant can mean that people actively switch off news sources exactly because they feel irrelevant and, sometimes, depressing; as a result they turn to entertainment or social media (Toff and Nielsen, 2018). The consequence for journalists is clear – they must recognise the complexities of audience tastes and preferences, focus on relevance, and avoid the trap of difficult to read analytics (Schrøder, 2019, p. 6):

> There are no simple recipes for meeting the relevance thresholds of news audiences. To the extent that journalists prioritise news stories with civic value, they should trust their instincts rather than relying on the unreliable seismograph offered by "Most Read" lists.

The challenge of making news content more relevant to young audiences in order to encourage higher levels of participation and civic engagement forms a crucial part of the "war on attention." Media literacy scholars Thinsz and Nordmark (2017) have observed, in their study of the Swedish context, that the problem is less a lack of content, than how to filter it. They contend that a focus on transparency in public service media might engage young people in journalism that through showing its workings earns trust and credibility.

But understanding audiences is only one step. To provide socially relevant news it is essential to re-establish connection to communities, to ensure the body of our journalists is as diverse as the people reported on, and to support local journalism. The next section tackles the first of these challenges, re-establishing connection with those in our own cultures who accuse journalism of being out of touch and aloof and listening with empathy to the voices of the marginalised and those caught up in conflict.

Building bridges

Journalism needs to be as close as possible to the voices of others. Proximity is a journalistic keyword, especially in the drive to engage audiences in the digital era (Ahva and Pantti, 2014). However, the exigencies of the 24/7 news cycle and stretched resources run counter to our ability to bear witness. The notion of "giving voice" is also contentious, with its connotations of a top-down, soothsaying elite. Documentary maker Mathew Charles works with indigenous communities in Colombia. In an interview for this book, he shared his belief that the concept of "giving voice" is "not only patronising but disingenuous" since:

> The vast majority of people and communities have a voice . . . the problem is we choose to listen to those who shout the loudest. By creating a space for the marginalised to be heard, we can begin to include stories, which provide a much more detailed picture of the truth.

Immersion in terms of being there (as opposed to the VR sense of the word) is crucial for authentic, credible storytelling. Vietnamese filmmaker and theorist Trinh Minh-ha urges us to stay close to the subjects of our stories, "speaking nearby, rather than speaking about," in other words, a speaking that does not objectify, does not point to an object as if it is distant from the speaking subject or absent from the speaking place (Minh-ha in Chen, 1992, p. 87). The journalist and author of *Voices from Chernobyl* Svetlana Alexievich (2006) goes further, taking herself out of the narrative so that the harrowing stories of the survivors of the nuclear disaster[10] speak for themselves. Their voices are heard clearly as they describe how each individual had been transformed from "a normal person" and dehumanised to become a "Chernobyl person."

Following the terror attacks in Paris and Nice in 2015, issues of voice were starkly evident, where journalists from mainstream French news outlets reported on the inhabitants of the suburbs or *banlieues* as if they were from a strange and foreign place, despite their proximity to the city. As Marsh (2016) identifies:

> Whole generations of marginalised French Muslims from north and west Africa grew up in the *banlieues*, but mainstream France never cared for their perspectives on anything . . . if you lived in the *banlieues*, you were voiceless and mostly invisible.

A magisterial air combined with a reliance on stereotypes led to mainstream media reporting that compounded division in an already fragile social context. *The New Yorker* journalist George Packer spent time in the *banlieues* with Mehdi Meklat, a writer at *Bondy Blog*, which was set up to give young journalists a chance to shape their own narratives. Meklat told him: "There are two parallel worlds" (Packer, 2015). Feeling voiceless and disconnected, Meklat and his contemporaries use vlogs and blogs[11] to get their own stories out, emphasising narratives of peace in order to debunk the fear narratives and stereotypical reporting of Parisian bi-nationals as a potential security threat. BBC foreign correspondent Fergal Keane believes that these issues of voice present crucial challenges for journalists whose "fundamental responsibility" is to avoid othering. He warns of the dangers of "seeing others through the prism of our own background, our own cultural pre-conceptions and often through stereotype" (Keane, 2018).

The ongoing Syrian crisis throws the importance of voice into sharp relief. The civil war that started in 2011 off the back of the Arab Spring uprisings across the Middle East has led to a major refugee crisis and human rights abuses, and nearly half a million people have lost their lives in the conflict.[12] The late Marie Colvin's final dispatch for *The Sunday Times* from the widows' basement in Baba Amr marked an important moment in showing the world the extent of the horrific genocide that Assad's regime was meting out on its own people. It is unlikely that the voices of those women would have been heard without Colvin's storytelling from inside the basement (Colvin, 2012). Likewise, the crisis in Eastern Ghouta, which at its peak in 2017 was described as "hell on earth," underlined the resourcefulness of desperate and frightened people in getting their stories out. One doctor quoted in *The Guardian* newspaper in a report out of Istanbul said, "We are standing before the massacre of the 21st Century."[13] There were no journalists in this enclave, close to the Syrian capital, Damascus, which, after six years of siege and attack, including chemical attacks by the regime, was subjected to deliberate daily bombardment early in 2017. Hundreds of people were killed and many more maimed in a matter of weeks. News organisations relied on bodycam footage from aid workers and rescuers, such as the White Helmets, to tell the story of Eastern Ghouta, sometimes foreign desks were able to connect with people on the ground via WhatsApp and Snapchat. This enabled us to hear the experiential first-person accounts (Coward, 2007) of normal people: bakers, lawyers, doctors working in hospitals. As the situation deteriorated and the aerial bombardment intensified, the only way to be safe was to go underground into basements. At this point, some of those trapped started to use mobile technology and social media to tell their own stories in their own words. Muhammad Najeem, a 15-year-old boy, used Twitter and video uploaded to YouTube to raise awareness of his horrific situation, accusing Assad of killing his childhood and venting his frustration with the silence of the international community: "It is difficult to describe with words what is happening now; it is genocide."[14]

The challenges presented to journalism by the issue of voice are manifold and complex. The journalist is relied on to provide an accurate and fair account, but there is also the question of the journalist's voice. The shibboleth of objectivity requires detachment, but audience engagement requires empathic, connected storytelling. These are not mutually exclusive, but at the same time, the journalist should never be the story, as Jon Snow reminds us.[15] If we are to avoid notions of "othering" and of "giving voice," perhaps we should focus more on listening, as discussed in Chapter 5 where Ivan Sigal describes how the mission of the participatory news website Global Voices involves listening to as wide a range of voices as possible. This brings us to consider the challenges of new journalisms that embrace diverse and inclusive approaches to storytelling.

A diverse workforce

The Grenfell Tower tragedy brought home how unrepresentative the British media are of those they are meant to serve. *The Guardian* newspaper columnist Owen Jones ascribes this partly to the decline of local newspapers, but also to the prevalence of unpaid internships and expensive postgraduate degrees in Journalism. Both routes into the profession are, he argues, prohibitively expensive for most young people (2019). A report by the British government's Social Mobility Commission found that journalists came second only to doctors in having the most privileged socio-economic backgrounds, including private education (2017, p. 17). These stark facts are played back into our popular culture through representations in television, film, drama, and literature, perpetuating the image of the white male middle class journalist championing free speech in the name of truth. British novelist and playwright Michael Frayn, who had started his career as a columnist on *The Guardian* and *Observer* newspapers, captured this elitism in a searing indictment of class structures in Fleet Street (the former home of the British press) in his 1967 novel *Towards the End of the Morning*:

> One by one and two by two the sober, responsible men emerged from the main door again to go out for lunch. The Foreign Editor, the Literary Editor, the Diplomatic Correspondent and the Rugby Football Correspondent made up a party to share a taxi to the Garrick.

That was, of course, rich satire, and things have indeed changed. But we can still read articles in Britain about how graduates from Oxford University's PPE[16] course continue to make up a significant proportion of today's leading media figures on television, radio, and in print (Beckett, 2017). A 2018 study by the National Council for the Training of Journalists (NCTJ) (Spilsbury, 2018) found that 90% of UK journalists are white (compared with 88% of the total workforce) while only 4% are classified as Asian/Asian British or Black/Black British (compared with 9% of the total workforce). It concluded that the lack of diversity was extreme in London where ethnic minorities live in greater numbers (and where the media is concentrated). In short, ethnic minorities remain significantly under-represented. The situation in the United States is no better. US newsrooms are more likely to be white and male than the general profile of labour in the country, although there are signs that the younger generation of American journalists is starting to show greater racial, ethnic, and gender diversity (Pew Research Center, 2018). According to the Pew analysis of American Community Survey data, more than three quarters (77%) of newsroom employees – reporters, editors, photographers, and videographers in the newspaper, broadcasting, and Internet publishing industries – are non-Hispanic whites. The comparable benchmark across all US industry is 65%.

Why does this matter? For US journalist, novelist, and academic Melissa Chadburn it is about equity and a society in which everyone can have a say in the narrative of society (2019):

> What I truly want is for other young black and brown girls in foster care to read the paper, and see their stories reflected back to them, for them to think they could be a journalist too, if they'd like. With parity comes a freedom to choose our own narrative. A freedom to shape the bigger story.

It comes back to the issue of personal relevance and connection. It is no surprise that in an age of populism audiences have turned their backs on the media, accusing journalists of being divorced from reality, too close to politicians, elite, cynical, unaccountable . . . the list goes on. The issue of diversity is a critical moral imperative if we are to "*talk with*" viewers and readers and not "*tell*" them. There is a hard economic point as well. Failure to engage audiences by being out of touch feeds the lack of trust and ultimately contributes to the financial crisis facing the news business. Teri Hayt, the executive director of the American Society of News Editors (ASNE), summed it up by saying that failure to care about diversity leads to a loss of audience share (Columbia Journalism Review, 2018).

Social media platforms – disruptive and destabilising

The fourth key challenge for journalism is to establish a more equitable relationship with social media platforms. Countless words have been written about the pernicious influence of social media on journalism, ranging from how they have sucked in advertising and undermined the traditional business of news to their use as a platform to spread fake news, hate speech, and disinformation by foreign powers trying to destabilise Western democracies. As Jon Snow says in the next chapter, while there is no reason to condemn the whole of the digital age to the waste bin, it certainly does have a dark side.

The task at hand in many Western nations is to redress the imbalance with social media networks which now, as noted earlier by the Reuters Institute, control access to audiences. This is vital because social media platforms' dominance in online advertising has been sucking the lifeblood out of traditional media outlets and, more recently, creating financial problems at the digital only players. This clearly has an impact on the ability of traditional media to carry out its role of civic engagement, particularly at the local level, and has been elevated to a level of such concern that it is now on the political agenda in several countries. The fear is that the trend of media retrenchment[17] accelerates into a downward spiral, with financially vulnerable organisations more open to pressure from politicians, advertisers, or the major social media platforms which can dictate their terms. BuzzFeed's Broderick is quite clear on the motivation of the digital giants such as Facebook, Google, and Apple. They are, he says, trying to make the Internet "a safe place for capitalism" and are contributing to the toxicity of public discourse; they have simply become too large. Increasingly, the various government-backed inquiries and commissions that have been set up are questioning whether the public good that is robust journalism can be left to the free market.

In the United Kingdom, the government-appointed Cairncross Review into the sustainability of the press has documented publishers' concerns that the relationship is excessively weighted in favour of the online platforms, that they do not share enough data with them, and that they are not subject to the same rules of accuracy and fairness (2019, p. 65). Both Google and Facebook guard their newsfeed algorithm closely. Indeed, in January 2018 Facebook changed its algorithm without advance warning to prioritise "meaningful social interactions," thus downplaying content shared by news and media publishers. None of the major platforms pay a publisher when they aggregate content and show only snippets with a link to the publisher's website (ibid, p. 68). As a result of this unequal equation, the Cairncross Review has recommended that online platforms should be placed under "regulatory supervision," saying the task of oversight is too important to leave entirely to the judgement of commercial entities (but note it has not gone as far as recommending outright regulation). At the same time, it proposes a menu of tax reliefs and direct financial support to sustain public interest journalism and places a specific emphasis on local news (ibid, p. 90). This does not go as far as some other countries in Europe; for example, newspapers in Norway receive state subsidy. But the Cairncross Review has certainly not been rejected out of hand and is now in the hands of government ministers who must decide whether to support the industry with hard cash. Steven Barnett, professor of Communication at Westminster University, has welcomed the proposals as potentially delivering more diverse, high quality journalism, particularly at the local level where it is most needed (2019). One of the most innovative recommendations which has received little attention is Cairncross's idea of setting up an Institute for Public Interest News, a dedicated body that would bring together publishers, the BBC, regulator Ofcom, academic institutions, and online platforms in an attempt to forge a partnership to ensure the future provision on public interest news.

Across the globe, we are seeing a similar process in which publishers are seeking to redress the balance against online platforms. But there are also signs that these plans can backfire. In Germany, changes to the 2013 copyright law granted news publishers the right to charge search engines and online aggregators for reproducing their content. The Cairncross Review recounts how a consortium of 200 German publishers led by Axel Springer told Google News it could no longer publish snippets of texts and images. Google complied and ran only headlines to limit its liability but over the first two weeks Axel Springer saw an 80% drop in traffic from Google News and reversed the decision (2019, p. 70). When publishers charged the platforms in Spain, Google simply shut down access to its aggregation service Google News. Both examples show the power of platforms such as Google. In the United States, media have mocked the way members of Congress have interviewed social media executives hauled in to give testimony, pointing out their ignorance of the digital landscape. Questioning has at times been hostile, and while there is a general feeling that "something must be done," US lawmakers appear hesitant because of First Amendment rights of free speech and for fear of harming Silicon Valley's economy or capacity to innovate. Concern has been less about the rights of US publishers than the spate of data breaches, not least the one revealed in 2018 where the data of 87 million users' Facebook profiles had been harvested by the consultancy firm Cambridge Analytica. In addition to that, the Senate Intelligence Committee released reports later that year showing how Russia weaponised social media during the 2016 presidential election campaign. At the time of writing, despite evidence mounting up against social media platforms, US regulation has yet to materialise.

New pedagogies – a partial route?

The fifth and final challenge resides with journalism education. If we are to explore new practices, we need to start in the academy (Zelizer, 2004) to ask whether new pedagogies can help in our quest for "new journalisms." In November 2018, we put this challenge, in an informal conversation session, to a group of media literacy scholars at the Media Education Summit in Hong Kong.[18] Several themes emerged: that pedagogy only offers a partial route through the current mess, since building external partnerships between the academy and industry is key, and as long as traditional values are endorsed in practice, any changes in pedagogy cannot gain traction. There was a clarion call for practice and pedagogy to move from "telling" to "talking with" models. Accreditation was seen as a potential "block to innovation," and journalism educators were urged to engage more closely with the media literacy movement. This latter point aligns with Stavitsky and Dvorkin's (2008) view that:

> Journalists must be active participants in the burgeoning media literacy movement, taking advantage of our channels of communication to explain, justify and when necessary, apologise.
>
> *(Stavitsky and Dvorkin, 2008, pp. 29–30)*

The delegates at the summit also encouraged journalism educators to work together in a critical re-evaluation of how we can best engage audiences (particularly young people) in an age of distrust, perhaps through experimentation with teaching innovative ways of storytelling. The ambition: a more connected and robust civic society, where journalism pedagogy is feeding a healthy and sustainable model of journalism practice. These are not insignificant tasks.

The dynamic and ongoing debate about rethinking journalism education (Mensing, 2010; Rosen, 2012; Gillmor, 2006) is evaluated elsewhere in this volume,[19] but the MES Conversation makes a rich contribution to the debate.

Building external partnerships

In the United States, Jay Rosen, working out of New York University, has long championed a model of journalism education that builds industry partnerships on the basis of utility, where his master's students make artefacts for news organisations (Rosen, 2012). This model is difficult to scale for large undergraduate programmes, but the key principle is striking: this "real world" environment seeks to avoid the production-driven approach to teaching journalism. Lighter, faster modes of publishing swept in with the digital age, and these need to be reflected in curricula (Rosen, 2011). In many journalism departments within universities in the UK multiplatform and converged newsroom practices have been embraced more readily, with some striking up external relationships based on propinquity or mutuality.[20] However, there is still work to be done, on both sides, to take the mutual exchange between journalism education and industry to the next level. Which leads us to the question:

To accredit or not to accredit?

There is a lively debate on both sides of the Atlantic about whether accreditation is a block to innovation. In the US, a number of leading J-Schools[21] have jettisoned accreditation: in 2017, Brad Hamm, the dean of Medill journalism school at Northwestern University articulated their rationale allowing accreditation to lapse: "As we near the 2020s, we expect far better than a 1990s-era accreditation organization that resists change – especially as education and careers in our field evolve rapidly" (Fain, 2017). In the UK, journalism programmes accredited by the National Council for the Training of Journalists (NCTJ) and the Broadcast Journalism Training Council (BJTC) or the Periodicals Publishers' Association (PPA)[22] face stringent requirements in terms of resources and the design and delivery of curricula. The accreditation question in the US settles around the tension between an input-driven accreditation body and the desire within J-Schools to be more output-focused. In the UK, the tensions between autonomy in curriculum design and industry council requirements lead to questions about whether accreditation is a block to innovation. Journalism education is caught between a rock and a hard place: accreditation is a recruiting tool, a quality hallmark that in a crowded and competitive Higher Education marketplace can separate the wheat from the chaff, but it puts a brake on quick response to the fast pace of industry change, and arguably makes it difficult for journalism educators to take a position in the vanguard of innovation.

Innovative and critical approaches

Educational spaces should provide a "safe space" for innovation and experimentation: the MIT Center for Civic Media and the Tow Center at Columbia provide compelling examples of learning environments where ideas can be generated, tested, and critically evaluated. Labs in universities. learning spaces that emulate the "third space" (Potter and McDougall, 2017) between home and institutions where there is slack for extra-curricular activity, play and experimentation are part of the effort to innovate. These spaces often facilitate inter-disciplinary approaches to journalism pedagogy. Similarly, bringing journalism education into the heart of media literacy pedagogies, with a sharp focus on multidisciplinary approaches (Lee, Kai and Chan, 2017), could help a shift towards a position of critical reflection whereby media literacy education moves away from problematising to offer routes through the mire. This is what Paul Mihailidis (2017) calls the "agency gap" between "concern and our capacity to act." He contests that the tools of media literacy have so far helped us to identify problems, not solutions:[23] a critical reimagining will provide educators with a sense of purpose that had been lacking. More active engagement should follow, but as journalism practice needs to abandon top-down approaches to "telling stories," seeking to re-engage audiences through incorporating diverse voices, so journalism education needs to adopt immersive modes of delivery where shoulder-to-shoulder replaces the transmission model.

"Talking with"

The teaching of journalism skills is often based on an apprenticeship model, where the newsroom becomes the classroom and where there is an element of "talking with," but with the lecturer adopting a classic "editorial style" role, there is still hierarchy and industry norms are at play in classes that mimic the "real world." Jarvis (2012) contends that a disruptive age offers opportunities for more radical rethinking from journalism educators. At California State University, Melissa Wall has trialled a "Pop-Up Newsroom" that:

- Creates temporary news operations around an event
- Uses personal media devices and social media tools
- Encourages students to build their own peer-to-peer networks for news dissemination

The model seeks to avoid traditional newsroom models that socialise journalists (Tuchman, 1973). It could also engender different modes of dialogue: as Wall (2017) explains, it is student led but does not produce student versions of professional news outputs, employing instead the concept of "liquid journalism" (Bauman, 2007; Deuze, 2006). Wall's pop-up experiment provides one example of a pedagogy that enables us to move from "telling" to "talking with."[24]

The MES Conversation provided some lively ideas for new pedagogies that might help us to sketch a route map to find new journalisms, if only to offer a partial route towards reimagining.

Conclusion

The five key challenges identified in this chapter provide a starting point for the reimagining of journalism that is needed to sustain democracy and rekindle civic engagement. One of the core messages coming out of the Salzburg Academy in recent years is that, despite what appears to be a sustained period of disruption, reimagining is not beyond our grasp. Indeed, the scholar Henry Jenkins, in his keynote to the academy in 2016, invoked the spirit of Harry Potter in quoting J.K. Rowling:

> We do not need magic to change the world. We carry all the power we need inside ourselves already. We have the power to imagine better.

The challenges as we see them and as set out in this chapter are:

- The need to understand audiences better and to interpret newsroom analytics without being seduced by the temptation of clickbait
- The need to re-establish a connection with the voices within our own communities and those of others through listening with empathy
- The need to build a genuinely diverse workforce, truly representative of society in which journalism can play its full part
- The need to redress the imbalance which gives social media platforms undue power and influence over audiences
- The need for new pedagogies that foster innovation and critical thinking to focus on civic engagement

Why does this matter? Why the need to reimagine? A hollowed-out journalism detached from publics and local voices reduces community engagement with local democracy, undermines journalism's ability to hold power to account, and leads to a debasement of public discourse.

Notes

1 President Trump has singled out news organisations and individual journalists for criticism, focusing particularly, though by no means exclusively, on CNN.
2 In 2015, the *Suedeutsche Zeitung* received a leak of 11.5 million documents relating to offshore investments which became known as the "Panama Papers"; a second leak to two reporters at the same newspaper about a year later included 13.4 million documents on a similar subject and became known as the "Paradise Papers."
3 According to Chief Executive Mark Thompson, *The New York Times* reported a "spectacular surge" in subscriptions in 2016 after the newspaper was attacked by Trump as a "failing" institution (2016). In Britain, *The Guardian* now has more than 500,000 supporters who donate a voluntary monthly sum (Viner, 2018).

4 The Leveson Inquiry into the culture, practice, and ethics of the British press was conducted in 2011–12 and led to an overhaul of the system of self-regulation of newspapers. Newspapers managed to avoid the imposition of government regulation despite a public outcry over the hacking of phone messages.

5 The BBC was one of the first major news organisations to set up a user-generated content hub, acting shortly after the July 7 bombings. Within 24 hours of the attack, the BBC had received 1,000 stills and videos, 3,000 texts, and 20,000 e-mails.

6 See Chapter 4 in this volume by Nicole Blanchett Neheli for a discussion of the use of analytics at local newspapers.

7 See Chapter 5.

8 BuzzFeed was founded in New York in 2006, the same year in which Twitter was launched, and is now a news organisation with a global news-gathering presence.

9 The *MailOnline,* the website of the UK newspaper the *Daily Mail,* has a monthly reach of nearly 30 million people.

10 The Chernobyl disaster was a nuclear accident that occurred on 25–26 April 1986 in the (now-abandoned) town of Pripyat in the northern Ukraine (at that time part of the USSR). It is known as the most disastrous nuclear power plant accident in history, in terms of human and financial cost. Thirty-one people died, many more were permanently affected by the contamination, and at least 15 people later died as an indirect result.

11 Widad Ketfi provides another example of the work of vloggers and bloggers in the *banlieues* of Paris. Available at: www.aljazeera.com/programmes/witness/2016/01/paris-voice-suburbs-160103095138746.html.

12 According to the World Bank, the death toll in Syria directly related to the conflict as of early 2016 is estimated between 400,000 (UN, April 2016) and 470,000 (Syrian Center for Policy Research, February 2016). More than 6.1 million people, including 2.5 million children, are internally displaced and 5.6 million are officially registered as refugees (UNHCR, September 2018). Available at: www.worldbank.org/en/country/syria/overview.

13 'It's not a war, it's a massacre': scores killed in Syrian enclave by Kareem Shaheen. (2018). Tuesday 20 Feb. Available at: www.theguardian.com/world/2018/feb/20/its-not-a-war-its-a-massacre-scores-killed-in-syrian-enclave-eastern-ghouta.

14 One of Muhammad Najeem's dispatches can be seen here. Available at: www.youtube.com/watch?v=5MvFs8tFcOc.

15 See Chapter 2.

16 Known universally as PPE, the undergraduate course combines Philosophy, Politics, and Economics.

17 Research for the Cairncross Review estimated that the number of frontline journalists in the UK has fallen to 17,000 from 23,000 in 2007.

18 The MES Conversation 2018: *New journalisms: Rethinking Practice, Theory and Pedagogy* hosted by Dr Karen Fowler-Watt, took place on Thursday, 1 November 2018, at the Media Education Summit 2018 at Hong Kong Baptist University.

19 See Chapter 7, K. Fowler-Watt, New journalisms, new pedagogies and Chapter 8, P. Mihailidis, R. Gerodimos, and M. Fromm. Civic intentionality and the transformative potential of journalism pedagogies.

20 Some journalism schools in the UK are located close to BBC newsrooms, others have mutual agreements with local/regional radio and TV stations and news organisations. Most are loosely based around industry placements and work experience, some form part of wider regional initiatives for the creative industries.

21 Northwestern and Berkley have allowed their accreditation to lapse. In the US, institutions are accredited every six years by the Association for Education in Journalism and Mass Education (ACEJMC). Read more here: www.poynter.org/business-work/2017/lapse-of-northwesterns-accreditation-sheds-light-on-fast-moving-world-of-journalism-education/.

22 The NCTJ also sets its "gold standard" diploma, whereby students on accredited courses sit professional exams as well as credit bearing modules for their honours degree. Available at: www.nctj.com/journalism-qualifications/diploma-in-journalism.

23 See also: B. Abreu, P. Mihailidis., A. Lee, J. Melki and J. McDougall. (2017). *International handbook of media literacy education*. New York: Routledge.
24 See also: E. Bennett. (2014). *How do journalism schools measure up as a training ground for newsroom innovators?* Available at: https://blog.wan-ifra.org/2014/07/17/how-do-journalism-schools-measure-up-as-a-training-ground-for-newsroom-innovators.

References

Ahva, L. and Pantti, M. (2014). Proximity as a journalistic keyword in the digital era. *Digital Journalism*, 2(3), pp. 322–333 [published online], 14 Apr. Available at: www.tandfonline.com/doi/full/10.1080/21670811.2014.895505?scroll=top&needAccess=true [Accessed 2 Mar. 2019].

Alexievich, S. (2006). *Voices from Chernobyl: The oral history of a nuclear disaster*. Translated by Keith Gessen. New York: Picador.

Barnett, S. (2019). The Cairncross review: Two cheers and two fears for the future of UK journalism. *The Conversation*, 13 Feb. 2019. Available at: https://theconversation.com/cairncross-review-two-cheers-and-two-fears-for-the-future-of-uk-journalism-111658.

Bauman, Z. (2007). *Liquid modernity*. Malden, MA: Polity Press.

Beckett, A. (2017). PPE: The Oxford degree that runs Britain. *The Guardian*, 23 Feb. Available at: www.theguardian.com/education/2017/feb/23/ppe-oxford-university-degree-that-rules-britain.

Bruns, A. (2003). Gatewatching not gatekeeping: Collaborative online news. *Media International Australia Incorporating Culture and Policy: Quarterly Journal of Media Research and Resources*, 107, pp. 31–44.

Bruns, A. (2011). News Produsage in a pro-am mediasphere: Why citizen journalism matters. In: Meikle, G. and Redden, G., eds., *News online: Transformations and continuities*. Basingstoke: Palgrave Macmillan.

Cairncross Review. (2019). *A sustainable future for journalism*. Available at: https://assets.publishing.service.gov.uk/government/uploads/system/uploads/attachment_data/file/779882/021919_DCMS_Cairncross_Review_.pdf.

Chadburn, M. (2019). Now is the time for equity journalism. *Literary Hub*, 27 Feb. 2019. Available at: https://lithub.com/now-is-the-time-for-equity-journalism/.

Chadwick, A., Vaccari, C. and O'Loughlin, B. (2018). Do tabloids poison the well of social media? Explaining democratically dysfunctional news sharing. *New Media & Society*, 20(11), pp. 4255–4274.

Chen, N. (1992). Speaking nearby: A conversation with Trinh T. Minh-ha. *Visual Anthropology Review*, 8(1), Spring.

Columbia Journalism Review. (2018). *This deepening division is not inevitable: The failing diversity efforts of newsrooms*. Available at: www.cjr.org/analysis/newsroom-diversity-failing-efforts.php.

Colvin, M. (2012). Final dispatch from Homs, the battered city. *The Sunday Times*, 19 Feb. Available at: www.thetimes.co.uk/article/final-dispatch-from-homs-the-battered-city-0ntg7xk3397 [Accessed 2 Mar. 2019].

Coward, R. (2007). *Me, me, me: The rise and rise of autobiographical journalism*. Inaugural lecture at Roehampton University, 15 May.

Deuze, M. (2006). Global journalism education. *Journalism Studies*, 7(1), pp. 19–34.

Deuze, M. (2012). *Media life*. Cambridge: Polity Press.

Fain, P. (2017). Quotes Brad Hamm, dean of Northwestern's Medill school of journalism, media and integrated communications in "J-Schools dump their accreditor". *Inside Higher Ed*, 3 May. Available at: www.insidehighered.com/news/2017/05/03/northwestern-and-berkeleys-journalism-schools-drop-accreditor-echoing-broader.

Frayn, M. (1967). *Towards the end of the morning.* London: William Collins.

Furedi, F. (2003). *Therapy culture: Capturing vulnerability in an uncertain age.* London: Routledge.

Gillmor, D. (2006). *We the media: Grassroots journalism, by the people, for the people.* 1st ed. Sebastopol, CA: O'Reilly media.

Harcup, T. and O'Neill, D. (2017). What is news? News values revisited (again). *Journalism Studies*, 18(12), pp. 1470–1488.

Hermida, A. (2010). Twittering the news. *Journalism Practice*, 4(3), 297–308.

Jarvis, J. (2012). Here's a blueprint for radical innovation in journalism education. *Nieman Labs*, 18 Sept. Available at: www.niemanlab.org/2012/09/jeff-jarvis-heres-a-blueprint-for-radical-innovation-in-journalism-education [Accessed 3 Mar. 2019].

Jenkins, H. (2016). *Civic imagination.* Keynote lecture at the Salzburg Academy on Media and Global Change, July 2016.

Jones, O. (2019). Let's give citizens free cash to save not-for-profit journalism. *The Guardian*, 13 Feb. Available at: www.theguardian.com/commentisfree/2019/feb/13/citizens-cash-not-profit-journalism-tax-relief.

Kakutani, M. (2018). *The death of truth.* London: William Collins.

Keane, F. (2018). *From where I stand.* Keynote lecture at Media Education Summit 2018, Hong Kong Baptist University, Hong Kong, 2 Nov. Available at: www.cemp.ac.uk/summit/2018/.

Lee, A., Kai, Z. and Chan, K. (2017). *Multidisciplinary approaches to media literacy, research and practice.* Conference publication Communication University of China and Hong Baptist University.

Marsh, K. (2016). *Terror, identity and the voices of the voiceless.* Lecture at Bournemouth University, 26 Feb.

McLuhan, M. (1964). *Understanding media: The extensions of man.* New York: McGraw-Hill.

Mensing, D. (2010). Rethinking (again) the future of journalism education. *Journalism Studies*, 11(4), pp. 511–523.

Mihailidis, P., (2017) 'Civic Media Literacies: Re-Imagining Engagement for an Age of Distrust", keynote at AMI Retreat 201, 3 September 2017 at *Journalism, Society and Politics in the Digital Media Era*, Cyprus University of Technology, Limassol, Cyprus.

Packer, G. (2015). The other France: Are the suburbs of Paris incubators of terrorism? *The New Yorker*, 31 Aug. Available at: www.newyorker.com/magazine/2015/08/31/the-other-france.

Pew Research Center. (2018). *Newsroom employees are less diverse than US workers overall.* Available at: www.pewresearch.org/fact-tank/2018/11/02/newsroom-employees-are-less-diverse-than-u-s-workers-overall/.

Phillips, A. (2012). Sociability, speed and quality in the changing news environment. *Journalism Practice*, 6(5–6), pp. 669–679.

Potter, J. and McDougall, J. (2017). *Digital media culture and education: Theorising third space literacies.* London: Palgrave Macmillan.

Plummer, K. (2001). *Documents of life 2: An invitation to a critical humanism.* Vol. 2. London: Sage Publications.

Reuters Institute for the Study of Journalism (2018). *Digital news report 2018.* Oxford: Reuters Institute for the Study of Journalism.

Reuters Institute for the Study of Journalism. (2019). *More important but less robust? Five things everybody needs to know about the future of journalism.* Available at: https://reutersinstitute.politics.ox.ac.uk/risj-review/five-things-everybody-needs-know-about-future-journalism.

Rosen, J. (2006). The people formerly known as the audience. *Pressthink*, 27 June. Available at: http://archive.pressthink.org/2006/06/27/ppl_frmr.html.

Rosen, J. (2011). What I think I know about journalism. *Pressthink*, 26 Apr. Available at: http://pressthink.org/2011/04/what-i-think-i-know-about-journalism/ [Accessed 3 Mar. 2019].

Rosen, J. (2012). *What should journalists be taught?* Lecture at City University, 21 June.

Sambrook, R., ed. (2018). *Global teamwork: The rise of collaboration in investigative journalism.* Oxford: Reuters Institute for the Study of Journalism.

Schrøder, K. (2019). *What do news readers really want to read about? How relevance works for news audiences.* Oxford: Reuters Institute for the Study of Journalism.

Social Mobility Commission. (2017). *Social mobility, the class pay gap and intergenerational worklessness: New insights from the labour force survey.* Available at: https://assets.publishing. service.gov.uk/government/uploads/system/uploads/attachment_data/file/596945/The_ class_pay_gap_and_intergenerational_worklessness.pdf.

Spilsbury, M. (2018). More jobs than we thought. *British Journalism Review*, 29(4).

Stavitsky, A. G. and Dvorkin, J. A. (2008). *Objectivity and balance: Conceptual and practical history in American journalism.* CPB research white paper. Available at: https://publicmediainteg rity.org/wp-content/uploads/cpb_ConceptualHistory_DvorkinStavitsky.pdf [Accessed 3 Mar. 2019].

Thinsz, G. and Nordmark, M. (2017). How to make media more relevant to younger audiences through higher participation. In: Lee, A., Kai, S. and Chan, K., eds., *Multidisciplinary approaches to media literacy, research and practice.* Beijing: Communication University of China Press.

Toff, B. and Nielsen, R. K. (2018). "I just Google it": Folk theories of distributed discovery. *Journal of Communication*, 68(3), pp. 636–657.

Tuchman, G. (1973). *Making news: A study in the construction of reality.* New York: Free Press.

Viner, K. (2018). Speech to Society of Editors conference. *The Guardian*, 23 November 2018. Available at: https://www.theguardian.com/gnm-press-office/2018/nov/23/ society-of-editors-annual-conference-katharine-viner-speech

Wall, M. (2017). Pop-up newsroom: Liquid journalism for the next generation. In: Goodman, R. and Steyn, E., eds., *Global Journalism Education in the 21st Century: Challenges & Innovation* (pp. 327–342). Austin, TX: Knight Center for Journalism in the Americas, University of Texas at Austin.

Zelizer, B. (2004). *Taking journalism seriously: News and the academy.* Thousand Oaks, CA: Sage Publications.

Zelizer, B. (2018). Resetting journalism in the aftermath of Brexit and Trump. *European Journal of Communication*, 33(2), pp. 140–156.

2

CONNECTED OR DISCONNECTED?

Jon Snow

Jon Snow, journalist, author and long-time anchor of the respected Channel 4 evening news bulletin, set off a period of introspection in the media with his frank assessment that journalists had become too comfortable with the elite. The personal perspectives presented in this chapter are drawn from his "in conversation" with an audience of students and faculty at Bournemouth University in April 2018.

THE GRENFELL TOWER FIRE

On 14 June 2017, a deadly fire broke out in the Grenfell Tower, a 24-storey block of flats in one of London's wealthiest areas. Seventy-two people died, more than 70 others were injured, and 223 people escaped. Amongst the dead were six members of the Choucair family and five members of the Hashim family who lived on the 22nd floor. The youngest victim was a 6-month-old baby, Leena Belkadi, who died in her mother's arms as she tried to escape. It was the worst residential fire in the UK since the Second World War, involving more than 250 firefighters and burning for around 60 hours until it was finally put out. Police and fire services believe the fire was started by a faulty fridge-freezer on the tower block's fourth floor, and the rapid spread of the fire has been attributed to the building's exterior cladding. The Grenfell Public Inquiry, set up by the government, opened on 14 September 2017. In her report to the inquiry, fire safety engineer Dr Barbara Lane identified the fire spreading vertically up the tower columns and "laterally along the cladding above and below the window lines (and) the panels between windows." The residents of Grenfell Tower had complained, for some time, that the building was at risk of

fire; in the aftermath, allegations of negligence were levelled at the management company (TMO) and the local council (Kensington and Chelsea). Protests and unrest grew, with journalists and media also being attacked as elitist
and absentee. A number of grass-roots activist groups emerged, including
Justice4Grenfell; community representative Ismail Balgrave[1] berated the media
for coverage that "validated" the slow response of government and claimed
that poor white and black people in the local community were "treated with
contempt" and felt "marginalised." In the months after the fire, co-author of
the Grenfell Community Action blog Edward Daffam[2] explained the problem
from the perspective of the residents of the tower:

> The reality is if you're on a housing estate it's indifference and neglect, two
> words that sum up everything about the way we were treated. . . . They
> weren't interested in providing housing services, keeping us safe, maintain-
> ing the estate. They were just interested in themselves.

A disconnected elite

The thing about Grenfell was that there were no local journalists, and I could not
understand why. The first thing you do when you go into a crisis in a place that you
have never been to before – and I had never been to the Grenfell Tower before – is
to look for local journalists who might know who lives there and what might be
going on, but there were none. The paper had closed due to a lack of advertising,
because if you were a small business in Kensington or Chelsea, you would advertise
online or on social media, but you would not bother to use a printed paper because
nobody reads one anymore. So that was of real concern, the fact that there was
nobody there who knew anything about the Grenfell Tower. And of course, none
of us had ever lived in a tower block. Whilst quite a high percentage of the popula-
tion lives in tower blocks, none of us seemed to be aware that actually they are not
run by local authorities. They owned them, had moral and legal responsibility for
them, but they did not actually maintain them. They were not involved in them, at
all. That was the case with TMO (the management company) who were nominally
running Grenfell Tower.

The other really interesting thing about Grenfell was that eight months before
the fire there was the warning from Edward Daffam, co-author of the Grenfell
Action Group blog, which nobody knew about, because there were no local journalists to know about it! He warned that there would be a fire and there would be a
catastrophe. I would go as far as to say that, if there had been a strong local publication in the area at the time, this tragic disaster could have been prevented. Then, we
would have been reading the action group's blogs. I did not read the action group's
blogs, because I had never heard of Grenfell Tower. I had driven past the group of
tower blocks on my way out of London, but I had never wondered what they were

or who they were. This is a real worry – you think about community and you think about society and you think about a country and you think about its people and then you discover that there is incredible disconnection from the roots upwards, and that was brought home to me by Grenfell in a big way.

These concerns were matched by the fact that the local authority, in one of the richest boroughs[3] in Britain (and probably in Europe), knew nothing about this tower in which people had perished. They knew very little about how it was being run; they knew very little about anything. It will be interesting to see whether democracy works effectively to remove all of the people who have had anything to do with all that has happened. I suspect not; I suspect that the fact that a tower burnt down in such an affluent area will be a matter of irrelevance (to those in positions of political power), but if the campaign to remove them is successful, then the Conservatives will have lost power in an area that they have run for 58 years.

Media framing

The dissonance evident in the Grenfell tragedy was exacerbated by the media's framing of the story as it unfolded. When I first arrived at the tower at about 5:30 am after the night of the fire, people were talking about overstayers, immigrants. This was not true at all; it was a very mixed community, all sorts of ethnicities, all sorts of classes, and some extraordinarily creative people, including a leading woman artist. As you would expect in a place in that location, there were some extremely talented and interesting people. They were not all white. It was a travesty initially to be describing them thus, in some ways almost to blunt the pain of what had happened, but I believe we soon put that right. This was all brought home to me, because I realised that I knew somebody in the fire: two months earlier I had been at an event with Bill Gates called "Debate Mate," which is a charity that brings schools together to debate against each other and I was a judge for the best floor speech in the 12–15 age range and a 12-year-old girl called Firdaws Hashim was absolutely outstanding. She wore a hijab, she clearly came from a Muslim family, she spoke lyrically, the construction of her arguments was absolutely spell-binding, and I had no doubt that she was head and shoulders above anybody else in that group. On the second day of the fire I was wandering around the "Missing" signs, and I saw her picture on the wall; I could not believe it was her, but it was. She and her entire family had died on the 22nd floor.

Media reports about the owner of the faulty fridge-freezer that started the fire also exacerbated the negative views of the media. It should be completely irrelevant, whose fridge it was; however, the tabloid newspaper, *The Daily Mail* was keen to deflect interest away from the institutional responsibility and the political responsibility onto someone who probably could not afford a decent fridge and had the misfortune to have a fridge catch fire, but you can have a fridge catch fire and it does not burn down a tower block. The responsibility for the fire resided elsewhere. This is bias. Bias is when you hunt down some way of deflecting from the truth. It is true, of course, he was the owner of the fridge that burst into flames, but that really was not relevant. It was perfectly fair to report it, but who was to know that a small fridge fire would threaten everybody in the building? So, the media framing was deeply problematic.

Finding voices in a vacuum

But the overriding challenge is, if there are no journalists in that space, how do you crack these issues, get into the story, and hold people to account? Then you have to start talking to real people, and real people are in enormous shock, a terrible state. That is when one of the most important words in journalism becomes <u>massively</u> important – and that word is empathy. You have got to put yourself into the position of the people who are suffering, people who have lost everything, people who have seen loved ones jump out of windows. I am in contact with a young 23-year-old man who carried his mother down from the top floor and whose father jumped out of the top (23rd) floor, and once you have heard that story and put yourself into that position, you begin to think how you could write this story, how you could report this story, because somehow, you have to get into it, inside the story you are covering and, in that sense, become thoroughly biased. This is a different sort of bias or partisanship: you are there in fact to represent the people who the state has failed. That sounds like a political statement; it is not, it is our job. Our job, as journalists, is actually to give voice to people who have no voice. I will return to discuss how we might strive for a more empathic journalism later in this chapter.

Raised consciousness?

One feature, post-Grenfell, that may only be temporary, is that we are possibly more conscious that we *ought* to be more connected to people with lower incomes. Certainly, I am aware of journalists making a more active effort to get a better spread of views and information and sources into their stories in order to be more inclusive. Inevitably human beings tend to gather together and talk with people they feel easy talking to because they have *shared lives*. This is the herd mentality that is problematic in journalism. I find myself doing the opposite, trying to talk to people who I would not necessarily find in my own social life. I think that is important.

THE WINDRUSH SCANDAL

Immigrants from Caribbean countries such as Jamaica and Barbados who were invited to live and work in the UK between 1948 and 1971 are referred to as the "Windrush generation." The term Windrush derives from the ship, MV Empire Windrush, which brought nearly 500 Jamaicans to the UK on 22 June 1948.

The Windrush scandal refers to a group of around 160 UK citizens who were either illegally deported or faced threat of deportation as a result of the government's immigration rules and quotas, which, in 2017–18 came to be called a "hostile environment" policy. When challenged, the government – and then Home Secretary Amber Rudd – repeatedly denied any awareness of Windrush deportations. Rudd was replaced by Sajid Javid, who, on 15 May 2018, admitted that at least 63 people from the Windrush generation, maybe more, could have been wrongly deported.

The fact that we are dealing now with the Windrush scandal[4] in the same period of time in which we dealt with Grenfell is shattering. I thought we had grown up, I thought we had moved on so that sort of thing could not happen again? The people who came over in that period of Windrush were not all on the boat; we use the boat to define people who came from the Caribbean to work to help to rebuild Britain and were given the right to live here forever. In 1971 a new act was passed to confirm that they could live here forever, and in 2018 we suddenly tell them they cannot, they are going to be removed, it is a "hostile environment." You could have read about this in the works of Dickens and you would have been shocked! Perhaps in the 19th century odious ogres would wander around the city saying, "Hostile environment, time you went home!" but not in the 21st century. It is unbelievable. It is our job, as journalists, to report this and to wake people up and tell them this is being done in their name: "A hostile environment has been set up in your name," and "we are going to be very hostile." I tweeted this morning (20 April 2018), perhaps it would be a good idea to have a little holiday from hostile environments and have a "bit of love" instead.

Triumphs for "old media"?

CAMBRIDGE ANALYTICA-FACEBOOK SCANDAL

Cambridge Analytica Ltd was a British consulting firm, specialising in data analysis and strategic communication. Set up in 2013, the company closed down its operations after the Cambridge Analytica-Facebook scandal was exposed in 2018 where the company was found to be illicitly harvesting the personal data from millions of Facebook profiles and using it for political purposes. A huge fall in Facebook's stock price and calls for tighter regulation followed, with Facebook CEO Mark Zuckerberg called to testify to the US Congress.

The scandal was exposed by *The Guardian* and *Observer's* investigative journalist Carol Cadwalladr, who worked with Channel 4 News and *The New York Times* to publish simultaneously on 17 March 2018. The whistleblower who was the source of the story, a former employee at Cambridge Analytica, Christopher Wylie, worked for a year with Cadwalladr and the team of investigative journalists to get the story out.

The scandal has had a significant impact, engendering debate about ethics and social media companies as well as political organisations and calls for greater protection and privacy rights for consumers.

Whilst it might be tempting to depict the exposure of the Windrush outrage and the Cambridge Analytica-Facebook scandal as a triumph for old style investigative journalism, I think we are mistaken to think of "old" and "new" media. The methods of transportation may have changed, but actually the job has been made easier; you can Google things. Before search engines it was hard work to gather information; you had to make phone calls, which was slow. In many ways, social media has enabled us to break through. Twitter is a tremendous journalistic device: the idea of being able to tweet columns from the *New York Review of Books*, which nobody read before, but which everyone picks up now, and it is even possible to disseminate your own findings. But what we did not know is that it can be put to extremely heinous and evil usages too. It is true that Cambridge Analytica-Facebook was broken by "old" media since it was the work of *The Guardian* and Channel 4 News, and it took investment of time and money, which is difficult to commit to.

There are many dedicated journalists who have slogged away for years at different stories and continue to expose truths. There is, however, a danger that people will not invest in in-depth journalism. They will continue to invest in journalism, but, although it is vital to do so, it is difficult to invest in the long-term investigations. It is this that we at Channel 4 News (and the BBC) can do that nobody else can do without collaboration, and we all need to collaborate, as the Cambridge Analytica-Facebook story has shown.

However, there is the challenge of eyeballs: nobody watches Channel 4 News – we only have 800,000 viewers – but we have 2 billion viewings a year on Facebook, 40% of which are in California. So, it is winning and losing. Cambridge Analytica was basically an organisation which harvested profiles, paying Facebook for access, not to sell advertising on this occasion, but to persuade you not to vote for certain candidates. In the US election, the organisation did not harvest profiles in order to get people to vote for Trump (that would have been an impossibility as you could not persuade people who did not want to vote for Trump, to vote for Trump). Trump was voted for by people who were so desperate about the lives they lived, and so aware through Facebook, and other social media, of the lives other people led, that for the first time, people who had never been out of their states, people who had no passport and would never have dreamt of having a passport, went out to vote. Basically, Cambridge Analytica found people who were vaguely interested in voting for his Democrat opponent, Hillary Clinton, and tried to persuade them not to vote for Hillary and all this "information" about her supposed crimes was poured into their various digital receptacles and it wilted the will of people to vote for her, that was the idea. In states where you literally only had to tip 70,000 votes in order to get her defeated, it worked. It was probably used in Brexit as well: in the referendum if even 2% or 3% of people were dissuaded from voting in a particular way, the only difference between Remain and Leave was 2%–3%. Obviously, there is dark activity online, but it does not condemn the whole digital age to the waste bin; the digital age has done journalism an enormous amount of good: access, ability to research fast, move fast outflank. We could not have done the Cambridge Analytica-Facebook investigation, or indeed Windrush, without the social network. We can now inhabit a world in our digital time, so as a journalist the challenges have never been greater, and the opportunities have never been greater. You can track down anybody basically, so just imagine what lies ahead.

Social media: the route to connectivity?

The difficulty is, all of this is happening against a backdrop of acute inequality, and trying to connect unequal people is difficult. Charities spend their whole time trying to connect people who have money with people who have nothing. It is an uphill job, and it is very difficult to persuade people that it is in their interests to be connected to somebody less fortunate than themselves. The present period that we are living through, in which, globally, the banking crisis is being paid for by the poorest people in the country, the cuts in local authority spending in the UK, the period of austerity which has kept wages down, has resulted in a profoundly unequal society. The digital age enables those people living in that unequal society to know just how unequal it is, because they can see the circumstances in which people much better off than themselves are living on a scale which they have never been able to see before, so it also makes for a profoundly unhappy society. Although we may be happy within our circles, I suspect there are a lot of people who, without knowing anything about Europe, for example, would have decided to vote "Leave" in order to upset those that they believe to be better off than them, to teach them a lesson. It can play in that way, there is no way of knowing where it will play in.

Social media also fails to offer routes to addressing the challenges of fractured communities presented by the Grenfell fire, since, in some ways, the digital age both facilitates and militates against building community. People are happier on their laptops than they are going to a meeting, so, as journalists, we have to resuscitate communities as much as possible. You can only really do that by having smaller administrative segments in society. Here is an illustration of the problem: currently in the UK the government is running education academies, rather than letting the local authorities run them. Education is definitely centrally driven in terms of deciding curriculum and so on, but a school is the hub of a community and it should be run by the community, i.e. the local authority, and the local authority should exist in small enough units to facilitate community. At the moment, we are, in Britain, beyond dispute, the most centralised government in Europe. Far, far too much is done by central government. The centralisation of power never does anybody any good.

Language barriers present another impediment to building understanding and creating connections. I do think that the paper monster that is Russia is partly a product of not being able to speak Russian. Clearly Mr Putin may not be the best-intentioned character, but they are human beings and they live lives, they live social lives, they love, they live, and they die, and it would be much better if we could talk the same language and understand each other for the better. However, whilst language barriers are there, at the same time I would not want to see anybody's culture eroded in order to embrace some language that the world understood better, so the Anglicisation of the world would not be an attractive idea at all. Google Translate is an amazing tool to find out quickly what we are all saying to each other: this is an example of where the Internet can help us build bridges and deepen our understanding.

Rethinking impartiality

Clearly it is essential, as a journalist, to understand the need to be impartial, but there are moments in life, and there are plenty of them, when you would not be doing the reader or the viewer a great service by being impartial. It is impossible to be impartial about the Windrush scandal; this is one of the most disgraceful episodes that I have ever known in the UK: the idea that people were given this pledge that if they came and rebuilt this country, they and their descendants would be able to live here forever and were then betrayed. They were betrayed in the most disgusting way. It is utterly shocking. I believe that in a situation like that you should let your bias go rampant, because you can hardly find the words to describe it. It is the most sordid, nasty, vindictive state of affairs. There are not words enough to describe it. And the suffering these people have been through, the money they have had to pay to try to redress not being able to get medical treatment, losing their homes. It is horrendous! There, I think, you have to let bias go. But here is the challenge: on the other hand, you have got to be sure that you are not so far from the viewers and the readers that they cannot cope with what is going on, so, as a journalist, feel it, believe it, row back and get into a position where you can make it quite clear that this is a grotesque moment, but understand that because the audience has not necessarily seen what you have seen, the reader and the viewer may need some help.

Another challenge is that one person's idea of factual reporting can be viewed by others as biased. The Israel-Palestine issue is problematic here: I believe that when I reported on Gaza in 2014 and was accused of bias,[5] I reported the facts and the facts were gruesome, so gruesome, that it looked like bias. The situation in Gaza is simply horrendous. Even now, in fact it is worse now. Because the power station was bombed during the war, there is no way of running the sewage system and the sea is full of shit, in the literal sense of the word. That simply is not acceptable.

Nothing has been done to alleviate it and they are besieged. Of course, it is a region in turmoil; there are attacks on the Israelis as well. It is an intractable and dreadful problem, but there are 2 million people on a completely isolated lump of land who are suffering greatly. Yemen is another example of a conflict zone where accusations of bias can be levelled at journalists. This is an absolutely disgraceful story in which our manufactured bombs are being purchased by people who are in the conflict and being deployed, and nobody turns a hair. Difficult. Am I biased about people being bombed with our bombs? Yes! I think that's a reasonable bias to have. But, you *have* to bring the audience with you and retain a connectivity with them. This is where facts are immutable. You have got to deal in facts. Facts are extremely important. The BBC and Channel 4 News have fact-checking units, which I believe are very important as fact-checking and *showing that you are fact-checking*, are important elements of any journalistic organisation. The digital age makes it easier to fact-check now than it was before, and you will not be accused of bias if you can produce enough facts. This also enables us to build trust in an age where we are not trusted by the public, in an age where they do not like us much. Fake news is not new, and there are many PR agencies whose stock in trade has always been a dash of fake news, just to disturb the system. The problem is that everybody is blaming the digital age for fake news, but the dissemination of fake news is a huge problem and we have to utilise the same media to combat it, to find really credible alternatives. This may seem a rather weak way to address a point that exercises us daily, but it is the dissemination rather than the existence of the fake news that is the problem as there will *always* be fake news.

Getting involved

In the context of the drive to be impartial and fact based in our reporting, I would like to explain what I mean by "being involved" and "getting involved." I return to the story of the young man who carried his mother down the stairs in the Grenfell fire. I told his story, as a journalist, but I also wanted to help him – this is what I mean by "being involved" and what that means, for this boy, who carried his mother down the stairs. It is an absolutely stunning story; 3 o'clock in the morning from the top floor, he carried his paralysed mother, who had a health condition, nothing to do with the fire, got to the 10th floor and really was not going to make it and he passed what he soon realised was an air pocket, he saw a black hole with the smoke hanging above it, and he came back and lay his mother down in the hole and then lay himself down and they gulped fresh air and they were then able to proceed further down the stairs. They reached the 7th floor and he was feeling his way forwards in the dark, walking over the dead bodies in the stairwell and found his hand connecting with the chest of a fireman coming up and they were rescued. A fireman and a firewoman rescued them and took them down. I asked him, after I had done the interview, what he wants to do, as he is 23. He said I really want to be either an aeronautical or a mechanical engineer in the car or the aeronautical industry. The previous week, on Channel 4 News, we had interviewed the head of

Volkswagen in Britain so we had that contact and so I wrote him an e-mail and asked whether he would ever take this guy on, saying, "I think he'd be very good, but he's obviously in a state of terrible shock and has an invalid mother." I received a fantastic letter back; I think at that moment in time everyone in the country wanted to help people in Grenfell Tower, and he pledged that there would be an opening for him. The problem is that we are a year on (in April 2018) and he is not really fit; he is so damaged psychologically and the mother is so dependent, he is not really able to take up the opportunity, but that is what I would talk about when I talk about "involvement."

As journalists, we have to prepare ourselves to talk to people who have suffered trauma, to listen to their stories, and this is where empathy is so important. To an extent you have got to try extremely hard and it is not that difficult when you are looking at a building like that and when you have spent hours looking at it, to put yourself in the position of the person. You can never completely live what they lived, in any way, but I think in your imagination you have to take a journey before you talk to the person, otherwise there is never going to be a point of connection. The same is true of any interview: if you are talking to a pensioner who has had a rough run in with local government, or whatever it is, you have to try and weave your way into the way things look from their point of view and interview them as if in some way you do fully understand what it is they are going through, and I believe that you do have to work very hard to achieve that. This is where empathy really comes into play, empathy is IT. It is the capacity to feel what it is they are telling you, to *feel* it. A lot of people in the old days used to say, "I don't get emotional, leave your emotions at the door." *Don't* leave your emotions at the door – get on with it. However, it is crucial that we, as journalists, never become the story. We can never be the story. We must never put ourselves at the front of the thing. What happens to you and me is irrelevant to the reader and to the viewer. They want to know what happened. In fact, I am often surprised that the fact that people see you on the telly every night means that they form an impression as to whether they want to talk to you or not, and I have found in the case of the Grenfell Tower, for example, that I have not had very much difficulty talking to people who were residents there. They are not interested in your class or colour, they are interested in your commitment to the story: Are you still interested? Have you done any more about it since it happened? Those are the sort of factors, I think, which win confidence. I do not think you can expect to dive in on a story that happens and then pack your bags and go. I think you have to come back again and use the contacts you made before to update, because almost invariably in all of these stories, it has not gone away and the issues that you raised on the first day (in this case, of the fire) are still "live" and still need to be pursued. In the end, we are trying to keep authority straight and if something like this happens, we cannot let them go until there has been redemption of some degree, so it could be years. The journalist should be the servant of society, rather than the master.

I am not sure how it is that journalists have become members of the elite, but I think, in part, it is the growth of university education. Twenty-five years ago, the idea of going to university to study journalism simply was not possible and there was a more diverse collection of people doing journalism. So, part of the issue is, I think, about education, which fosters upward social mobility: 50% of young people now get to university and certainly when I was young, if you met a journalist they were very often working class, not university-educated, and would be walking around their patch, or on a bike looking for stories and would be a *local* journalist.

At the time of this conversation event, in April 2018, we were marking various anniversaries: the Grenfell fire, of course (June 2017); the suicide bombing at the Manchester Arena, which killed 23 people (22 May 2017); and the terror attack on Westminster Bridge, where six people lost their lives (22 March 2017). These stories must always be kept in the public consciousness; they never go away because the people who are affected live on and their lives evolve. Here is an example from my own journalistic practice: I was in Manchester the morning after the bombing and I was in the main square, at a bit of a loose end, because I really was not sure how we were going to move the story on for that evening's news programme. A man came up to me in terrible distress, whose wife had been killed in the bombing. Of course, your first instinct is that you want to interview him – but he was beyond interviewing – and I took him for tea in a little café and we talked for a couple of hours and then he left. Two days later (I had obviously left him my contact details) he told me he wanted to do an interview and so I did an interview with him. Now this year, I went back to Manchester and we talked again, and I realised that there were many areas of his life that had not been addressed by the system at all. There were all sorts of unfinished things about his home and his family, and so I think the way you move it on is actually once again to hold power to account for what has, or has not, been done. I think we need to praise when things have been done and when things are a lot better than they were last year. But of course, sadly that does not happen very often.

Being connected

If empathy is the route to connectivity, we also need to consider the potential impact on the journalist of reporting the traumatic experiences of others. If empathy is important, crying is important, and if you are overwhelmed emotionally by what you see, you should cry. I would urge people to cry. Just go off quietly and indulge what you are feeling and reckon with it and then pull yourself together and get on with it. I think grief, shock, trauma is best dealt with initially by you, by embracing it and accepting it, accepting that "I am horrified. I have seen something so bad, **what** have I seen? Yes, I have seen . . ." And you lay it out and you exorcise it to some extent. I think that hoping that third parties are somehow going to help you six months' later is not a helpful way of approaching it. We should not be too "po-faced" about journalism, because it is an emotional experience; you will be subjected to things which you would never normally be exposed to, but I think you should accept that you have had an abnormal experience and then either cry or if it's worse than that, talk to somebody, not even necessarily a specialist, but just say: "I have seen something bloody awful and I need to talk." I think that this ena-bles us to be connected and to continue to do our job. Autobiographically, I deal with trauma and seek balance in various ways: I do watercolours, I play the piano, and I have the occasional good meal. I have a lovely wife and a few daughters and a sort of a life. And I ride a bicycle. I ride a bike everywhere. In fact, I would advocate every journalist needs a bike. That is a terrible thing to insist, but in all honesty – particularly in the local situation – a bike is absolutely fantastic, and it is the reason I have often gotten stories, because nobody else could get there on time, especially in London, where traffic is a nightmare, just because of the bike.[6]

Afterword by the editors

Some of the issues raised by Jon Snow in this chapter formed the basis for the Cairncross Review into a sustainable future for high quality journalism. Its findings were published on 12 February 2019. The review highlighted two areas of public interest news that "matter greatly" and whilst "often of limited interest to the pub-lic . . . are essential in a healthy democracy":[7]

1   Investigative and campaigning journalism, "especially investigations into abuses of power in both the public and the private sphere." This journalism is defined as "high-cost" and "high risk."
2   Reporting on the daily activities of public institutions, which it calls a "hum-drum task." This also captures "discussions of local councils or the proceedings in a local Magistrates Court." Local newspapers are highlighted as "a particu-larly important component of news coverage" since broadcasters tend to oper-ate regionally.

The review drew on evidence from a range of academic studies. One from the UK[8] highlighted a significant drop in court reporting between 2012 and 2016, showing a decrease of 30% in the national press and 40% in the regional press. Two large-scale studies in the United States found that the existence of local newspapers keeps local governing bodies in check and makes them more efficient, as they are effectively audited and monitored by the local press, acting as a watchdog. UK aca-demics Moor and Ramsay, also cited in the report, agree. They describe journalists as "scarecrows" whose very presence in a local area acts as a threat against abuses of power by keeping "the powerful" in check. However, others (Howells, 2015) argue that it takes more than the survival of a paper to safeguard healthy civic engagement as the journalists who report on a community also need to live within it.[9] This has resonance for the Grenfell Tower tragedy, where the only journalist writing about the area lived in a different part of the country. The compelling conclusions of the review validate, without reservation, the news industry's "important democratic function that supports participation in local and national society and safeguards the public-interest by reporting on the activities of the powerful and the workings of the state" (Cairncross, 2019).

Whether it will in any way address the deficits and dissonance that Jon Snow describes in this chapter remains to be seen. Depressingly, Cairncross says that it "seems improbable" that the market will eventually provide resources to nurture local journalism, with lack of reader engagement providing a major obstacle.

So, we need to look for other ways to engage publics and to sustain journalism's democratic function of speaking truth to power. This chapter also calls for journalism to reflect society more accurately, arguing that evidence of a more diverse and inclusive workforce could help to combat the allegations of "elitism" levelled against journalists. Diversity and inclusivity could foster heightened awareness of the voices within communities (see the Grenfell community action blogs that were being written before the deadly fire). This could, in turn, mitigate a reliance on reporters who "parachute in," snatch a quote or two and depart, leaving in their wake individuals and communities who still have all the issues to deal with that were there before the news-gathering machine arrived. Journalism is not social work, but reporters can stay around for longer to listen and to care and they can return to highlight inequities and problems once the headlines have faded. This is important if we are to engage our audiences.

Allied to the need for a more diverse journalism is the imperative to incorporate as wide a range of voices as possible into our storytelling. We need to avoid going to the same, tried and tested sources (this also compounds the elitist issue) and to broaden the scope of our storytelling, always seeking the human dimension and building relationships (as evident in the example of Snow's reporting after the Manchester arena attack).

Finally, we have to tell the stories of others with empathy and to work very hard to put ourselves as close to their experiences as we can in our reporting. In this chapter, Snow declares that "empathy is it." The Windrush scandal and the Grenfell tragedy indicate that, in the past few years, empathy has taken a back seat, that the *zeitgeist* is one of hostility and selfish individualism where power is not held effectively to account and journalism has been negligent in its civic duty. Moreover, social media has not delivered the connections that we hoped it might. This chapter, with its various calls to action, seeks to find a route out of the disconnectedness towards greater connectivity, while understanding that it will take a feat of *human* endeavour to get us there.

Notes

1 Ismail Balgrave's heated exchange with a Sky News reporter can be seen here. Available at: www.youtube.com/watch?v=qcJPlkqOYX0.
2 Edward Daffam is a social worker who lived in Grenfell Tower for 20 years. He escaped from the fire and is now a member of Grenfell United: the main group representing survivors and bereaved of the fire. He has been campaigning on housing issues since 2009.
3 Borough status is purely honorary and granted by royal charter to local government districts in England, Wales, and Northern Ireland. It does not give any additional powers to the council or those who live there.
4 See more on the Windrush generation. Available at: www.channel4.com/news/topic/windrush-generation.

5 Snow's reporting aroused debate about impartiality between media news executives. Available at: www.haaretz.com/was-it-okay-for-anchor-to-show-his-stripes-on-gaza-1.5264158.
6 This chapter draws on Jon Snow's talk in 2018 but is not verbatim. The conclusions for this chapter were written as reflections after the event by the books co-editors, Karen Fowler-Watt and Stephen Jukes in February 2019.
7 The Cairncross Review was set up by the UK government as an independent review led by Dame Frances Cairncross into a sustainable future for journalism. Its findings were published on 12 February 2019. Available at: www.gov.uk/government/publications/the-cairncross-review-a-sustainable-future-for-journalism.
8 This refers to research conducted by Brian Thornton at University of Winchester, UK.
9 The *UK Press Gazette* provided a helpful guide to the Cairncross Review to draw out findings that were not highlighted in the report's summary. Available at: https://pressgazette.co.uk/cairncross-review-key-facts-and-findings-you-might-have-missed/ collated by Freddy Mayhew, 22 Feb. 2019.

References

Howells, R. (2015). *Journey to the centre of a news black hole: examining the democratic deficit in a town with no newspaper*, Unpublished PhD thesis, Cardiff University quoted in Mayhew, F., 2019. Cairncross review: Key facts and findings you might have missed. Available at:https://pressgazette.co.uk/cairncross-review-key-facts-and-findings-you-might-have-missed/ collated by Freddy Mayhew, 22 Feb. 2019.

The Cairncross Review: A sustainable future for journalism. 2019. Available at: www.gov.uk/government/publications/the-cairncross-review-a-sustainable-future-for-journalism.

3

JOURNALISTS IN SEARCH OF IDENTITY

Stephen Jukes

This chapter considers the challenges that journalists face in terms of their own identity in an age in which they are viewed with distrust.

> *The film of the year in 1976 was "All the President's Men," in which Robert Redford and Dustin Hoffman gave us the journalist-as-hero role model, which would prove very resilient over the decades to come.*
>
> — *Alan Rusbridger*

Introduction

The film *All the President's Men* depicted *The Washington Post*'s fearless reporting that brought down US President Richard Nixon and, in turn, inspired a generation of journalists. The 1976 thriller, with its dashing young stars, received critical acclaim and contained all the elements of classic journalism: seeking the truth, holding power to account, and protecting the identity of a mysterious yet powerful source in the shape of "Deep Throat." As the former *Guardian* editor Alan Rusbridger observed in his recently published autobiography (2018), that one film gave us a lasting impression of what it means to be a journalist. The film may have presented a romanticised view of the newsroom and the reality may have been much messier, but the fact remains that four decades ago few people had serious doubts about the role of a journalist. *All the President's Men* captured in just 138 minutes the ideology, values, and ethos of journalism in its classic 20th century form. Today, in an era of social media, fake news, citizen journalism, and user-generated content, the lines have become decidedly blurred and the answer to the question "What does it mean to be a journalist?" is no longer clear.

This chapter explores how journalists today are searching for their identity – both professional and personal – in an age in which they are no longer viewed as heroes but are attacked as "enemies of the people" or, as the current US President Donald Trump would have it, are denounced as "fake news" or the "opposition." As *All the President's Men* suggests, the narrative had once been relatively simple and coherent. By the 1930s, the Anglo-American discipline of journalism had been codified as a profession: stable values, principles, and practices had been established across many diverse nations and cultures, particularly within the powerful and dominant Anglo-American news industry. But the recent period of social media disruption has fragmented that monolithic culture in the same way as the prevailing objectivity paradigm that captured many of journalism's core values has been subjected to increasingly robust and virulent challenges. The result has been growing antagonism between many professional journalists fighting a rearguard action to protect their boundaries and the "citizen journalists," bloggers, and purveyors of social media who maintain that traditional journalism is failing the public. That antagonism burst into the public spotlight following the tumultuous US election campaign in 2016 that saw Donald Trump installed in the White House and, in the same year, the controversial UK referendum over membership of the European Union. Partisan and populist reporting of both campaigns and a furore over the phenomenon of fake news have been accompanied by an unprecedented decline in public trust of traditional media organisations and journalists themselves.

This chapter argues that it is time to re-conceptualise what it means to be a journalist and calls for a more flexible model that moves beyond the analysis that has focused on the clashes of rival "us and them" camps and pitted "real journalists" against "amateurs." It proposes a model that sees journalists as members of a community of networked practice in which we recognise that not only actual *practice* but some of the normative *values* of the past are changing. It also argues that it is time to shift the focus of analysis away from the newsroom culture of the large "legacy" news organisations and concentrate instead on the individual journalist and how he or she relates to others, reflecting the reality of today's casualised labour market (symptomatic of the "gig economy")[1] that often sees young journalists working for start-ups or on a freelance basis. The chapter explores elements of current practice which are challenging core values of objectivity and detachment, autonomy and impartiality, charting the way normative values are slowly but surely shifting. It specifically focuses on four areas of change: the rise of emotion in news journalism, the prevalence of personal branding by journalists, the failure of norms of balance, and how the taboo of collaborative working has been broken in an era of big data leaks.

The coherent narrative of journalism begins to break down

Professions often erect boundaries around their activity to protect themselves from intruders, and journalism is no exception (Carlson and Lewis, 2015). There is, however, one clear difference. Unlike, for example, law or medicine, journalism does not require its practitioners to take exams or belong to a specific industry association. Instead, its boundaries are defined through practice, discourse, and values, with journalists consistently engaging in "boundary work" to cultivate a distinct logic that sets them apart from other fields (Waisbord, 2013, p. 10). Journalism had until recently enjoyed a long and stable development in many countries (Deuze and Witschge, 2018, p. 2). That occupational ideology was founded on common values and practices that in Britain and the United States date back to the late 19th century and are deeply rooted in shared concepts such as objectivity, impartiality, and freedom from bias. These are, in turn, informed by a powerful common narrative, reinforced by such films as *All the President's Men* (and more recently the films *Spotlight* and *The Post*),[2] that journalism's role is to support democracy, hold power to account, and uncover the truth. Zelizer has described journalism as an "interpretive community" in which journalists self-referentially develop a shared discourse and interpretation of events which defines the profession (1993, p. 221). In the early 20th century it was important, for example, for journalists to set themselves apart from the emerging profession of public relations. That, in turn, led to the journalistic values of autonomy and independence from commercial influence. This catalogue of normative values has often been questioned by both journalists and academics alike (Bell, 1996; Cunningham, 2003; Maras, 2013) but until recently had stood the test of time. Indeed, some academics have described these values as having almost talismanic status (Richards and Rees, 2011).

However, we are now clearly witnessing a transition from what was a more or less coherent industry to a highly varied and diverse range of practices (Deuze and Witschge, 2017, p. 2) with an increasing array of actors. The resulting debate, played out in the academic world of Journalism Studies and in the world of journalism itself, has led to the establishment of two broad camps – those who maintain that there is a core body of journalistic practices and values that must be upheld to regain trust in the profession; and those who argue that the disruption wrought by social media should be enthusiastically embraced and traditional boundaries should be contested or broken down. Conceptually, this assumes that there is a central core of immutable values that make up journalism and an outer fringe of activities where the boundary of what is, or is not, considered to be journalism is contested.

Proponents of the core body of normative values tend to argue that sticking to tried and tested principles of fact-based journalism is essential if public trust is to be regained in the profession. I have argued earlier that it should come as no surprise that when faced with disruption, aggressive competition, and financial pressures, journalists at established "legacy" news organisations such as the BBC, Reuters, and the Press Association should be pushing back and highlighting values that had served the news industry well for the first 150 odd years of its existence (Jukes, 2018). In an organisation like the BBC this has resulted in an increased emphasis on fact-checking and the relaunch of its "Reality Check" desk. There are some early indications that this strategy might be bearing fruit. A 2018 survey by the Reuters Institute for the Study of Journalism illustrates that trust in the legacy news brands has stabilised at 44% (as opposed to much lower values for news found on social media), although rebuilding that trust means starting from very low levels. There are also signs that consumers seeking a trusted brand are willing to pay for news, confirming the old adage that good (firmly grounded) news sells. News outlets such *The New York Times* and *The Economist* have seen subscriptions rise, benefiting from what has been called a "Trump bump" as readers seek out critical reporting. Somewhat more surprisingly, *The Guardian* newspaper's campaign for voluntary subscriptions to support its journalism is showing signs of success, with more than 500,000 people donating each month (Viner, 2018). Proponents of the opposing camp have argued that it is time to embrace wholeheartedly the periphery, focusing on the potential democratising impact of social media and its benefits to news journalism (Allan, 2013; Bruns, 2003, 2011). They maintain that by doing so journalism will experience a renaissance, with the Internet providing access to more sources, citizen journalism providing additional material, and multimedia formats offering new means of connecting to an audience anywhere at any time in what is a participatory culture (Jenkins, 2014).

Against this backdrop of tension and at times outright antagonism, some scholars have sought to revisit the entrenched culture of journalism and propose new models and ways of thinking about what it is to be a journalist. The disruption of social media has led to reinterpretations of the boundaries of journalism (Carlson and Lewis, 2015) and a search for new ground that breaks the dichotomy of the "us and them" camps (Deuze and Witschge, 2017). Above all, the concept of "hybrid journalism" has come to the fore as traditional boundaries become blurred and as Journalism Studies confronts the tendency to focus on a stable and homogenous understanding of the journalistic field (Witschge et al., 2018). Theoretical frameworks that suggest homogeneity prevent us from doing justice to the dynamic and diverse nature of today's journalism practice although, as Witschge et al. argue, the term hybridity in itself needs further definition (ibid, p. 2). The danger here is that is becomes an all too easy shorthand term to try to overcome the binary dualities of professional and amateur journalist. It is here that the concept of hybridity goes beyond an "either/or" choice of, for example, objectivity versus subjectivity, and allows for a "both/and" fluid combination. At the same time scholars have started to recognise that the newsroom-centric approach to Journalism Studies, with its focus on legacy organisations and hierarchical news structures, is problematic. This has meant that those journalists operating at the margins of those organisations and their spaces – for example the large number of freelancers, bloggers, or start-up news outlets – can be overlooked (Wahl-Jorgensen, 2009). It is here that it is useful to view today's journalism as a "community of networked practice," drawing on Zelizer's earlier concept of journalists as an interpretive community (1993) and recent ideas of networked journalism (Beckett and Mansell, 2008) that are more inclusive and better reflect today's working patterns. In a networked environment, the old linear processes of journalism are replaced by ones in which there is constant communication and interaction with information and in which the space occupied by the producers and users of news is continually being negotiated.

These approaches point the way to a more fluid and realistic understanding of contemporary journalism that eschews the false binary choices that have been so commonplace in narratives of values and identity. They recognise that journalists are taking on new roles and in doing so are *de facto* renegotiating boundaries.

How changing practice is challenging and shifting values

This chapter therefore seeks to explore the concept of journalism as a community of networked practice through concrete examples of the way in which journalists are working in today's digital media landscape. This can admittedly only be a selective snapshot in time since the shape of journalism, and with it the journalist's identity, are continually being negotiated and renegotiated. But the analysis of practice shows that some of the values and ideological certainties of the past are slowly but surely shifting as what is acceptable in today's networked community is reinterpreted. Sometimes this is done with eyes open as a clearly defined decision; at other times there is an underlying dissonance between the (often normative) values still professed through discourse and the type of journalism actually being practised on the ground. The following sections of this chapter explore four distinct areas of practice in which the rules have, until now, been clear: emotion, autonomy, balance, and collaboration.

The inexorable rise of emotion

Despite the rearguard action being fought by some legacy news organisations to highlight the "objectivity paradigm" and detached, fact-based journalism, there are clear signs that what Richards and Rees described as the taboo around emotion (2011) is finally being broken down. While objectivity and subjectivity are by no means binary opposites, there has been a long history of awkward tension between journalism's normative values of objectivity and the everyday practice that sees the harnessing of emotive words, opinions, and images to engage the audiences of news. Journalists' professional ideology sits uneasily with the need to "sell" a story to the public. On the one hand, codes of objectivity, based around concepts of detachment and impartiality, have been a core part of the journalistic discourse and value system that helps define the profession and identity of the individual journalist. Yet on the other hand, today's news media is infused with raw emotion and the old adage "if it bleeds, it leads" holds true more than ever; that news must be visual is an intrinsic value of modern journalism, from print to television (Domke, Perlmutter and Spratt, 2002). In practice, while journalists traditionally derogated emotion and valued dispassionate and disembodied impartiality, they evolved an effective work-around – quite simply they "outsourced" the emotion a story needed by quoting the emotions of those being interviewed. This technique, called the "strategic ritual of emotionality"[3] by Wahl-Jorgensen (2013), allowed the injection of emotion into stories to gain the attention of audiences while upholding on the face of it the objectivity paradigm since the emotions expressed were not those of the journalist.

However, today's combination of digital disruption and societal change is leading to the erosion of this normative practice, to a direct injection of the journalist's own emotions into stories and a rise of what can be termed an "affective dimension" in journalism. While it is tempting to ascribe such change solely to social media, new technologies, and the financial crisis facing many news organisations, it is impossible to ignore the wider cultural phenomena and impact of broader societal shifts of the past 50 years, including the "therapy culture" (Furedi, 2003) and the "affective turn" of the 1990s. Plummer, for example, argues that in what is a postmodern or late modern turn, we are now part of an autobiographical society where "life stories" are everywhere (2001, p. 78). The audience expectation is that journalists will put more of themselves into stories, sometimes sharing their emotions. Research into life stories is personal, emotional, and embodied work (ibid, p. 213). Coward contends that today's media increasingly rely on visual, emotional stories and personal voices (2013). She argues that media consuming audiences want real-life experience, "with all details, especially all the emotions and feelings straight from the protagonists' mouths" (ibid, p. 3). That reflects the normative technique of outsourcing emotion referred to above. But at the same time, the journalist's *own* experiential first-person narrative is becoming ubiquitous and can sometimes be seen as having a veracity that is closer to the "truth." This in turn is reflected in a demand for what has become the holy grail of authenticity articulated in the rise since the 1980s of Reality Television and real-life documentaries such as, in the United Kingdom, Channel 4's *Benefit Street* or the BBC's *The Mighty Redcar*.[4]

The technique of outsourcing emotion arguably held up until the attacks of 11 September 2001, which represented the biggest challenge to the objectivity paradigm for the US media since Vietnam. Many forms of US media engaged in highly jingoistic coverage (much as British media did during the Falklands War in 1982) and adopted the Bush administration's language of the "War on Terror." News anchors wore lapel pins with the Stars and Stripes, and statistical analyses of broadcast and text content have shown an overwhelming preponderance of pro-administration sources. Analysing 9/11, Sreberny has argued that the combination of what was a global media event watched live by millions on television and the outpouring of emotion created an "affective public sphere" (2002, p. 221). The everyday taken-for-granted norms of journalism were shaken in rushed opinion and emotion, driven by trauma (ibid). Other academics have identified a series of triggers, which can lead to the disruption of the objectivity norm and increased injection of emotion. Schudson, for example, cites three typical scenarios (2002, p. 40): first, in moments of tragedy, journalists tend to assume a pastoral role, characterised by hushed, reverent tones of television and radio presenters and is evident at times of political assassination (e.g. President Kennedy in 1963), state funerals, or the mourning of victims; second, in moments of pubic danger, whether from terror attacks or natural disaster (such as Hurricane Katrina in 2005) journalists tend to offer practical advice (e.g. disseminating a public health campaign) and communicate their solidarity; and finally, in moments of threats to national security (e.g. the botched American invasion of the Bay of Pigs on Cuba in 1961) journalists tend to willingly withhold or temper their reports.

But the real watershed was the advent of social media in the first decade of the 21st century which unleashed a tidal wave of user-generated images that now dominate today's news reporting. As Sontag observed before the event nearly two decades ago, public attention can often be steered through images and we have entered into a period of hyper-saturation of images (2003, p. 94). Major stories from our recent past graphically illustrate how the use of images is creating a more emotionally laden news file and how some journalists, in practice, are being sucked into this atmosphere, injecting their own opinion and emotion into coverage. Technologically, two major stories of the post-9/11 era in 2013 – the first major chemical weapons attack on the Damascus suburb of Ghouta and the ISIS-inspired killing in London of the off-duty British soldier Lee Rigby – are light years away from the attacks on the Twin Towers. In both cases, mainstream news media relied on user-generated content to provide the core material for their news stories. Nabila Ramdani, a French-Arab journalist who worked extensively in Syria, recounted how her contacts in the country sent her almost contemporaneously video footage of children dying in Ghouta from the effects of nerve agents (2013). The extent to which social media and citizen journalism are now embedded in our news culture and practice was illustrated in May of the same year when Rigby was hacked to death in broad daylight outside his barracks in London. Rigby's two assailants calmly engaged passers-by in conversation, waiting to ensure that they were captured by mobile phone footage before the arrival of the police. Similarly, when Amedy Coulibaly took hostages in a Paris supermarket in the wake of the 2015 Charlie Hebdo massacre, he came armed not just with a Kalashnikov but also a GoPro camera strapped to his torso. He tried (but failed) to e-mail footage of his attack, including his killing of three shoppers, from a computer in the supermarket. These stories illustrate how media the emotive images have become deeply embedded in our everyday life, even at the level of terror. As Deuze observes (2012, p. 261), people nowadays know that everything they do in life could be recorded, archived, edited, redacted, and publicised on a continuous basis – it is a world that lives in the moment of recording itself. It is as if the very technology of modern media is creating an affective proximity, as Kavka says (2008, p. 3), foreclosing distance and blurring the lines between lived and mediated forms of reality. Papacharissi (2015, p. 52) applies similar logic to social media such as Twitter where the "always-on" nature of the medium produces an "ambient information sharing environment." There are then times when reporters are sucked into this emotional environment and break with normative values of detachment. When ISIS gunmen rampaged through Paris in November 2015, killing 130 people, journalists descended on the French capital from across the world. The BBC's Graham Satchell, an experienced correspondent reporting "live" from Paris on breakfast television the day after the attacks, injected his own opinion into the script, only to break down in tears on camera. Standing in front of a fountain strewn with flowers in memory of the dead, he stated: "Last night ... the Eiffel Tower was lit up in red, white and blue, which I think is a sign of hope." Afterwards, he said in a Twitter post he was mortified at his behaviour (the discourse and practice of journalism are in this case very different). But his Twitter followers were full of praise for the human emotion and empathy he had shown, further illustrating how today's consumers of news expect their correspondents to wear their feelings on their sleeve. Reporters are no longer just expected to show authority but also personality. As Anne Perkins, the former deputy political editor of *The Guardian*, wrote the next day (2015):

> Viewers and listeners want a human account of a human experience conveyed with superhuman fluency and accuracy. They want to be able to empathise not just with the victims, but with the reporter, their guide through the victims' experience. Satchell's emotional crisis was enthusiastically received by viewers. Yet while I have every sympathy with him, I do wonder what will come next.

That critical comment reveals the deep divisions between those who cling to the normative values of objectivity and detachment and those who believe that embracing emotion is not only expected but also legitimate. The ground is shifting in favour of the latter.

The journalist as a brand and marketing agent

A second fundamental normative value that is being challenged in this networked environment is the journalistic culture of independence or autonomy from commercial interests. Linked to the rise of emotion discussed above, this development also owes much to cultural and organisational shifts that are coursing through business and society. As consumers of news now expect journalists to show their personality and a "human face," some journalists have been actively building their brand and carefully managing their identity through social media platforms such as Twitter and Facebook. But in fact, their practice of "personal branding"[5] goes further than that, with some journalists crossing, wittingly or unwittingly, a previously recognised boundary line and effectively engaging in marketing activity to promote and support their news organisation.

The Anglo-American norms of journalism that developed in the 19th century dictated a clear separation between the business of news and reporting of news, often known in the Western culture of journalese as a "Chinese Wall." For Coddington, that separation is so fundamental that it is simply known as "the wall" (2015, p. 67). Crucially, as long as newspapers prospered, journalists were able to believe that they had succeeded in building a wall between "church and state" (ibid, p. 70). This often manifested itself through physical separation: the newsroom and business sides of a newspaper were on separate floors. As one of the contributors to this volume *New Journalisms* has observed elsewhere, the Canadian Press news agency still has two distinct entrances on the same street in Toronto, one for journalists and one for business staff (Blanchett Neheli, 2019). But today, a practical problem lies in the dire financial straits faced by news organisations. And while the journalist may be the essential unit of ethical agency, he or she does not operate in a vacuum – many are employees of large corporations, the primary aim of which is to maximise the return to shareholders (Richards, 2004, p. 119). In this difficult environment, it hardly comes as a surprise that journalists are under pressure to help their employers garner online clicks and, in practice, become part of what used to be considered a marketing role. Some scholars have asked whether it is time to reconsider whether the wall is ripe for renegotiation (Artemas, Vos and Duffy, 2018, p. 1004). But in fact, there is clear evidence that it is already being renegotiated and quietly breached.

One of the main tools that has emerged for the construction of a journalist's identity is Twitter, now with more than 335 million users worldwide. This provides an ideal platform to gain visibility, credibility, and prestige (Barthel, Moon and Mari, 2015, p. 2). Molyneux, Holton, and Lewis argue that journalists engage in three levels of "branding" through their use of Twitter: promoting the self, their employer's news organisation, and the institution of journalism at large (2018, p. 1386). It follows that such branding is a product of several pressures that journalists, their organisation, and their occupation are facing (ibid, p. 1391). Their study of US journalists found that 58% of their tweets included elements of branding. My own investigation of ten top UK lobby correspondents in the Houses of Parliament showed that all of them used Twitter in one way or another to promote their own work, that of their colleagues, and their news organisation (Jukes, 2019). ITV's chief political correspondent Robert Peston, for example, has developed a cult of personality through his use of Twitter and during the party-political conference season in September 2018 28% of his tweets or retweets promoted either his political talk show on television, his blogs, or other commentaries. The same trend was also apparent with top newspaper lobby correspondents. *The Guardian's* joint political editor Heather Stewart used 31.6% of her tweets or retweets to promote her own stories or those of her *Guardian* colleagues. In one tweet, Stewart, who attended the Labour Party annual conference in Liverpool, commented:

> I am bloody proud to work for the paper that exposed the Windrush[6] scandal, which Jeremy Corbyn spoke about so movingly in his conference speech yesterday. Just saying.

The codes of conduct under which such journalists operate – either as public service broadcasters or newspaper reporters – tread a narrow line between pointing out the risks of social media to normative values of objectivity while at the same time allowing some freedom of expression and recognising that consumers of news are interested in the human face of their journalists. "Social media," the BBC's guidelines say, "is all about personality and being human" (2015). *The Telegraph's* guidelines (2018) go even further. On the one hand they stick to the normative discourse about independence from commercial interests or those of advertisers. But on the other hand, they suggest a subtle shift in the boundary of what is now acceptable practice, stating:

> It is entirely appropriate, and indeed essential, that editorial staff understand and contribute to the commercial success of the Telegraph.

None of the political journalists interviewed as part of that research felt they were crossing a line into commercial activity by developing their own brand or promoting their news organisation (Jukes, 2019). One newspaper correspondent said:

> We are all in a war for ears, a war for eyeballs, we are all trying to make our pieces more attractive and persuasive and it is therefore my job. I am not measured by how many clicks I get but the company is trying to build subscriptions. . . . I feel it is my job to get people to look at my stuff and to promote the work of the paper – that's what pays my bills.

This analysis and those of others (Barthel, Moon and Mari, 2015; Brems et al., 2017; Lough, Molyneux and Holton, 2017; Molyneux, 2015; Molyneux and Holton, 2015; Molyneux, Holton and Lewis, 2018) show clearly that journalists today accept the practice of personal branding as second nature – a far cry from the aloof detachment that might have been typical of a journalist's identity even two decades ago. What is interesting in this case is that not only has practice changed on the ground but that the discourse around journalism has also shifted. For some journalists, the desire to create a public identity has led them to engage without criticism in what in the recent past would have been frowned upon as marketing activity.

How the norm of balance is failing the public

One of journalism's greatest challenges over the past few years, and one that is also dislodging previously stable notions of values and identity, has been the rise of populism, nationalism, and, at times, downright xenophobia. The election of President Trump in 2016 and the Brexit referendum campaign in the United Kingdom during the same year showed the Anglo-American model of journalism to be seriously flawed. It revealed media cultures that were elitist, out of touch, and, in some cases, wedded to normative values of balance that failed to capture the real story and at times gave credibility to frankly outlandish views. More than two years on, these failings are slowly being recognised and the concept of balance is rightly one of the norms that is under increasing scrutiny. For Zelizer, the US and British press failed to serve the electorate in the Trump and Brexit campaigns, exacerbated in part by a fixation with method and collusion with power (2018, p. 149). It is, she argues, time for an "immediate reset" (ibid, p. 152).

While the concept of balance is deeply ingrained in the psyche of Anglo-American journalism, and particularly in the case of British public service broadcasters regulated by Ofcom, it is also highly problematic. The value of balance has deep roots, being one of the core components of the objectivity paradigm set out by David Mindich in his influential 1998 account *Just the facts – how objectivity came to define American journalism*. In theory, the concept is designed to root out bias in reporting by ensuring all sides to an argument are heard. According to Entman (1989), balance aims for neutrality, requiring reporters to represent conflicting sides in any serious dispute and provide both parties with roughly equal attention. But therein lies the problem. It was laid bare during the Balkans wars of the 1990s when CNN's Christiane Amanpour, at the height of the bloody civil conflict, voiced her concerns about false balance and called for a reappraisal of objectivity, saying that this meant giving all sides a fair hearing but *not* treating all sides equally. Objectivity, she argued, had to go hand in hand with morality. She returned to the topic in 2016, saying that much of the media was "tying itself up in knots" trying to differentiate between balance, objectivity, neutrality, and crucially, the truth. She added (2016):

> We cannot continue the old paradigm, we cannot, for instance keep saying, like it was over global warming, where 99.9% of the science, the empirical facts, the evidence, is given equal play with the tiny minority of deniers. . . . I believe in being truthful, not neutral. I believe we must stop banalizing the truth.

But this is exactly what broadcasters in the United States and United Kingdom did during the respective election and EU referendum campaigns of 2016. As a consequence, it was for Zelizer one of the worst periods for Anglo-American news, providing two profound disruptions of the elite consensus on which much of the shared journalism culture rests (2018, p. 146). Journalism failed to engage meaningfully with the events (ibid, p. 140).

Not only were the US networks rooted in the normative methodology of balance, the financial crisis coursing through the media made coverage of Trump irresistible. A network like CNN had made its name with breaking news, but breaking news does not happen every day – until, that is, the Trump election campaign. The former reality TV star, with his outspoken anti-establishment views and electric campaign rallies, was a godsend to broadcasters and advertisers alike. As *The New York Times* wrote after the election: "CNN had a problem, Trump solved it" (2017). While broadcasters could argue they were being balanced in their election coverage, their finances were rapidly improving – it was like broadcasting the Super Bowl every day. The US media analysis company mediaQuant calculated that Trump received the equivalent of $5.0 billion in free media coverage. According to Nielsen Research, the Fox network recorded the best quarter in the history of 24-hour cable news in the first three months of 2017. For CNN, it was the best quarter for 17 years. Emphasising the slavish drive for balance, US coverage focused almost exclusively on the "horse race" between Trump and his Democrat rival Hillary Clinton, with policy issues taking up only 10% of reports.

The same problem with what has now become labelled "false balance" was present throughout the EU referendum campaign. Few would expect balance of any kind from Britain's newspapers, which for many years have been highly politicised (well outside the confines of their leader columns or "op-ed" pages). This was graphically illustrated in the campaign in which many right-wing "Leave" campaigning newspapers demonised immigrants and refugees and *The Daily Mail* served up the headline "*Enemies of the People*" when three judges ruled that parliament should have the final say in beginning the process of Brexit. Britain's public service broadcasters, including the BBC, are subject to clear rules in how they cover such political campaigns and have been widely perceived to have failed to distinguish between the values of balance and impartiality. A study by Cushion and Lewis of television coverage during the ten-week campaign found that broadcasters maintained a strict adherence to a binary balance between Leave and Remain actors and issues, with journalists reluctant to contextualise or challenge the tit-for-tat claims and counter-claims (2017, p. 208). In a similar analysis to that applied to the Balkans wars by Amanpour, the authors argue that journalists needed to adopt an evidence-based approach to impartiality in which they independently explored the veracity of claims and had the editorial freedom to challenge them (ibid). In theory, UK broadcasters need to uphold the concept of "due impartiality" under Ofcom rules in news and current affairs programming, a concept that goes beyond strict balance between opposing sides in an argument. But while broadcasters recognise that this goes beyond just giving all views equal airtime, what was served up was effectively a notion of "stop watch" balance. The Cushion and Lewis analysis concludes that most broadcasters, including the BBC, ITV, and Channel 4, were "doggedly even-handed" in balancing the statistical claims of the Leave and Remain campaigns (ibid, p. 217). Predictably, in the aftermath of the historic vote to leave the EU, the BBC was widely criticised by the losing Remainers for giving too much credence to claims by Leave. The BBC's then director of news, James Harding, dismissed this charge of false balance or equivalence, saying the news operation had been keenly aware of the risk (2016). But few of the BBC's critics were convinced, least of all the British public; one Ipsos MORI poll conducted just before the vote found that less than one third of those questioned felt well or very well informed. It is hard to see how the concept of stopwatch balance can still serve the public in an age when political campaigns can be so driven, and at times manipulated, by the use of social media.

Breaking the taboo around collaboration

In the past, the discourse and practice of journalism has given pride of place to exclusivity – the "scoop" – and competition. But over the past few years a combination of factors has conspired to break down traditional resistance to collaboration, in turn opening up new avenues for investigative journalism. A flood of information now confronts journalists, not least from data leaks of sensitive security or financial data. These have led mainstream news organisations to pool their resources as they sift through material for multiple stories. The stories that became known as the Panama and Paradise papers could not have been produced in anything like the same speed by one newsroom.[7] That has become essential not just because of the sheer volume of data, but because newsrooms have been depleted by the financial crisis facing journalism; one organisation just cannot deal with long-term complex investigations (Sambrook, 2018, p. 1).

Collaboration is, of course, far from new. The Associated Press came into being in 1846 because US newspapers couldn't afford to cover the Mexican-American

War (Lewis, 2018, p. 5). At times of war news organisations have often pooled cov-erage, either because of the risk to their journalists or because governments waging wars have insisted on it to exercise control. But news thrives on competition and while journalists naturally collaborate with their sources to secure stories, they are notoriously possessive about owning the actual news they have produced. Return-ing to the start of this chapter, Bob Woodward and Carl Bernstein certainly did not share the identity of their Watergate source "Deep Throat" with rival newsrooms. Journalists are ready to, and have, gone to jail rather than naming their source. Equally, in the early days of news websites during the late 1990s many traditional newspapers held back exclusive stories from the web to preserve their scoop (and prevent rivals copying it) until the overnight print editions were published. Those days are long gone, with live breaking news blogs now routine; scoops simply play out these days in real time but the instinct is still to strive for exclusivity, a culture that stretches from junior reporters to editors and the business executives running a news organisation.

The change in attitude towards collaboration has much to do with the shift towards a networked news environment. But it suddenly gained momentum over the past few years thanks to the overwhelming size of recent data leaks – the Panama Papers alone consisted of 11.5 million documents, 4.8 million of which were e-mails and constituted the biggest data leak to date. The Munich-based *Sueddeutsche Zeitung* shared the material with the International Consortium of Investigative Journalists (ICIJ) in Washington, DC. The collaboration was able to bring together more than 400 journalists across six continents, including in the United Kingdom from *The Guardian* and BBC. The subsequent exposure of wide-spread tax evasion and financial and political corruption was equally global in its reporting and earned the team a coveted Pulitzer Prize. The international scope of such stories also makes it impossible to cover them from the perspective of one news organisation, but in his analysis of the Panama Papers Sambrook stresses that the deeply ingrained competitive instincts of each partner are still very much alive and need to be carefully managed in a collaboration. Here, the ICIJ played the role of a trusted and neutral intermediary, nurturing partnerships in a non-competitive way (2018, p. 28). Sambrook added:

> A neutral partner – such as a non-profit news organisation or jointly owned joint venture – can play a valuable role in managing tensions and potential conflicts of interest between partners. In the end, one trusted party has to make decisions and hold other partners to account.

In the case of both the Panama and Paradise papers, the ICIJ was also able to pro-vide and develop the technology needed to handle the volume of data (ibid, p. 37).

There will inevitably be tension among consortium members about when news should be released as they try to coordinate between the conflicting interests of daily and weekly publications, online operations, and broadcasters. But in an era when news organisations are struggling to maintain resources to handle complex international stories, collaboration is proving to be a valid approach to advance investigative journalism when it might otherwise not be possible.

Conclusion

If there ever was a monolithic culture of Anglo-American journalism, it is today truly fragmented. In many key aspects, the discourse of who journalists are and what they do has remained remarkably consistent in the face of social media disruption. But beneath the surface, the day-to-day practice of news-gathering and production has changed substantially and, with it, some of the normative values that grew out of the 19th century.

This chapter has argued that it is time to recognise some of these changes, either because they are an inevitable development in today's networked media environment, or because they represent better ways of achieving journalism's core mission of seeking the truth and holding power to account. Part of that is the recognition that the old hierarchies of news production and employment practices are changing in a casualised labour market where very few journalists now have only one or two employers in their lifetime and can look forward to a pension. That means that Journalism Studies needs to shift its focus away from sole concentration on legacy news organisations and the traditional newsroom to embrace the pure online players such as BuzzFeed and the HuffPost as well as start-ups and freelancers working from short-term contract to short-term contract.

Some of the changes of practice explored in this chapter have become normalised and can no longer be categorised as a "challenge," such as personal branding and a journalist's willingness to promote his or her own stories and news organisation. The separation of news and the business of news, or "church and state," has been diluted and with it the identity of the journalist as an aloof outsider. The inevitable consequence is that journalism is more exposed to pressures of the business. When it comes to emotion, the age-old tension between normative values of detachment and the need to engage audiences remains, but there is an increasing acceptance by journalists, and an expectation from viewers and readers, that showing emotion is no longer taboo. The furore over coverage of the US presidential election and EU referendum campaign has led to a widespread consensus that journalism needs to jettison simplified notions of balance and take seriously its duty to apply principles of due impartiality that require critical assessment of claim and counter-claim. And in the face of dwindling editorial resources and the need to manage large data leaks, news organisations have discovered that collaboration can pay dividends for investigative journalism and complement the cut-throat competition that has always lain at the heart of the news industry.

Today a journalist's identity is ever shifting. Sometimes the narrative of what it is to be a journalist changes in lockstep with practice – simplified notions of balance have run their course, and collaboration is essential in an age of big data leaks. At other times the narrative remains doggedly entrenched but actual practice shifts – emotion is no longer taboo, and promoting your own work and news organisation is seen as natural and common sense in hard times. It is hardly surprising in today's turbulent media landscape that the notion of a journalist's identity is no longer as clear as it was in the heyday of Woodward and Bernstein.

Notes

1 The term has been adopted to describe features of today's labour market which is characterised by the high number of short-term contracts or freelance work (as opposed to permanent jobs).
2 The 2015 film *Spotlight* tells the story of *The Boston Globe's* investigative reporting team as it tracked down cases of child sexual abuse by Roman Catholic priests in the Boston area; the 2017 film *The Post* dramatises the story of *Washington Post* journalists and their fight to publish the "Pentagon Papers," classified documents about US involvement in the Vietnam War.
3 This is a reference to Gay Tuchman's phrase the "strategic ritual of objectivity" which she coined in her seminal 1972 paper Objectivity as Strategic Ritual: An Examination of Newsmen's Notions of Objectivity.
4 *Benefit Street* was a controversial 2014 documentary series which focused on the lives of residents of a street in Birmingham where 90% of the occupants were on social benefits. *The Mighty Redcar* was a 2018 series by the BBC marketed as a "real-life soap opera" depicting the lives of young people in the northern town after the closure of its steel works.
5 Branding is understood as the action of differentiating an individual, entity, or product from others (Murphy, 1987).
6 *The Guardian* broke the story of the UK government's mistreatment of the so-called Windrush immigrants to Britain who had arrived from the Caribbean in the years after World War II. Windrush referred to the name of one of the ships that arrived in London from Jamaica in 1948.
7 In 2015, the *Sueddeutsche Zeitung* received a leak of 11.5 million documents relating to offshore investments which became known as the "Panama Papers"; a second leak to two reporters at the same newspaper about a year later included 13.4 million documents on a similar subject and became known as the "Paradise Papers."

References

Allan, S. (2013). *Citizen witnessing: Revisioning journalism in times of crisis*. Cambridge: Polity Press.
Amanpour, C. (2016). *International press freedom awards*. Committee to Project Journalists, 22 Nov. Available at: https://cpj.org/awards/2016/christiane-amanpour.php.
Artemas, K., Vos, T. P. and Duffy, M. (2018). Journalism hits a wall: Rhetorical construction of newspapers' editorial and advertising relationship. *Journalism Studies*, 19(7), pp. 1004–1020.
Barthel, M. L., Moon, R. and Mari, W. (2015). *Who retweets whom: How digital and legacy journalists interact on Twitter*. Tow Center for Digital Journalism. Available at: http://towcenter.org/research/whoretweets- whom-how-digital-and-legacy-journalists-interact-on-twitter/.
BBC. (2015). *Social media guidelines for staff*. Available at: http://news.bbc.co.uk/1/shared/bsp/hi/pdfs/26_03_15_bbc_news_group_social_media_guidance.pdf.
Beckett, C. and Mansell, R. (2008). Crossing boundaries: New media and networked journalism. *Communication, Culture & Critique*, 1(1), pp. 92–104.
Bell, M. (1996). *In harm's way*. London: Penguin Books.
Blanchett Neheli, N. (2019). *Metrics and analytics in the newsroom: An ethnographic study exploring how audience data are changing journalistic practice*, doctoral dissertation, Bournemouth University.

Brems, C., Temmerman, M., Graham, T. and Broersma, M. (2017). Personal branding on Twitter: How employed and freelance journalists stage themselves on social media. *Digital Journalism*, 5(4), pp. 443–459.

Bruns, A. (2003). Gatewatching not gatekeeping: Collaborative online news. *Media International Australia Incorporating Culture and Policy: Quarterly Journal of Media Research and Resources*, 107, pp. 31–44.

Bruns, A. (2011). News Produsage in a pro-am mediasphere: Why citizen journalism matters. In: Meikle, G. and Redden, G., eds., *News online: Transformations and continuities*. Basingstoke: Palgrave Macmillan.

Carlson, M. and Lewis, S. (2015). *Boundaries of journalism: Professionalism, practices and participation*. London: Routledge.

Coddington, M. (2015). The wall becomes a curtain: Revisiting journalism's news-business boundary. In: Carlson, M. and Lewis, C., eds., *Boundaries of journalism: Professionalism, practices and participation*. London: Routledge.

Coward, R. (2013). *Speaking personally: The rise of subjective and confessional journalism*. Basingstoke: Macmillan International Higher Education.

Cunningham, B. (2003). Rethinking objectivity. *Columbia Journalism Review*, July–Aug. Available at: www.cjr.org/feature/rethinking_objectivity.php?page=all&print=true.

Cushion, S. and Lewis, J. (2017). Impartiality, statistical tit-for-tats and the construction of balance: UK television news reporting of the 2016 EU referendum campaign. *European Journal of Communication*, 32(3), pp. 208–223.

Deuze, M. (2012). *Media life*. Cambridge: Polity Press.

Deuze, M. and Witschge, T. (2017). Beyond journalism: Theorizing the transformation of journalism. *Journalism*, 19(2), pp. 165–181.

Domke, D., Perlmutter, D. and Spratt, M. (2002). The primes of our times? An examination of the "power" of visual images. *Journalism*, 3(2), pp. 131–159.

Entman, R. M. (1989). How the media affect what people think: An information processing approach. *The Journal of Politics*, 51(2), pp. 347–370.

Furedi, F. (2003). *Therapy culture: Capturing vulnerability in an uncertain age*. London: Routledge.

Harding, J. (2016). A truly balanced view from the BBC: Don't blame us for Brexit. *The Guardian*, 25 Sept. Available at: www.theguardian.com/commentisfree/2016/sep/24/dont-blame-bbc-for-brexit-false-balance.

Jenkins, H. (2014). Rethinking 'rethinking convergence/culture'. *Cultural Studies*, 28(2), 267–297.

Jukes, S. (2018). Back to the future: How UK-based news organisations are rediscovering objectivity. *Journalism Practice*, 12(8), pp. 1029–1038.

Jukes, S. (2019). Crossing the line between news and the business of news: Exploring journalists' use of Twitter. *Media and Communication*, 7(1).

Kavka, M. (2008). *Reality television, affect and intimacy*. London: Palgrave Macmillan.

Lewis, C. (2018). Tear down these walls: Innovations in collaborative accountability research and reporting. In: Sambrook, R., ed., *Global teamwork: The rise of collaboration in investigative journalism*. Oxford: Reuters Institute for the Study of Journalism.

Lough, K., Molyneux, L., & Holton, A. E. (2017). A clearer picture: Journalistic identity practices in words and images on Twitter. *Journalism Practice*, 12(10), 1277–1291.

Mahler, J. (2017). CNN had a problem, Trump solved it. *New York Times Magazine*, 24 Apr. Available at: www.nytimes.com/ 2017/ 04/ 04/ magazine/cnn-had-a-problem-donald-trump-solved-it.html.

Maras, S. (2013). *Objectivity in journalism*. Cambridge: Polity Press.

Mindich, D. (1998). *Just the facts – how objectivity came to define American journalism*. New York: New York University Press.

Molyneux, L. (2015). What journalists retweet: Opinion, humor, and brand development on Twitter. *Journalism*, 16(7), pp. 920–935.

Molyneux, L. and Holton, A. (2015). Branding (health) journalism: Perceptions, practices, and emerging norms. *Digital Journalism*, 3(2), pp. 225–242.

Molyneux, L., Holton, A. and Lewis, S. C. (2018). How journalists engage in branding on Twitter: Individual, organizational, and institutional levels. *Information, Communication & Society*, 21(10), pp. 1386–1401.

Murphy, J. M., ed. (1987). *Branding: A key marketing tool.* London: Palgrave Macmillan.

Papacharissi, Z. (2015). *Affective publics: Sentiment, technology, and politics.* New York, NY: Oxford University Press.

Perkins, A. (2015). The sight of a reporter expressing emption is a sign of the times. *The Guardian*, 18 Nov. Available at: www.theguardian.com/commentisfree/2015/nov/18/reporter-emotion-bbc-graham-satchell-paris-attacks.

Plummer, K. (2001). *Documents of life 2: An invitation to a critical humanism.* Vol. 2. London: Sage Publications Ltd.

Ramdani, N. (2013). Assad is a war criminal, but an attack will do nothing for the people of Syria. *The Observer*, 31 Aug. Available at: www.theguardian.com/commentisfree/2013/aug/31/syria-assad-warcriminal.

Reuters Institute for the Study of Journalism (2018). *Digital news report 2018.* Oxford: Reuters Institute for the Study of Journalism.

Richards, B. and Rees, G. (2011). The management of emotion in British journalism. *Media, Culture & Society*, 33(6), pp. 851–867.

Richards, I. (2004). Stakeholders versus shareholders: Journalism, business, and ethics. *Journal of Mass Media Ethics*, 19(2), pp. 119–129.

Rusbridger, A. (2018). *Breaking news. The remaking of journalism and why it matters now.* Edinburgh: Canongate Books Ltd.

Sambrook, R. (2018). *Global teamwork: The rise of collaboration in investigative journalism.* Edited by Richard Sambrook. Oxford: Reuters Institute for the Study of Journalism.

Schudson, M. (2002). What's unusual about covering politics as usual. In: Zelizer, B. and Allan, S., eds., *Journalism after September 11.* London: Routledge.

Sontag, S. (2003). *Regarding the pain of others.* London: Penguin Books.

Sreberny, A. (2002). Trauma talk: Reconfiguring the inside and outside. In: Zelizer, B. and Allan, S., eds., *Journalism after September 11.* London: Routledge.

The Telegraph. (2018). *Editorial and commercial guidelines.* Available at: www.telegraph.co.uk/about-us/editorial-and-commercial-guidelines/.

Viner, K. (2018). Guardian has received support from one million people. *Society of Editors*, 5 Nov. Available at: www.societyofeditors.org/soe_news/guardian-has-received-financial-support-from-one-million-people-says-katharine-viner/.

Wahl-Jorgensen, K. (2009). On the newsroom-centricity of journalism ethnography. *Journalism and Anthropology*, pp. 21–35.

Wahl-Jorgensen, K. (2013). The strategic ritual of emotionality: A case study of Pulitzer Prize-winning articles. *Journalism*, 14(1), pp. 129–145.

Waisbord, S. (2013). *Reinventing professionalism: Journalism and news in global perspective.* Cambridge: Polity Press.

Witschge, T., Anderson, C. W., Domingo, D. and Hermida, A. (2018). Dealing with the mess (we made): Unravelling hybridity, normativity, and complexity in journalism studies. *Journalism*, 20(5), pp. 651–659.

Zelizer, B. (1993). Journalists as interpretive communities. *Critical Studies in Mass Communication*, 10, pp. 219–237.

Zelizer, B. (2018). Resetting journalism in the aftermath of Brexit and Trump. *European Journal of Communication*, 33(2), pp. 140–156.

PART II
New practices

4

CAN ANALYTICS HELP SAVE LOCAL NEWSPAPERS?

Nicole Blanchett Neheli

This chapter explores the effects of digital production on journalistic values, focusing on how a growing reliance on metrics and analytics is impacting editorial decision-making in local newsrooms. It posits how effective use of audience data might help such newsrooms survive.

Introduction

On the face of it, the *Bournemouth Daily Echo*, housed in a majestic Art Deco building close to the sandy beaches of a small English seaside town, and *The Hamilton Spectator*, operating in new-build offices in an industrialised city southwest of Toronto, Canada, would appear to have little in common. The two local newspapers are more than 3,500 miles apart and operate in completely different cultural and social environments. But geography aside, the two newspapers on different sides of the Atlantic share a similar challenge – they are both grappling with the disruption to "legacy" news organisations wrought by digital production and social media, and both are trying to come to terms with a rich new source of data about their readers in the shape of comprehensive newsroom analytics.

This chapter explores, through the perspective of these two local newspapers, how the use of newsroom analytics is changing the fabric of what makes local, local, and how such changes are challenging definitions of journalism and the traditional values associated with it. Almost every local newsroom is facing a critical shortage of money, resources, and time – and that's if they're lucky enough to still exist. Local, legacy newspapers, particularly, have been decimated by an onslaught of closures and mega-media mergers. Typically, they have fewer bodies to cover what were previously considered local news staples, such as the courts and city council. Many that have survived are still figuring out how to replace lost print revenues and manage shifting means of content consumption. Once, there was a finite local focus, target audience, and delivery mechanism. Now, ingrained routines are being transformed by a market opened wide by the Internet, shared resources, the expectation of multiplatform coverage, obligatory self-promotion and branding on social media, and the influence of metrics and analytics.[1]

The chapter uses an ethnographic approach to explore from within the newsroom how the two local newspapers, *The Hamilton Spectator* and *Bournemouth Daily Echo*, are working to carve out a future in an exasperatingly fluid media landscape.[2] Both are developing practice to use metrics and analytics in a way that aligns with the goals of a much larger collective, negotiating who and where their audience is, and working at a relentless pace to meet output demands. Can the use of analytics give fresh insight into the audience and help save local newspapers from their seemingly steady decline? Or is the lack of time and training to use audience data contributing to an erosion of journalistic values? My research shows the answer to both questions is complex. However, by comparing and contrasting these two organisations, the chapter aims to further understanding of the effects of digital production and how a growing reliance on metrics and analytics is impacting local newsrooms.

Local news matters

The importance of local journalism is widely recognised (Radcliffe and Ali, 2017). However, due to cuts that have gutted coverage of civic institutions, such as school boards and city halls (Greenspon, 2017), and the sweeping loss of local news agencies (Abernathy, 2016), there is a dearth of local news (Wardle and Derakhshan, 2017; Newman, 2018). Referring to a lack of reporting on issues that resulted in London's Grenfell Tower fire that killed 72 residents, Feller (2017) described local newspapers as "toothless" because they are "published against the odds with no money and few staff" (p. 14). Although there are government initiatives to shore up local coverage in both England and Canada (Rispoli and Aaron, 2018),[3] there are many common issues faced by local news organisations working to make the jump to digital, often operating within a much larger media conglomerate. The long list includes: using editorial strategies and content management systems (CMS) that frequently work better for the collective than individual outlets; difficult-to-meet website targets set by head office; a reliance on social media despite recognising the inherent shortcomings of doing so; cost cutting leading to closures and layoffs; the fact that the overwhelming majority of revenue still comes from print (Jenkins and Kleis Nielsen, 2018); and the dramatic shrinking of print revenue and audiences (Cornia et al., 2017; Thurman and Fletcher, 2017).

Defining the target audience, along with content creation and promotion, has also become much more complicated than it used to be in local newsrooms. Some local offices write or promote stories to be consumed on an international scale – an "anyone anywhere" demographic that can be in contrast to more specifically local content created for their traditional platforms of delivery. On a less expansive scale, some local newsrooms develop more nationally focused stories in order to build scale or use regional content from other partners within a media conglomerate to keep web pages active and cycle ad impressions, broadening their traditional local focus. Even if newsrooms maintain strictly local breadth, or a hyper-local focus online, they might still be part of a larger conglomerate or organisation that operates on a national/international scale and sets traffic targets (Blanchett Neheli, 2019). Typically, though, there is a lot less local coverage on local news websites than one might expect (Napoli et al., 2018; Buchanan, 2018).[4]

The loss of a local focus on many local websites is just one example of the wider impact of the use of metrics and analytics on journalistic practice (Anderson, 2011; Bright and Nicholls, 2014; Tandoc, 2014; Schlesinger and Doyle, 2015; Bunce, 2017; Björkman and Franco, 2017). In an effort to grow the digital audience traffic metrics are the most commonly used (ICFJ, 2017). This is despite a resurgence of the paywall (Madrigal, 2017), more talk of subscription models (Newman et al., 2018), and mounting evidence that the data they provide are unreliable (Read, 2018). Because such metrics are easily understood and accessible, they often "become proxies" for "journalistic ideals" (Ferrer-Conill and Tandoc, 2018, p. 12). Widely popular stories are also seen as more valuable because pushing pageviews increases the cycling of ad impressions[5] (Cohen, 2018; Christin, 2018; Nelson, 2018). This can result in local newsrooms posting content with little relevance to their communities (Blanchett Neheli, 2018) and falling victim to media logic, where processes are designed around ease of production and attracting eyeballs versus promoting informed discourse (Altheide and Snow, 1979).

Compared to my own experience working in a local newsroom, the pace of production now borders on absurdity, something referred to as "churnalism" (Davies, 2008, p. 59), or "factory" or "assembly-line" (Carey, 2009; Cohen, 2015) news production. There is less original reporting (Phillips, 2010; Lee-Wright, 2012; Le Cam and Domingo, 2015) and, often, an "emphasis on profits over civic responsibility" (Marwick and Lewis, 2017, p. 47). On the newsroom floor, this can result in a stark difference in the narrative between what journalists say they do or feel they should do to uphold traditional values and what they actually do or are able to do because of the demands of their daily routines,[6] something that is blatantly evident looking at the journalists working in the newsrooms discussed in this chapter.

Two local newspapers in flux

The Hamilton Spectator has been in publication for almost 200 years; however, the struggle to cover its community is growing increasingly difficult. *The Spectator* operates under the umbrella company of Metroland Media (parent company TorStar), and there have been widespread cuts across the organisation.[7] There has also been widespread centralisation of services in order to deflect operating costs. This was evident at *The Spectator* where Metroland's copy-editing team[8] managed the content of more than a hundred Metroland publications, with on average, each person handling eight items per hour. On a busy day, the team processed 1,200 pieces of content. *The Spectator's* digital team ran *thespec.com* and websites for two other publications, *The Waterloo Region Record* and *Guelph Mercury*. Its press also printed all or part of a number of other papers and community weeklies and *The Spectator* operated as a flyer printing and distribution hub for Metroland.

The *Bournemouth Daily Echo*, in production since 1900, is also run under a much larger umbrella group, Newsquest, owned by the US-based Gannett Inc., which was also centralising services. The *Echo* was printed at another Newsquest outlet in Weymouth, and extra space in the *Echo*'s underutilised building was rented out as a source of revenue, as was done at *The Spectator*. Like Metroland, Newsquest had created a centralised editing team but later cut it to save costs, leaving reporters and newsroom managers at the *Echo* also doing the job of copy-editors (or "subs"). One editor said those working on the news desk could look at/edit "well over a hundred stories a day." At the time of my observation, a plan was also being implemented to eliminate production staff by having reporters use tools such as page templates to "streamline" production. All reporters also contributed to multiple publications.[9]

Limited resources, multiplatform delivery, the need to supply multiple versions of stories and live coverage of events, such as court trials via Twitter, and having a social media presence resulted in increased workloads for staff in both newsrooms. Both newsrooms also had shared CMSs that were not necessarily best suited to promote content in their local environments and allowed limited control on how to position stories. Both also used analytics systems/dashboards and had monitors showing a variety of metrics hanging in the newsroom. They also both had traffic targets. At *The Spectator*, there were monthly pageview website targets, compiled to meet a goal of annual growth. At the *Echo*, every reporter story posted on the web was expected to reach a benchmark of 2,500 pageviews, and staff on the newsroom floor consistently discussed the pressure to meet unique-user targets.[10]

Deuze and Witschge describe the number of layoffs in journalism as "astounding" (2017, p. 6), and this was evident at both local newspapers in this study, struggling to produce sufficient content after drastic reductions in staff. One reporter at *The Spectator* said there were only about a third of the reporters left in the newsroom compared to when she started six years ago,[11] and all reporters discussed the pressure to deliver multiple versions of stories and/or complete more feature-style or investigative stories while still contributing daily content. Participants at both sites of study often held multiple roles. For example, at the *Echo*, the business and technology editor/reporter was also responsible for writing nostalgia stories, the local history section, did general reporting, and, as required, helped run the news desk.

Reporters at the *Echo*, on average, were expected to write ten stories a day (of varying sizes) and, as outlined earlier, do much of their own production work. At the time of my observation, Newsquest's editorial development director Toby Granville said no reporters had been "cut." However, journalists working in the newsroom noted that within the past two years seven had been lost through attrition and had not been replaced. Another reporter, who was described as integral to the newsroom, resigned during one of my visits because of what was described as the "relentless" pace of the job and could not be replaced due to further budget cuts. After my observation, a part-time reporter was let go. Despite assertions that changes in the newsroom had no negative impact on the work of reporters, those working in the newsroom had a different viewpoint. One journalist described himself as "massively disillusioned." He readily accepted the business needed to evolve due to loss of revenue but said at some point how cuts to the newsroom were impacting quality journalism had to be considered in order to "keep standards." Otherwise, it would be a "downward spiral" and they would no longer be able to hold decision makers in the community to account.

Despite noted similarities, the two sites of study had significant differences in management structure and environment. At *The Spectator*, there was a chief editor and separate managing editors of print and online. At the *Echo*, there was one senior manager, responsible for print and web content who performed the job of both the managing and news editor, positions that were once separate but amalgamated as a cost saving. At *The Spectator*, the vast majority of participants expressed confidence in the quality of journalism but significant apprehension about continued revenue shortfalls and the fact that they saw no clear plan for the future – concerns voiced within a newsroom scattered with empty desks and offices. At the *Echo*, where there were also revenue concerns and empty desks, there seemed more hope of a future for the paper, but greater distress over how the sacrifices needed to save the business were impacting the actual journalism.

The impact of metrics and analytics

There were similarities but also significant differences in the use of audience data between the two newspapers. The concept of dayparting, or aiming to post content at the time of day when it would be most read (Hanusch, 2017), was recognised in both newsrooms. Every digital editor also acknowledged the importance of a photo when posting content on the website or promoting a story in social media in order to expand reach, and that such photos were not always available, or of good quality, due to a growing reliance on reporters to supply pictures. There was also growing understanding of the importance of mobile and reaching readers on multiple platforms. However, the use of metrics and analytics was more widespread and ingrained in practice at the *Echo* than at *The Spectator*.

At *The Spectator*, metrics were primarily used to decide where to place content on the website and perform promotional or, in other words, real-time or short-term, gatekeeping (Blanchett Neheli, 2018) as opposed to deeper analysis of audience data to assist with the development of content. Digital editors incessantly "enhanced" content to improve the traction of stories/get more views by changing the picture or headline, or its position on the website, or, conversely, "de-selected" (Tandoc, 2014) stories, removing them from prominent or "locked" positions on the website if they were not garnering views. Outside the digital team, little importance was placed on the use of analytics, and, in interviews, many expressed concern that using audience data to help make editorial decisions would impinge upon journalistic values.

At the *Echo*, although metrics and analytics were used to manage website content, there were not enough staff to perform the constant surveillance and enhancement to stories on the website that was seen at *The Spectator*.[12] Stories were often left in the same position for several hours on the home page regardless of traffic metrics,[13] and although similar enhancement strategies were used, they were not implemented at the same frenetic pace. In Bournemouth, analytics were often used more for developmental gatekeeping, or, in other words, the longer-term planning of coverage and story selection. The use of analytics in relation to story development for both print and web content became a focus at the *Echo* starting in the autumn of 2016 with the implementation of a Newsquest pilot project called "the data driven newsroom." According to Newsquest's editorial development director Granville, the pilot was designed to get reporters to adapt content based on "what readers want to read" and avoid doing stories that "under-perform" in terms of pageviews.[14] This was done through daily, in-depth analysis of story presentation and promotion with an aim to further develop popular subjects. Multiple journalists from the *Echo* agreed that the initial implementation of the pilot led to better coverage of local issues and less "churnalism." However, although Granville said the protocols instituted during the pilot project were still being followed, including morning meetings with reporters to discuss their analytics and how they might be used in story selection, during the period of my observation, in September 2017, those working in the newsroom said there was no time to follow such protocols. One journalist said deeper analysis of audience data was "out the window" because of staffing cuts. Referencing the use of analytics, an *Echo* reporter said, "When you're in a busy newsroom those slightly more strategic approaches to anything are the first casualty of business."

Churnalism and chasing traffic: a negotiation of time and values

The pace of work at the *Echo* was exemplified by one reporter. When she arrived in the morning, before she even sat down at her desk, the managing editor asked her to add a quote in one story and then add it to the story queue of one of the weekly publications. When told a different story also needed work, she replied that she was waiting for a response and the current version in the system could change significantly. She was then told she needed to update yet another story and was then assigned a new story regarding possible legal trouble for a local businessperson. About an hour later, as she was furiously typing away at her desk, she was asked to take yet another assignment to which she replied, "Yeah, all right" – much less enthusiastically than her responses to the first set of requests. And then, a short time later, she was asked to make a call on a traffic accident.

The managing editor said that although they tried their best to cover the courts and local council they increasingly relied on press releases. An *Echo* reporter said sometimes it was a case of "churn, churn, churn" and there was "relief" when she received a press release written by a former journalist as it could just be "put through" without any editing. Another had developed his own strategy for a ten-minute edit of press releases to ensure, despite so many of them being used, that the

Echo still looked like a "proper paper." This included "shoving" in the quotes that were provided in the press releases rather than trying to get his own, explaining he would likely get the same quotes anyway. Although an efficient, and perhaps necessary, methodology in order to meet the high output demands at the *Echo*, such practice is not "journalism."[15]

The negotiation of journalistic values at *The Spectator* was most evident in practice exhibited by its digital team. As one reporter noted, "The web team knows that the more clicks we get, the more advertising dollars we get and I think that sort of guides their decision-making." An editor said pageviews and advertising impressions were basically "synonymous." As such, and because of traffic targets set by head office, pageviews were a priority and the target audience was expanded to anyone anywhere. The expansion of the target audience, compared to the local focus of *The Spectator*'s print product, led to discord in the newsroom. As one reporter said, "It particularly bothers me when it's stuff we're just picking up from somewhere else, crime stuff in the United States or something that has nothing to do with Hamilton." In response to this concern, another editor said a "great" local story would "trump" everything in terms of popularity on the website, but most local stories were not "great" because they were only important to a "handful of viewers" compared to viral stories that did "remarkably well" in terms of garnering pageviews.

Contrary to *The Spectator*, the hyper-local focus of the print version of the *Echo* extended to the website, to the extent that web editors put up disclaimers on stories not directly related to their catchment area. This was to head off reaction on the paper's active Facebook page, where the audience was vocal in criticising news considered clickbait because it was outside the *Echo*'s local range. As another illustration of how local their coverage was, the managing editor said "they had a bit of a laugh" when another Newsquest outlet, approximately 25 miles away, used one of the *Echo*'s stories about a traffic accident[16] in Bournemouth. He was critical of the other newsroom for breaking the boundary of "local" coverage to get "a few more thousand pageviews."

The digital divide of editing practice

Decisions in relation to what content should go in the print and/or web publications of each newsroom were dealt with quite differently. The chief editor at *The Spectator* said they used significant amounts of external content online that were too "inconsequential" for the newspaper because, in basic terms, the primary goal on the website was to garner traffic and the primary goal of the newspaper was to inform the community. All of the original local reporting produced by reporters was posted to the website for the practical purpose of increasing the flow of stories and to support the narrative that, despite what might be promoted on the website, *The Spectator* still supplied a breadth of online local coverage. However, local stories, generally, were not changed/optimised for web publication and if not locked into a prominent position could be difficult to find due to the large volume of material flowing through the site[17] and a limited search function.

At the *Echo*, though, there was acknowledged and observed effort to make stories posted on the website presented in a manner better suited to the online audience. Also, based on analytics, stories written for the paper that were perceived as having little chance of garnering clicks were not posted on the website,[18] unless they were of great import to the community, for example, a local political story with significant ramifications. As a result of data analysis, at the time of my visit to the *Echo* in autumn 2017, this meant that for both print and web fewer/less involved stories were being done on education and council meetings, more detailed stories were being done on planning applications, and stories on subjects such as road safety might only go in the paper.

Although there may not have been the same constant level of enhancement to web stories and tracking of pageviews at the *Echo* as there was at *The Spectator*, there were comparable pressures. One digital editor at *The Spectator* noted she would post content that made her "cringe" if she knew it would receive lots of pageviews. She said she continually attempted to strike a balance between being "true to the craft" of journalism and giving the audience what it wanted, which also aligned with meeting targets. One digital editor at the *Echo* said the worst pressure was experienced at the end of the month because they relied on breaking news to meet targets and there was no guarantee there would be breaking news in the required timeframe. If they were still short of targets with no breaking story in sight, although she would not resort to posting clickbait, she would promote something "less newsworthy" if there were a chance it would boost the numbers and bridge the target gap.

Cohen documented the potential of analytics to "undermine journalistic autonomy" (2018, p. 9) and Bourdieu noted that the impact of external constraints can create "structural processes" (2005, p. 45) which make journalistic choices "totally preconstrained." Although Schudson posited that journalism's dependence "on the drama of events that neither state nor market nor journalists can fully or even approximately anticipate or control" (2005, p. 219) helps to ensure journalistic autonomy, evidence from this research suggests the pressure to meet traffic targets in the face of a slow news cycle can have the opposite effect.

Negotiating the value of a story and the definition of a journalist

One reporter believed the pressure to meet targets increased the value of the story of "a hamster with two heads" that could "wipe the floor" with a story that took a long time to put together and was important to the community, but could be seen as less valuable in terms of getting "the figures." The dichotomy between effort, quality, and perceived popularity was discussed by multiple journalists. As one reporter at the *Echo* said,

> It does make you think, if I'm putting in a lot of effort into doing something that I think is a quality news story and that's not well-received online, in terms of our business and how analytics are affecting journalism output, I may feel like I shouldn't focus on those kind of more quality stories, but that

is what you kind of set out to do rather than just bits that take 10 minutes to put together.

Although she felt that the use of analytics, overall, had improved the quality of stories done at the *Echo*, one journalist was worried their use was changing the types of stories covered by local newsrooms, saying:

> I do think that a lot of stories don't get covered by papers because they're not in the best interest of your analytics and I think that the stuff that local newspapers do is unique. So, no one else is going to magistrates' court. No one else is going to go to that council meeting or report on it, but sometimes that's not done because people have got their mind on their analytics.

Because of metrics and analytics, the value of the content created by reporters was also being re-evaluated at *The Spectator*, where online stories were locked into a line-up, monitored, or enhanced based on their perceived ability to build traffic. One editor said reporters expressing concern their original content was not getting promoted or was bumped by, for example, a press release, was more about reporter expectations clashing with the online reality:

> If you're a reporter, how does that fit into your sense of value to the organisation or what you've been sort of led to believe your whole working life that your content is the most valuable – and on any given day it might not be?

Social media: beauty and the beast

The need to increase the reach and visibility of stories equated to new expectations for reporters to promote their work on social media at both sites of study, and to provide coverage of events, for example, using Twitter. Newsquest's editorial development director said, ideally, he wanted reporters to "become almost entrepreneurs and market their own content." Reporters at *The Spectator* also referred to being encouraged to build a "brand" on social media. However, there were recognised drawbacks. A digital editor at *The Spectator* said social media was "the beauty and the beast" because it generated more people coming in to the site, but people coming in to the site via social media consumed little content. In a coincidental use of a fairy-tale metaphor, an editor at the *Echo* described Facebook as a "poison chalice." Although they had successfully built a thriving Facebook community where they interacted with the audience and often found valuable stories, when *Echo* readers were "unhappy they let you know en masse." As a result of such interactions, the digital team at the *Echo* had come to the conclusion that there was "good" and "bad" traffic. They believed the only way to build a loyal audience was to avoid alienating readers and potential readers:

> If people are reading a story because they find it interesting, that's what we want. If they're reading a story and are criticising us for the way we've

handled that story, we don't necessarily think that's particularly good traffic, because they may not return on that basis.

Digital editors would also tone down newspaper headlines for the online version of *Echo* stories as a "sensationalist" or "clickbaity" headline might draw more views but was also more likely to generate divisive discourse within their online community.

Regardless of the fact that analytics protocols instituted by head office were not being followed at the *Echo*, analytics and metrics were still being used by all editorial staff, to varying degrees, to determine the selection of stories covered and how they would be treated. At *The Spectator*, however, those working primarily in print had little use for data because, as Usher found, "the relevant social group that would be likely to create a traffic-focused meaning for metrics is the managers" and if that is not done in a "considered way" journalists have no "relevant context to understand the new metrics technology as measurement for quantifying and selecting news" (2013, p. 19). Outside of the Chartbeat monitor hanging in the newsroom, analytics information was available to but not actively shared with *Spectator* reporters, and their observations of the web team's fixation with pageviews did little to provide evidence of how analytics could be used to enhance editorial decision-making. However, despite this, some reporters at *The Spectator* expressed a desire to have access to analytics, or be shown how to better understand the analytics they could access in order to better manage their time to avoid "trying to do a little bit of everything in the hopes that something will turn out well but . . . diluting the final product."

A spectrum of practice

The two case studies in this chapter, and evidence from the larger study from which data were derived (Blanchett Neheli, 2019), provide significant evidence that journalists/newsworkers generally agree on normative journalistic values, such as the importance of verified information and the production of original content that tangibly benefits a particular community – and they measure their work against such values. But it was clear that economic pressures result in a spectrum of normative practice that can be impacted by a number of factors depending on a newsworker's particular position within an organisation. At *The Spectator*, promoting content of little news value in an effort to build the audience was embedded in meeting pageview targets/cycling ad impressions. This pressure to meet targets was felt by digital editors, who received regular analytics reports and contributed to meeting website targets. However, reporters, who worked under a different direct supervisor who saw little merit in the way metrics and analytics were being used, often held little regard for audience data. This difference in understanding, and the different editorial bar for the posting and promotion of digital content,[19] caused conflict within *The Spectator* newsroom.

At the *Echo*, despite growing concerns the coverage of relevant local issues could be hampered by the pressure to produce content in conjunction with traffic goals, overall, there was wide ranging acceptance of the value of analytics in helping make editorial decisions that fell in line with reader expectations. Participant observation and interviews would suggest this was largely due to the consistent message of the importance of analytics from the top down in the *Echo* newsroom. There was no question, at any level, as to whether there was value in analytics, just differing opinions on whether there was enough time to use them effectively. And, although there were different strategies in what to post online and in print, these strategies were based on what readers might read online, and content that was considered important to the community was still optimised for online consumption. This was posted regardless of potential pageviews and, sometimes, in the case of advertorials/supplements, content considered relevant to the community was promoted regardless of outside authorship. However, there was widespread acknowledgement that the habitual use of press releases, although in conflict with journalistic ideals, was essential in order to meet increasing production demands due to loss of staff, demands which also directly impacted the quality of content created by reporters.

Conclusion

The Hamilton Spectator, despite revenue pressures and no clear plan how to bridge the gap between the loss of print revenue and future digital revenue, continued to produce investigative, award-winning work with long-term, significant impact[20] and digital editors had a mechanised strategy to promote website content. However, a lot of time was spent promoting content that had nothing to do with *The Spectator's* community. This was even though, according to shared data looking at a longer view, *The Spectator's* audience clearly preferred local content.

As further evidence of the marketability of local content, the *Echo* was able to garner almost double the pageviews of *The Spectator*[21] during a similar timeframe despite a smaller target audience and with its hyper-local focus. At the *Echo*, the majority agreed that efforts to establish protocols in relation to analytics helped improve local coverage online and in print, and were helping with the management of limited resources. The *Echo* also offered evidence of the benefits of building an online community, including choosing civil discourse over clickbait in online narratives and making a continuous effort to connect with the audience online. According to Newsquest senior management, streamlining workflows was ensuring the paper's future and supporting existing and new print publications. However, there was a negative shift towards factory-style journalism and despite an effective plan to develop the deeper use of analytics, no one had time to properly implement that plan.

If you could take best practice from both newsrooms, the ideal would be to use proven promotional strategies to showcase the original work of local reporters online and use deeper analysis of data to determine what stories engage the audience in the long term, and communicate with the audience directly to help interpret the data and uncover relevant issues within the community. This strategy would focus production on areas of audience interest while finding innovative ways to build engagement surrounding stories of import, thereby building audience trust. However, in order to cover such stories and ensure relevance within the community being served, it is also essential that reporters are given the resources they need to act as journalists.

As with many local newsrooms, though, a significant issue for *The Spectator* and *Echo* is their lack of control to pivot in response to reader needs or create strategies specific to their communities because instituted corporate policies, such as traffic targets, are designed to build profit, not quality and/or relevance. Such strategies, along with shared CMSs, are also selected because they can be shared at all outlets in a conglomerate, even though they might not be ideal for any of them. It is clear that centralisation of services offers savings. But at what cost? If larger media groups are interested in boosting profits, irrespective of good journalism, they need to consider the long-term economic benefits of allowing individual organisations to develop single-site strategies that build relevance within a community, alongside goals that might benefit the larger collective, such as shared copy-editing or printing presses.

When it comes specifically to the use of audience data, metrics and analytics are neither good nor bad, nor do they compel a choice between building profit or building community. Their usefulness and their impact on journalistic production are determined by the way in which they are used. Slavishly following volume metrics will not save any newspaper, local or otherwise. A longer view of data provides the best perspective – and the best way to ensure fulsome interpretation of data, and therefore relevance, is by giving readers a chance to interact with, contribute to, and submit feedback on coverage. This interaction makes local newsrooms and the stories only they can generate irreplaceable because, as described by a former reporter and digital editor from *The Spectator*, it creates "that vital sense of community that every community needs . . . a place to talk about themselves, to see themselves, to form their story as a place." And that is what will save local journalism.

Notes

1 Metrics are units of measurement that reflect a specific element of audience behaviour; analytics encompass the analysis of audience data as a means of performance appraisal on existing content and the development of hypotheses to improve audience engagement in the future; analytics systems are platforms specifically designed to aggregate, display, and assist in the reporting and analysis of audience data (Blanchett Neheli, 2018).
2 The data are taken from a larger study of newsrooms (Blanchett Neheli, 2019).
3 See also Chapter 1 for references to recommendations made by the Cairncross Review aimed at ensuring a sustainable future for the UK press. These focus specifically on the need for local news.
4 As will be discussed later in the chapter, though, what is in the newspaper can be more "local" than what is in the website. This is also reflected at regional outlets of Norway's public broadcaster NRK, where radio and television still cover stories considered too "local" for the website (Blanchett Neheli, 2019).
5 Meeting the demands of advertisers is not the only factor in expanding the scale of the audience, as seen at NRK, where regional offices nationalised stories to increase pageviews and the metric was often used as a measure of a story's value despite the fact the public broadcaster was almost entirely government-funded (Blanchett Neheli, 2019).
6 Difference in conceptions of the role of a journalist compared to actual performance was also noted by Hanitzsch and Vos (2017), Welbers et al. (2016), and, specific to the use of analytics, Vu (2014).

7   This trend was exemplified in 2017 when TorStar and another Canadian media-chain, Post Media, struck a deal to swap 41 local newspapers. However, this deal was made with a plan to shut down 36 of those papers in order to improve the chances of survival for the papers that remained open. Almost 300 employees were laid off as a result of this exchange (Watson, 2017). At the time this chapter was written, the transaction was being investigated by Canada's Competition Bureau (Evans, 2018).

8   The team was made up of four part- and eight full-time staff with a combination of eight in total working per shift.

9   As of January 2018, the *Echo* staff, 21 full-time and two part-time employees, produced *The Bournemouth Daily Echo* and four other weekly papers, including all content creation, production/layout, and copy-editing, and supplied content for a monthly, glossy-magazine.

10   Although the Newsquest manager of the *Echo* said the pageview benchmark existed, he denied the existence of unique user targets, saying there was only unspecified "expected growth."

11   At the time of my research, there were about 50 full- and some part-time staff at *The Spectator* with approximately 30 to 35 of those being "content producers."

12   At the time of my observation, *The Spectator's* digital team (managing three websites but with *thespec.com* being the primary focus) was comprised of two early morning editors (one who had multiple other duties and primarily worked on *The Record* website), two more who arrived at around 10 am, and another who worked an evening shift. At the *Echo*, there were two members of the digital team who used to focus solely on the website and managing multiple Facebook pages but were now completing their digital duties part time in order to take on other responsibilities.

13   After the time of my observation, a new initiative called "ACE" (audience and content editors) was being implemented aimed at enhancing/changing content more frequently on landing pages in order to increase traffic.

14   This is in complete contrast to a study on the Newsquest-run *Northern Echo* (MacGregor, 2014) where there was "web-print conflict" (p. 30), print took priority, and metrics/analytics had "no influence on story choice or presentation" (p. 25).

15   For example, if measured against Shapiro's (2014) essential elements of journalistic activity.

16   Participants at both *The Spectator* and *Echo* noted that car traffic/accident stories, generally, received high pageviews.

17   Content was curated from other Metroland outlets, news agencies such as The Canadian Press and Associated Press, and other media outlets *The Spectator* had agreements with, such as *The Washington Post*.

18   An example given of a story that would not be used on the website was coverage on a birthday concert for a community group as similar stories had previously received negligible views.

19   After my data collection, *The Spectator* was shifting to more of a subscriber-based model with less focus on pageviews, though there were still pageview targets.

20   Including investigative work on the impact of income on health care (*The Hamilton Spectator*, 2011) and concussions in football (*The Hamilton Spectator* and *The Canadian Press*, 2018), and stories related to everyday reporting, such as restricting journalistic access to open courtrooms (Clairmont, 2018).

21   Acknowledging the caveat that *The Spectator* operated with a partial paywall and the *Echo* had none.

References

Abernathy, P. M. (2016). *The rise of a new media baron and the emerging threat of news deserts*. Chapel Hill: Center for Innovation and Sustainability in Local Media, University of North Carolina.

Altheide, D. and Snow, P. (1979). *Media logic*. Beverly Hills, CA: Sage Publications.

Anderson, C. W. (2011). Between creative and quantified audiences: Web metrics and changing patterns of newswork in local US newsrooms [online]. *Journalism*, 12(5), pp. 550–566. Available at: www.academia.edu/10937194/ [Accessed 20 Feb. 2017].

Björkman, F. and Franco, S. (2017). *How big data analytics affect decision-making: A study of the newspaper industry* [online]. Available at: www.diva-portal.org/smash/get/diva2:1110878/FULLTEXT01.pdf [Accessed 22 Feb. 2018].

Blanchett Neheli, N. (2018). News by numbers: The evolution of analytics in journalism. *Digital Journalism*, 6(8), pp. 1041–1051.

Blanchett Neheli, N. (2019). *Metrics and analytics in the newsroom: An ethnographic study exploring how audience data are changing practice*, PhD thesis, Bournemouth University, Bournemouth.

Bourdieu, P. (2005). The political field, the social science field, and the journalistic field. In: Benson, R. and Neveu, E., eds., *Bourdieu and the journalistic field*. Cambridge: Polity Press, pp. 29–47.

Bright, J. and Nicholls, T. (2014). The life and death of political news: Measuring the impact of the audience agenda using online data [online]. *Social Science Computer Review*, 32(2), pp. 170–181.

Buchanan, C. (2018). Disrupting the local: Sense of place in hyperlocal media. *The Future of Local News* [online]. Available at: http://futureoflocalnews.org/portfolio-item/disrupting-the-local-sense-of-place-in-hyperlocal-media/ [Accessed 28 May 2018].

Bunce, M. (2017). Management and resistance in the digital newsroom. *Journalism*, https://doi.org/10.1177/1464884916688963.

Carey, J. (2009). *Communication as culture: Essays on media and society*. New York: Routledge.

Christin, A. (2018). Counting clicks: Quantification and variation in web journalism in the United States and France. *American Journal of Sociology*, 123(5), pp. 1382–1415.

Clairmont, S. (2018). The spectator kicked out of open courtroom. *thespec.com* [online], 8 Aug. Available at: www.thespec.com/opinion-story/8805652-the-spectator-kicked-out-of-open-courtroom/ [Accessed 9 Aug. 2018].

Cohen, N. S. (2015). From pink slips to pink slime: Transforming media labor in a digital age. *The Communication Review*, 18(2), pp. 98–122.

Cohen, N. S. (2018). At work in the digital newsroom. *Digital Journalism*, 6(4), pp. 1–21.

Cornia, A., Sehl, A., Simon, F. and Kleis Nielsen, R. (2017). *Pay models in European news* [online]. Oxford: Reuters Institute for the Study of Journalism. Available at: www.digitalnewsreport.org/publications/2017/pay-models-european-news/ [Accessed 21 Jan. 2018].

Davies, N. (2008). *Flat earth news*. London: Vintage.

Deuze, M. and Witschge, T. (2017). Beyond journalism: Theorizing the transformation of journalism [online]. *Journalism*. Available at: http://journals.sagepub.com/doi/full/10.1177/1464884916688550 [Accessed 3 Mar. 2017].

Evans, P. (2018). Competition bureau searches post media and Torstar offices in probe of newspaper deal. *CBC.ca* [online], 12 Mar. Available at: www.cbc.ca/news/business/post media-torstar-competition-bureau-1.4572960 [Accessed 6 May 2018].

Feller, G. (2017). Who demands answers now? *British Journalism Review*, 28(3), pp. 13–18.

Ferrer-Conill, R. and Tandoc Jr, E. C. (2018). The audience-oriented editor: Making sense of the audience in the newsroom. *Digital Journalism*, 6(4), pp. 436–453.

Greenspon, J. (2017). *The shattered mirror: News, democracy and trust in the digital age* [online]. Ottawa: Public Policy Forum. Available at: https://shatteredmirror.ca [Accessed 26 Jan. 2017].

The Hamilton Spectator. (2011). Spec code red series wins two major accolades. *The Hamilton Spectator* [online], 15 May. Available at: www.thespec.com/news-story/2203388-spec-code-red-series-wins-two-major-accolades/ [Accessed 22 Nov. 2018].

The Hamilton Spectator and The Canadian Press. (2018). Spectator writer wins national newspaper award. *The Hamilton Spectator* [online], 4 May. Available at: www.thespec.com/news-story/8589669-spectator-writer-wins-national-newspaper-award/ [Accessed 22 Nov. 2018].

Hanitzsch, T. and Vos, T. P. (2017). Journalistic roles and the struggle over institutional identity: The discursive constitution of journalism. *Communication Theory*, 27(2), pp. 115–135.

Hanusch, F. (2017). Web analytics and the functional differentiation of journalism cultures: Individual, organizational and platform-specific influences on newswork. *Information, Communication & Society*, 20(10), pp. 1571–1586.

International Center for Journalists (ICFJ). (2017). *The state of technology in global newsrooms* [online]. Available at: www.icfj.org/sites/default/files/ICFJTechSurveyFINAL.pdf [Accessed 10 Oct. 2017].

Jenkins, J. and Kleis Nielsen, R. (2018). *The digital transition of local news* [online]. Oxford: Reuters Institute for the Study of Journalism. Available at: www.digitalnewsreport.org/publications/2018/digital-transition-local-news/ [Accessed 30 Apr. 2018].

Le Cam, F. and Domingo, D. (2015). Gatekeeping practices in French and Spanish online newsrooms. In: Vos, T. and Heinderyckx, F., eds., *Gatekeeping in transition*. New York: Routledge, pp. 123–140.

Lee-Wright, P. (2012). The return of Hephaestus: Journalists' work recrafted. In: Lee-Wright, P., Phillips, A. and Witschge, T., eds., *Changing journalism*. Abingdon: Routledge, pp. 21–40.

MacGregor, P. (2014). Siren songs or path to salvation? Interpreting the visions of web technology at a UK regional newspaper in crisis, 2006–2011. *Convergence*, 20(2), pp. 157–175.

Madrigal, A. (2017). Prepare for the new paywall era. *The Atlantic* [online], 30 Nov. Available at: www.theatlantic.com/technology/archive/2017/11/the-big-unanswered-questions-about-paywalls/547091/ [Accessed 15 Dec. 2018].

Marwick, A. and Lewis, R. (2017). *Media manipulation and disinformation online* [online]. Data and Society Research Institute. Available at: https://datasociety.net/output/media manipulation-and-disinfo-online/ [Accessed 13 May 2017].

Napoli, P. M., Weber, M., McCollough, K. and Wang, Q. (2018). *Assessing local journalism: News deserts, journalism divides, and the determinants of the robustness of local news*. Sanford School of Public Policy. Available at: https://kjzz.org/sites/default/files/Assessing-Local-Journalism_100-Communities.pdf [Accessed 18 Dec. 2018].

Nelson, J. L. (2018). The elusive engagement metric. *Digital Journalism*, 6(4), pp. 528–544.

Newman, N. (2018). *Journalism, media and technology trends and predictions 2018*. Oxford: Reuters Institute for the Study of Journalism. Available at: https://reutersinstitute.politics.ox.ac.uk/our-research/journalism-media-and-technology-trends-and-predictions-2018 [Accessed 20 Jan. 2018].

Newman, N., Fletcher, R., Kalogeropoulos, A., Levy, D. A. and Kleis Nielsen, R. (2018). *Reuters digital report 2018* [online]. Oxford: Reuters Institute for the Study of Journalism. Available at: https://reutersinstitute.politics.ox.ac.uk [Accessed 14 June 2018].

Phillips, A. (2010). Old sources: New bottles. In: Fenton, N., ed., *New media, old news: Journalism & democracy in the digital age*. Los Angeles, CA: Sage Publications, pp. 87–101.

Radcliffe, D. and Ali, C. (2017). *Local news in a digital world: Small-market newspapers in the digital age* [online]. Tow Center for Digital Journalism. Available at: www.amic.media/media/files/file_352_1368.pdf [Accessed 22 Nov. 2017].

Read, M. (2018). How much of the internet is fake? Turns out, a lot of it, actually. *New York Magazine* [online], 26 Dec. 2018. Available at: http://nymag.com/intelligencer/2018/12/how-much-of-the-internet-is-fake.html [Accessed 28 Dec. 2018].

Rispoli, M. and Aaron, C. (2018). Local government funds local news – and that's a good thing. *Nieman Lab* [online]. Available at: www.niemanlab.org/2018/12/government-funds-local-news-and-thats-a-good-thing/ [Accessed 13 Dec. 2018].

Schlesinger, P. and Doyle, G. (2015). From organizational crisis to multi-platform salvation? Creative destruction and the recomposition of news media. *Journalism*, 16(3), pp. 305–323.

Schudson, M. (2005). Autonomy from what? In: Benson, R. and Neveu, E., eds., *Bourdieu and the journalistic field*. Cambridge: Polity Press, pp. 215–223.

Shapiro, I. (2014). Why democracies need a functional definition of journalism now more than ever. *Journalism Studies*, 15(5), pp. 555–565.

Tandoc Jr., E. C. (2014). Journalism is twerking? How web analytics is changing the process of gatekeeping. *New Media and Society*, 16(4), pp. 559–575.

Thurman, N. and Fletcher, R. (2017). Has digital distribution rejuvenated readership? Revisiting the age demographics of newspaper consumption. *Journalism Studies*, pp. 1–21.

Usher, N. (2013). Al Jazeera English online: Understanding web metrics and news production when a quantified audience is not a commodified audience. *Digital Journalism*, 1(3), pp. 335–351.

Vu, H. T. (2014). The online audience as gatekeeper: The influence of reader metrics on news editorial selection. *Journalism*, 15(8), pp. 1094–1110.

Wardle, S. and Derakhshan, H. (2017). *Information disorder: Toward an interdisciplinary framework for research and policy making*. Council of Europe. Available at: https://rm.coe.int/information-disorder-toward-an-interdisciplinary-framework-forresearc/168076277c [Accessed 1 Oct. 2017].

Watson, H. (2017). Torstar and postmedia swapped 41 newspapers and are closing most of them. *J-Source: The Canadian Journalism Project* [online], 27 Nov. Available at: http://j-source.ca/article/torstar-postmedia-swapped-41-newspapers-closing/ [Accessed 28 Nov. 2017].

Welbers, K., Van Atteveldt, W., Kleinnijenhuis, J., Ruigrok, N. and Schaper, J. (2016). News selection criteria in the digital age: Professional norms versus online audience metrics. *Journalism*, 17(8), pp. 1037–1053.

5

CONNECTING PUBLICS THROUGH GLOBAL VOICES

Ivan Sigal

This chapter looks at new practices arising from the Internet and considers routes towards greater connectivity through the Global Voices project.

Global Voices: mission and values

The genesis of Global Voices comes out of a series of conversations that happened at the Berkman Klein Center for Internet and Society at Harvard University in 2004. It grew out of communities that work in the open culture, open knowledge, and free software movements. Many of us live in networked societies, and we have a digital accompaniment or persona to everything that we do in public life. In the early to mid-2000s, the number of people blogging – by which I mean a generic term for people communicating online or conversing online before the days of active social media communities – was significant, but it had not reached the scale that we see today. Global Voices was able to identify people who were living in one country and writing about it with an imagined audience in other countries. These individuals were performing the functions of explaining, or contextualising, their lives for other audiences, often in English. For example, a writer from Iraq was writing in English, because there was not, at that time, a significant blogging community in Arabic. Such individuals were already performing the function of explaining their communities to the rest of the world – at least to the English language world – and by co-ordinating, linking, and organising their work Global Voices was able to innovate by approximating the role of foreign correspondents. This process of removing the layer of journalism between the local authorial voice and the reader is called *disintermediation*, which is at the heart of the theory of networked societies.[1]

When Global Voices began, it was possible to identify and follow many of the people in the world who were working in this way – there were hundreds, maybe thousands. Global Voices was able to build an index of what we called bridge bloggers. Three or four years later, that was no longer possible, first as blogging took off and then as Twitter, Facebook, and other social media platforms started to re-mediate the open web through the lens of social media applications. By the time I joined Global Voices in 2008, four years after its inception, to help set up an independent legal entity separate from the Berkman Center, we already knew that blogging as the primary form of participatory media was on the decline. In those years, we started talking about the lack of utility of the term "blogger," large and significant audiences were online in all the major languages in the world, and the role of blogs in bridging between languages was starting to feel less necessary, because there were so many other modes of expression. Many of the functions that blogs had played were disaggregated into social media platforms and mobile had kicked in. In 2005–6, anyone with their own blog would often write on it multiple times a day. By 2008–9 some of that energy would be diverted into Twitter for shorter posts, using the blog for longer pieces, focused more for a specific community and less for a platform. Facebook started building groups, the newsfeed, and various tools for blogging-like activity, and we also saw the growth of Reddit and other platforms for dialogue. Eventually, by the early teens of the 21st century, private and difficult-to-search group chat apps such as WeChat, Telegram, WhatsApp, and other platforms had emerged. The Internet became consolidated into this generation of applications, resulting in a concentration of power, voice, and resources. This was accompanied by the fragmentation of a loosely joined set of publics that were searchable and linked at the level of the Web, rather than at the level of the application. The outcome was a fragmentation of online discussion into applications and a remediation of audiences by web applications.

Throughout all of those trends, GV has sought to make a simple, and perhaps obvious, point that the potential for the democratisation of expression in online spaces is not going to happen unless people act according to those ideas. The Internet was never inherently a democratising force in the sense of governance or distribution of power; rather it was democratising in terms of the lowering of the costs of access and enabling all of us to simultaneously run a mini broadcaster or an archive and share that with the world. But just because that potential is embedded in the system, it does not mean that we will use it in that way. This is why it is important to say that the breathless assertions made ten years ago about the radical restructuring of society for some positive effect were overstatements and misunderstandings. Technology is not the subject; we humans as users and citizens have considerable agency, and technology is the object. Likewise, today, the demonisation of platforms is also an overstatement: once again, it is humans looking to displace our behaviours and our agency onto the agency of the social media platforms. This is not to say that the platforms in the past few years are blameless. It is clear and evident that their choices – such as algorithmic sorting and the growth of programmatic ad technology – have led to quite negative effects. At the same time, it remains our collective choice to use them for our communications.

Throughout, Global Voices has sought to embody the democratic potential of the Internet. This means focusing on questions of attention, on voice, on what stories we hear, how these are framed, and what it means both for the people writing them, and for the communities for whom a story matters. At Global Voices, we are attentive to different forms and processes of public expression, of public speech and public writing. We seek to understand the relationship between the creation of technologies and their affordances, and modes of expression. We have for many years debated which words really resonate for us in terms of our mission and values. For example, currently there is a rush of concern about a perceived lack of trust in media. Is there trust in the news media, is there trust in institutions, and if not, why not? Is information credible? And what is the validity or basis of that credibility? We have instead chosen to focus on the term "integrity," because integrity captures the visibility of a process: where information comes from, how much we know about it, what we do not know about it, what our position is with relation to it. Likewise, the term "transparency" is not as useful for us as the term "legibility" – seeing the structure of creation, production, and dissemination.

Through all this we are trying to do something which is both simple and complicated: to actualise the democratic potential of online communities. In the 2000s this was difficult because not many people were doing it – participation and disintermediation seemed novel. At that time, mass media outlets, given their dominant presence, wanted to work with us as they sought to use the outputs of bloggers in their reporting.[2] Today we are presented with a different set of problems. The scale of online assets, the number of voices and perspectives, and, increasingly, the automation of online expression, whether it is for malign or benign purposes, means that people with resources are once again dominant in online spaces. People without resources have to work through the platforms to achieve a significant voice in networked societies and remain subject to their policies and priorities.

A new practice?

It is complicated to answer the question whether Global Voices is – or was, at the time of its inception – a new practice. The news economy, the mass media economy is a political economy, which means that in many countries the production of media is intertwined with other goals – explicitly political goals. This can be manifest in political parties that support media production because they seek to promote positions or influence. Elsewhere we might see media promoted, bought, or created by groups who seek state or economic capture and use their media outlets as tools for their personal benefit, or use media to leverage some interest. A lot of money goes into media that does not have a rational economic purpose. This is important to mention because when we say the "mainstream media" we are actually talking about many different activities.

In the past few decades, we have seen two interesting trends regarding money:

1   Starting in the 1980s and into the '90s, we saw a movement away from private ownership of media companies and towards publicly held media coupled with the financialisation and globalisation of media industries. Media outlets were therefore less beholden to single markets and are increasingly part of conglomerates. They are expected to generate consistent returns for their shareholders in ways that might not be conducive to the production of stories in the public

interest. Over time, this trend has arguably degraded the quality of some kinds of mass media, such as television news, and some digital first media outlets.

2   In the last six years, investments by venture capital firms have supported a class of digital first media outlets such as Vice, Vox, HuffPost, and BuzzFeed. In the last year, many of them failed to meet their revenue targets for digital advertising and have flat, or slow, audience growth. The markets may not be able to sustain all of them. Many of these companies have multiple brands in multiple markets and languages. They have created interesting effects, flooding markets with a deluge of stories, and betting that media companies can reach exponential readership, as technology companies seek exponential returns by rapidly scaling user growth. The underlying idea is that exponential growth in eyeballs will drive advertising growth, such that media companies become a source for data that can be sold to advertising markets.

These two financial trends have significantly shifted what mass media are in many countries in the past decade. We may be arriving at another inflection point. In the United States, around 2,000 journalists affiliated with digital media outlets were recently laid off as a result of those missed revenue targets. Many of those digital media companies were able to use their venture capital money to buy attention in social media. As a volunteer network of writers and translators, Global Voices never had those resources. At the same time, worldwide, we have seen more support for the growth of non-profit, investigative reporting; membership models; and subscriptions. We are seeing multiple attempts to strengthen the connection between media and their audiences.

The one thing that is not elastic is attention. As we leverage money in the contest for attention, it becomes more challenging for any one group to "win the Internet" for any extended period of time. Many compelling projects have launched, made a splash, and then failed to sustain themselves due to this relentless hunger for stories engendered by the flow of capital. Sometimes we see alignments with civic interests, but as often as not we see attempts to align our publics towards markets.

This is important context, because from a Silicon Valley and from a mass media perspective scale is treated as a value. For Global Voices scale is not a value, but a function. Scale is not necessarily good or bad but is in the service of some normative value. Some of the civic values we support do not easily scale. Conversations do not usually scale, editorial processes do not easily scale, especially stories about people and relationships, which will always need some degree of editing.

The Global Voices editorial process includes stories written in one language and then translated into many others. Those stories need multiple layers of engagement. The process of writing them is itself a conversation that has value for the participants in terms of creating understanding or knowledge. Thus, our work often sits at the scale of community. It has certainly had mass effects, for example around the Arab uprisings or while covering Russia, as our reporting both had mass audiences and shifted the way that others reported stories. However, the primary, salutary effect is often at the level of community. Our audience is not insignificant, at 50–60 million pageviews on our site, and re-publication by hundreds of partners and others, but it is much smaller than that of media conglomerates.

In considering whether Global Voices is a new practice, we certainly began something new online, although the notion of disintermediation has many precedents in media history, from community radio to mediated town hall discussions. Our work in online spaces is reflective of those practices. The Internet is an accelerant, and transformative in the sense that it affords opportunity to build communities and links, not just by geography or real-world connectivity, but by proximity. Internet connectivity allows us to quickly identify common interests with others. This mass awareness effect is true for all of us. It is important that these qualities are not attributed to any one Internet-based project, however. Global Voices is oriented toward those affordances of the Internet.

Over the past year, we created a deliberative process to more carefully define what we mean when we say "community" and to discuss how we make decisions. Our decision-making process had primarily been based on consensus, but consensus is challenging for a community distributed across dozens of countries and dozens of languages, with people who have many different interests, skills, and educations. We decided to discuss how we talk about what we know, what we assume, how we frame our stories, and who we listen to. As we worked on the model, we realised that if we could model deliberation for ourselves, we might also create an alternative approach that could be useful for others.

An early, major shift in the history of Global Voices, made over a decade ago, was to recognise that the idea of listening to people online was no longer rare or novel. We decided that, instead, we needed to look at what stories we are paying attention to, what we mean by representation, and to understand the meta-effects of millions of people conversing on a huge variety of technology platforms. We moved away from the notion that listening to someone in another part of the world without the mediation of a media outlet is itself newsworthy. This introduced a new level of complexity into our work. It has all sorts of challenging and fascinating effects that we can contend with. As many have become aware that social media companies prioritise scale over the safety and wellbeing of their users, we have seen a renewed appreciation for the value of direct connections and conversations found with slower, community-oriented Internet-based media. Global Voices has never really moved away from that position, but there are cycles and there are trends, and it is a truism that commercial media will always seek scale.

Two other resurgent trends are investment in non-profit media and the awareness that publics and states can support public interest media that markets may not support. Public interest journalism and other forms of civic-minded knowledge production are not necessarily capital-maximising. If we want them, then we need to fund them in some way, or accept a lower rate of return for them. Underlying all of that is the fact that governments recognise the power of citizen voice and collaboration in online spaces, and that has made the work of Global Voices considerably more difficult.

New challenges

In this context, the challenges are several:

1   The idea of reporting stories out of social media and other online spaces has become significantly more complex since the rise, not just of social media, but of algorithmic sorting of stories by social media companies. The primary challenge of algorithmic sorting and the personalisation of the news is that we no longer have the assurance that we are all seeing the same information, and thus may not have a common basis of understanding to discuss and debate public interests. To achieve that common understanding, we first need to have conversations about what we know. That creates another layer of complexity, another layer of time, another layer of analysis.

2   The shift of online conversation into private social media spaces such as Whats-App and Telegram groups means that it is difficult – or impossible – to search for, document, or link to and share many online conversations. Our goal is to demonstrate the integrity of our information sources, and with these closed social media environments we need to do more work to contextualise stories and establish facts.

3   There is much more noise in our information systems. Disinformation and misinformation are aspects of that noise but do not necessarily constitute the primary problem. Algorithmic sorting creates the conditions for disinformation to thrive. There is also a great deal of informational flotsam and jetsam designed to grab our attention. When trying to write stories based on people's interests, we often have to wade through a mass of distracting content to find the ideas that matter. For our contributors, this effort is time consuming and sometimes daunting.

4   The web applications we are discussing tend to reward sensationalism in the stories that they promote. They privilege attention, extreme views, and rapidity over accuracy. More reasoned, complex, nuanced views do not play particularly well in social media contexts or in mass media contexts. Subtlety has not been of value for much of the history of news production.

5   Many of the people who write with us live in authoritarian and semi-authoritarian states, and also in quite a few democracies, where online expression is increasingly regulated. We have to be cognisant of legal contexts, ensure that our writers are safe, and avoid publishing material that could cause them harm.

1–5 together mean more work to produce a smaller number of stories, more attention to risk, more systems, and slower processes. We had been trying to deal with those dynamics incrementally, responding to challenges as they arise. In 2018, we decided that this incremental approach was not going to get us to where we need to be. We are looking to make large, strategic shifts in how we work and in order to do that we decided to have a serious conversation with the community of people who write Global Voices stories.

Those of us who oversee Global Voices act as stewards or custodians. We call ourselves Global Voices after all. We are not trying to be charismatic leaders or to promote ourselves. We serve our mission. We therefore asked ourselves, where does the moral authority to make these decisions actually sit? The answer is with the community, but the community is highly diversified and global, so how do we talk to each other about what those shifts might be? That led us to the idea of a deliberative council, a public and open discussion with our members about future directions for the organisation.[3]

The issues and the process

Traditionally it is very difficult to move away from a consensus-based model of decision-making and many movements (especially activist groups) struggle to find new models for their deliberation. We decided to take up the challenge: the model that we evolved aims to ensure that everyone who wants to participate is able to do so, with a baseline of knowledge for the discussion, so that they can have input to the issues in an informed way. We then shared a set of polls with clearly structured questions to elicit their preferences in four key areas. The process had several stages:

a   The creation of a community council: since 2004, Global Voices has had more than 6,000 participants, and between 1,000 and 1,200 people contribute each year as writers, translators, editors, and technologists. We wanted to include all active members (within the last five years) who were interested in the governance of GV in a model that would work whether we had 50 or 500 people involved. One hundred ninety-one participants joined the community council.

b   Identifying the four key areas for deliberation. For each of the four issues we had a two-week deliberation period in which the 191 participants read an issue paper offering a set of five different models for the future, where we are, what works, and what does not work. There was a week of deliberation on private channels and Zoom chats and then we took a poll.

   The polling method was constructed in an interesting way with the support of a Prague-based civic tech company, D21. The system that they devised enabled polling that did not just record choice or yes/no but allowed participants to choose both positive and negative votes, to show polarity as well as preference. This provides a rich data set (Figures 5.1a–d).

   The four issues and associated polling questions were:

1   Should we *narrow the focus of our content or should we expand it?* What are the options available to us? In the poll we shared sets of values and activities and asked:

   •   Which of these values are most important for our editorial model to represent?
   •   Which of these editorial activities would you most want to participate in?
   •   What, for you, best defines a successful editorial effort?

GV Consultation Poll 1: Topic Focus

Global Voices

Which of these values are most important for our editorial model to represent?

NUMBER OF VOTERS: 94

1. Amplifying underrepresented and misrepresented voices	57 FOR 0 AGAINST	57
2. Credibility and accuracy	47 FOR 0 AGAINST	47
3. Bridging and connecting diverse audiences	36 FOR −1 AGAINST	35
4. Contributors from many places and backgrounds	32 FOR 0 AGAINST	32
5. Influence and impact	28 FOR −6 AGAINST	22
6. Freedom of contributors to choose what they work on	21 FOR −4 AGAINST	17
7. High Quality Writing	19 FOR −6 AGAINST	13
8. Relevance of stories to a global audience	16 FOR −6 AGAINST	10
9. Personal development of contributors	8 FOR −11 AGAINST	−3
10. Wide range of topics	13 FOR −17 AGAINST	−4

Which editorial activities would you most to want to participate in?

NUMBER OF VOTERS: 94

1. Translation	45 FOR −2 AGAINST	43
2. Research	44 FOR −2 AGAINST	42
3. − − 4. News features (standard GV posts)	41 FOR −3 AGAINST	38
3. − − 4. Finding and sharing leads and story ideas	38 FOR 0 AGAINST	38

FIGURE 5.1   Results of a 2018 poll of the Global Voices community council for input to help create a new model.

5. Advocacy campaigns	31 FOR / -2 AGAINST	29
6. Covering citizen media	25 FOR / -3 AGAINST	22
7. Writing personal narratives	27 FOR / -7 AGAINST	20
8. Data journalism and visualization	23 FOR / -8 AGAINST	15
9. Social media promotion	20 FOR / -8 AGAINST	12
10. — — 11. Photography and sourcing photos	8 FOR / -4 AGAINST	4
10. — — 11. Podcasting	13 FOR / -9 AGAINST	4
12. Breaking news	10 FOR / -15 AGAINST	-5
13. Graphics	2 FOR / -11 AGAINST	-9
14. Video production	4 FOR / -14 AGAINST	-10

What, for you, best defines a successful editorial effort?

NUMBER OF VOTERS: 94

1. Read by policymakers, journalists, academics and other influential audiences	53 FOR / 0 AGAINST	53
2. Bridges audiences from different countries and languages	45 FOR / 0 AGAINST	45
3. Produces concrete change in the world	34 FOR / -4 AGAINST	30
4. Republished or quoted in mass media	21 FOR / -3 AGAINST	18
5. Generates strong engagement on social media	13 FOR / -5 AGAINST	8
6. Read by partners and colleagues in our field	6 FOR / -4 AGAINST	2
7. Generates high traffic to articles	11 FOR / -10 AGAINST	1
8. Read and celebrated by GV community	1 FOR / -14 AGAINST	-13

FIGURE 5.1 (Continued)

Which editorial topic model most appeals to you?

NUMBER OF VOTERS: 94

1. Designated topic	60 FOR -6 AGAINST	54
2. Hybrid	50 FOR -7 AGAINST	43
3. GV Classic	29 FOR -14 AGAINST	15
4. Rights & access	25 FOR -12 AGAINST	13
5. Platform	13 FOR -23 AGAINST	-10

POWERED BY (D21) WWW.D21.ME

FIGURE 5.1 (Continued)

2 Should we consider *different approaches to professional engagement*? Should we offer more opportunity for paid work? Should we require certain jobs be done only by professionals? Should we radically de-professionalise and become only volunteers? In the poll we asked:

- Should inclusiveness continue to be our primary value with regard to the composition of our community? Or should we require contributors to have higher levels of proficiency and specific types of knowledge in order to participate?

The answers to these questions would help us determine:

- Whether we should be a community primarily dedicated to learning and growing our own skills and knowledge, whether our primary aim is to inform and engage an external audience, or whether the solution is designing programs that allow us to manage the tension between these goals.

Then as we look ahead we ask ourselves:

- When it comes to the skills, knowledge, and diversity of our community and our outputs, what is most important to us? What do we most want to achieve?

3 *Organisational structure*: should we de-centralise or centralise authority? Should we create regional authorities, chapters, or a membership organisation?

In the poll we considered:

- The question of decision-making and authority within Global Voices: Should we decentralise decision-making and governance, or should we centralise it further?

These choices would determine:

- Where decision-making authority resides for our policies and activities. They will also influence the ways we grow and change, and our ability to raise and distribute funds.

Looking ahead, we asked ourselves:

- When it comes to organisation, which structure will best serve our values and goals and help us succeed in our efforts?

4   *The funding question* – until the end of 2018 we had bans on categories or classes of funding: advertising, government support, most corporate money. We are exploring alternatives that would allow us to have a more flexible approach to funding while still retaining our independence of action and thought. In the poll we asked whether:

- Choosing a different ethical framework for funding could allow us to maintain or even strengthen our independence, while also expanding opportunities for new revenue.
- The choices we make about funding sources strongly influence our ability to support and expand our work and reach the goals we set for ourselves.

As we look ahead, we asked, when considering funding

- Which sources will best serve our values and goals and help us succeed in our efforts?

These were the outcomes and the clear decisions for change:

1   *Topics and focus.* We explored models from designating or narrowing topics to creating a platform in which anybody could write about anything. A system of designating topics was the clear winner. We will therefore come up with alternative ways for people to design and focus their stories with more intentionality. Designated topics does not mean coverage of a narrow set of topics, but we are going to build a system to encourage focus. We also learned that people contribute to Global Voices primarily to make an impact in the world, rather than to educate others. We defined principles for Global Voices stories:

   i   Equality of representation
   ii Originality
   iii Bridging and connecting cultures and languages
   iv Integrity

2　Following on from Item 1 is the question of *where to situate our work on the spectrum of amateur-professional contributions*. Here we also looked at a range of options: the most popular was finding more ways for people to participate. This means everything from more paid opportunities to leading research projects or in-depth projects (where there might be some paid opportunities), to being able to contribute piecemeal – leads, story ideas, tips – without having to write full stories, without having to promote. Rather than define categories or classes of contributor, we are talking about behaviours and roles. Take myself as an example: due to my background, I still have substantial expertise on the former Soviet Union and Asia, but I have not lived in those communities for a long time, so while I am still fluent and conversant in those issues, I am not necessarily up to date enough to write stories about them anymore. But I can still help: I can promote stories, I can make contacts, I can find leads, I can edit, and I can contextualise and evaluate. However, for Latin American stories, my role is mostly to listen, promote, and be attentive, but I do not really have much to offer in terms of story production there because it is not my area of expertise.

　　Items 1 and 2 together are looking at an editorial funnel – more open spaces for idea generation, topic generation, and research generation – that then ties to a fundraising process for some stories and topics that can lead to some paid opportunities.

3　*Organisational structure* – whether we should centralise or de-centralise authority and management of our activities. The most popular choice is a membership model. Within the community there are contributors who are interested in the long-term health and governance of Global Voices, who can apply to be members of a standing council that will consider and support everything from ethics and principles to pitching for project management.

4　*Funding.* The clear winner is a model we call the Ethical Organisation. We prioritise independence from external agendas and reject funding that seeks influence regardless of the source. As a result, we will no longer need to block different types of funding by category but by whether or not they will have influence over our independence. We could potentially take some kinds of advertising, some kinds of governmental support, and some kinds of corporate support, as long as the relationship does not unacceptably obligate us and as long as there is no reputational harm. We are writing a public ethics statement to share with our funders that will form the basis for our relationships with them and this protocol will help us to decide what kinds of funds are appropriate.

Conclusions

The council process gave us new energy and it showed us how many people are really invested in the survival and prosperity of Global Voices as a project. That is very heartening. It suggests that we do have a path and a place that will rest with people who want to invest their energy. We have long espoused the ideal that online spaces are spaces for conversation and for people to learn from each other – through sharing stories across cultures and languages. The deliberative process showed us that we can still do this ourselves.

For years we have been discussing questions of scale and how to grow. Scale could mean that one story gets 15 million readers, or it could mean that there are 15 million separate conversations. Those are both models of scale. I wanted to know if we could come up with a method of talking to each other that would work whether 50 or 500 people were involved. Could we make meaningful decisions? If we could not do it, we certainly could not ask others to do it!

In a sense, we went back to a basic idea of people talking to each other, to try and understand something about the world and about each other. That was enduring and worth doing for those of us involved. It also highlighted for me this is what we *should* be doing. That might not mean a mass audience; it might mean a relatively small number of people working around some issues, but if we do that many, many times, that is another kind of scale. What this actually means in terms of activities is still nascent, but we have many ideas. It is sustainable and meaningful to the extent that people keep doing it – it is the idea that, like a democracy, a community media system or group or concept is a practice – it is not an end. It is a way of being in the world. It is a way of acquiring knowledge. It is a way of retaining relationships. Whether in Global Voices or in some other context, this is a way of building meaning in societies: how we talk to each other, what we talk about, what we choose to privilege, who we listen to, who we are attentive to, how we organise our power relations – this tells us how we organise our societies. Global Voices for me has become one way to think about how we organise our lives. This is both an immodest goal and something exceedingly simple. We are not claiming that there is an answer, or a conclusion. We are not claiming that technology is going to fix our problems. We are building a practice of being attentive to the concerns of others and questioning and critiquing received knowledge. Journalism is part of civic life, not a practice that is separated into a professional niche. We need professional journalism, but – as we have shown at Global Voices for nearly 14 years – others can also play that role and, through their storytelling, make a significant contribution to civic knowledge.

Notes

1 See, for example, M. Castells. (2014). The impact of the internet on society: A global perspective. *MIT Technology Review*, 8 Sept. Available at: www.bbvaopenmind.com/en/articles/the-impact-of-the-internet-on-society-a-global-perspective/.
2 In 2010, the BBC teamed up with Global Voices to "present a different range of perspectives and commentary from around the world." Available at: www.bbc.co.uk/blogs/theeditors/2010/03/superpower_bbc_and_global_voic.html [Accessed 24 Feb. 2019].
3 In February 2019, Sigal discussed the process in a podcast made for journalism.co.uk. You can listen here. Available at: www.journalism.co.uk/podcast/how-global-voices-is-asking-their-contributors-to-inform-some-of-their-biggest-decisions/s399/a734071/.

Further reading

Castells, M. (2014). *The impact of the internet on society: A global perspective.* MIT Technology Review, 8 Sept. Available at: www.bbvaopenmind.com/en/articles/the-impact-of-the-internet-on-society-a-global-perspective/.

Global Voices. Available at: https://globalvoices.org.

Granger, J. (2019). Interviews Ivan Sigal. Podcast. *Global voices asks its contributors to make its strategic decisions instead of a boardroom,* 1 Feb. Available at: www.journalism.co.uk/podcast/how-global-voices-is-asking-their-contributors-to-inform-some-of-their-biggest-decisions/s399/a734071/ [Accessed 27 Feb. 2019].

Zuckerman, E. (2013–2015). *Digital cosmopolitans. Why we think the Internet connects us, why it doesn't and how to rewire it.* New York: W. W. Norton & Company.

6

IMAGES

Reported, remembered, invented, contested[1]

Susan D. Moeller

This chapter evaluates how photojournalists visually report news. It also examines why political partisans challenge the veracity of news images and documents how bad actors misrepresent news images to manipulate audiences for political and economic ends.

Introduction: the truth demands our attention

We live in times when covering the news is dangerous. As I was writing this chapter, I read the news of Victoria Marinova, a Bulgarian journalist who was raped and murdered following her reporting on an investigation into political and corporate corruption. Marinova's death occurred four days after the assassination of journalist Jamal Khashoggi at the Saudi Arabian consulate in Istanbul. Khashoggi, a Saudi dissident and a columnist for *The Washington Post*, had been sharply critical of Saudi Arabia's crown prince Mohammad bin Salman.

We live in times when free expression around the world is under threat. As I was writing this, I read of the Burmese court that sentenced to seven years in prison two Reuters reporters, Wa Lone and Kyaw Soe Oo, who were investigating the mass murder of ten Rohingya men. I further read that Nobel Peace Prize laureate Aung San Suu Kyi, Burma's civilian leader, denied that the case limited freedom of the press in Myanmar. "They were not jailed because they were journalists, they were jailed because . . . the court has decided that they have broken the Official Secrets Act," she was quoted as saying (Smith, 2018).[2]

We live in times when private companies are "making profound choices about the contours and the boundaries of political expression." As *New Yorker* writer Evan Osnos wrote about Facebook (2018):

> What are the bounds of free speech? What do we actually want to be able to have, and what do we consider to be out of bounds? What is, in effect,

shouting fire in a crowded theater, and what is legitimate provocative, unsavory speech?

These questions are increasingly in the hands not of jurists or legislators, journalists or philosophers, Osnos reminded, but of Facebook's "engineers, the people who created this incredibly powerful application." As he mused: "It has to make a person uneasy to know that there is now a company which is capable of deciding not only what kind of information it's going to suppress but also which kind of information it's going to promote."

We live in times when faked photos go viral. A photo of Emma González, one of the students who survived the Marjory Stoneman Douglas High School mass shooting, was doctored to show her ripping up the US Constitution. The faked image was first tweeted by a popular alt-right account, then retweeted over 65,000 times. Another photo, of a rescue attempt in the wake of Hurricane Florence, was altered to show President Trump floating in a raft extending a red "Make America Great Again" hat to a flood victim. That faked photo was shared on Facebook more than a quarter of a million times.

Yet we also live in times when the world can be witness to abuses in a far corner of the world – if the world chooses to look. Consider the photographs taken of starving Yemeni children by *New York Times* photographer Tyler Hicks. The photographs of the dying and the dead were not taken lightly nor published without considerable thought. As *Times* editors wrote to explain, this is the job of journalists to bear witness, give voice to those who are otherwise abandoned, victimised, and forgotten (2018). They added:

> The images we have now published out of Yemen may be as unsettling as anything we have used before. But there is a reason we made this decision ... we felt it would be a disservice to the victims of this war to publish sanitized images.

They felt strongly that the story of Yemen had to be told but understood that it could not be told in words alone:

> Yes, Tyler's images are hard to look at. They are brutal. But they are also brutally honest. They reveal the horror that is Yemen today. You may choose not to look at them. But we thought you should be the ones to decide.

A few months before the Yemen story appeared late in 2018, *The New York Times* began a new branding campaign with the slogan: "The truth demands our attention. Read. Watch. Listen."

We, the public, need to reflect on that statement: "The truth demands our attention."

Why should readers of *The New York Times*, or any news outlet actually, expect – or perhaps hope – that "the truth" can be discovered and then communicated via photos, words, audio? (*The* truth, by the way, not just *a* truth.)

Consider just the second of those admonitions: to "Watch." Consider the truth of visual reporting. Really, isn't the notion that truth can be found in images that one can *watch* or *see* somewhat 20th century? (Or even 19th century?) Given the 21st century's wholesale manipulation of images via technological tools as well as by the ever-Machiavellian technique of framing the news, is it reasonable to think that photographs even can report *a* truth, much less *the* truth about the world?

Yet there are some, the photographers and editors of *The New York Times* among them, who would argue that it is reasonable. News photographs *can* report truths. Journalists work hard, sometimes with their lives on the line, to bring the truths that they themselves witness to the public at home watching and listening and reading. The different stories told in photographic news coverage are not (always or even mainly) because of intentional bias or partisanship or incompetence. Differences arise because each photographer takes a different – and cannot avoid taking a different – angle of vision on the world.

Consider a tweet in 2018 by photographer Benjamin Sorenson, a tweet that reproduced two photographs, taken by others, of the same event: the return of the flag-draped coffin of US Senator John McCain, a decorated war veteran and former P.O.W., to Andrews Air Force Base outside Washington, DC, for burial in late August 2018. Sorenson tweeted the following (2018):

> *Example #1257 of why political photographers are the best. They all take photos locked into same positions and each come up with something unique that tells the story.*[3]

You don't have to be cynical (or even sceptical) about the media's portrayal of the world to see the differences in the two photos reproduced in Sorenson's tweet as well as to celebrate those differences. One photo, by Saul Loeb, shows eight members of the military, of visibly different races, in the dress uniforms of different branches of the armed forces, labouring together to bring the coffin from the airplane to the waiting hearse. The second photo, by Tom Brenner, makes it plain that the ceremony is happening at dusk; the eight men are saluting the casket that has been just loaded into the hearse. The foreground is shadowed, except for the casket's flag, luminous in the light in the interior of the hearse. Labouring together. A luminous flag. Different portraits of the moment as well as of the man being commemorated. *The* truth? Perhaps not. But certainly, both are truths.

Consider what photography is, in all its permutations – video, still images, even "live" photos and gifs, etc. Photography is the visual medium with the longest association with news coverage. But photography by many standards is just another artistic medium, with much in common with painting, sculpture, architecture, graphic design, music, theatre, and dance. Like those arts, photography captures, interprets, and, at times, changes the world. The creativity of painters, musicians, actors, and dancers is celebrated, whether these artists are realistic in their descriptions of the world or are impressionistic or even hallucinogenic in their explorations. Across nations and cultures, people understand that the arts describe and translate but also re-examine the world, whether that art is representational, simply emotive, or entirely preoccupied with aesthetics: colour field paintings or per-cussive rhythmic compositions. Photographers, even news photographers, are like artists but for different, if overlapping, audiences. When photographs matter, it is because they tell truths, sometimes great truths. "The camera is an instrument that teaches people how to see without a camera," said famed Depression-era photog-rapher Dorothea Lange (cited in Meltzer, 2000, p. vii).

This is a media literacy lesson. Media literacy teaches students of all ages that even given photography's need for a camera lens – and the automatic ways that that lens can be activated – there are always, at base, human decisions involved in what images are taken and shown. (Just as media literacy lessons teach that there are human decisions involved in the algorithms that serve up online search results, for example.) A deep dive into media literacy should also remind us that photography's necessity for human input is not a negative. Or at least it is not always negative; at least it does not have to be.

The power of images has always derived from their content and aesthetics, but also from their emotional force, which is as much to say, as from their humanity. As Vietnam War photographer Don McCullin has said (2019): "Photography for me is not looking, it's feeling. If you can't feel what you're looking at, then you're never going to get others to feel anything when they look at your pictures."

This can be stated as a fact: in ways both large and so small as to be near-invisible, there is a human hand (and a human mind) behind all photographic reproduction. And that is one signal reason why photography has had the power that it has. In our era of rampant technological and digital innovations that are outstripping our abilities to keep ethical pace with their implications, that continued intercession of humanity is, potentially at least, a good thing. To make that potential good, what is needed is to recognise that *photography must tend to all of humanity*, even as it also searches for ever smaller, faster, sharper, pixel-laden, bokeh–enabled, low-light-receptive camera technologies.

In our era, perhaps in every era, images play (are *made* to play) multiple roles – some beneficial, some toxic – in the news and journalism ecosystem. Even in our hyper-sophisticated times, it is worth reflecting on how individuals and groups are *reporting* the world via images, why images have become the way that events are *remembered*, how *invented* images have become a potent political tool, and why par-tisan conflict is *contesting* the meaning of even fact-based (indexical) images.

Reported images

Journalists believe it is their ethical obligation to tell the truth as they under-stand it: to be accurate, to be fair. But always they are aware that they are making choices of what to report and how to report. So, too, is that subset of journalists, the photojournalists. Photographers do not, cannot objectively capture world events; photographers have to edit events for our present and future consumption. As pho-tographer (and PhD economist) Sebastiao Salgado has bluntly noted (2008): "You photograph with all your ideology."

Consider this hypothetical scenario: something major is happening, somewhere in the world. Imagine it is a meeting of world leaders. Photographers have gathered and are literally circling the event. Each photographer is of necessity shooting from a slightly different space around the table of leaders. Each has set up with slightly different equipment; each has made slightly different technical adjustments to their cameras. Each photographer is additionally, of course, distinctive in age, nationality, political perspective, gender presentation, religion, race, and ethnicity – not to mention personality and even height. The climactic moment in the meeting comes – perhaps it is a moment of confrontation between two major heads of state – and a flurry of pictures is taken. Then let's say, in our hypothetical case, that all those photos are pooled and made available to the world's media. Next, let's stipulate that none of those images have been altered from their RAW form, they all are *true*, as taken. But all are different: literally in who is in each photo but also in the micro-expressions captured from the different angles of vision. The event is the same, but the look of the event, in each photo of it, is different.

Here is the question. You are a photo editor for a major news outlet from your country. To illustrate your news outlet's lead story of this event you need to select a single image. Which one do you pick to tell the story of the event? Do you pick the photo that includes your own country's world leader in the image, even if she or he was not one of the two leaders in the direct confrontation? Do you pick a close-up of the confrontation between the two sparring leaders or a wide angle that emphasises the reactions of those other leaders looking on? Do you pick a photo that shows the angriest expressions or a photo that shows the more pacific ones? Do you pick a vertical that will fit well on your outlet's mobile phone app, or perhaps you want a close-up that will read well on a small screen? What prompts your choice of image?

You are aware, as a photo editor, that every single photo you are looking at is accurate. But you are also aware that any single image is a selective (but not fake) accounting of the event. No one image tells the whole story; every image captures the event from a singular perspective.

That observation prompts you as an editor to consider: is there any way that your news outlet's photographic representation of this event can be entirely truthful? If not, if you feel that your image is slightly more favourable to one side of the encounter, do you try and "balance" that image with the headline, or the photo caption, or with the story's lead sentence, or with a sidebar story that takes another angle on the encounter? Or is the entire decision process, and event, just one quick story among dozens across your desk that day, and you do not really have the time to sweat such details as "What is truth?" For you, "Which photo?" has to be a ten-second decision, then you need to move on to editorial judgements about the next story. You are not being paid to examine the philosophical questions of truth. Your job is to pick the most compelling photo, so *your* news outlet's audience will click on your story out of the thousands of stories on politics, sports, and celebrities that are shrieking to be looked at.

This hypothetical challenge is actually not hypothetical. It is a challenge faced daily by news outlets. Choices of what photographs to take and which ones to publish are perennial concerns and never more so than when the truth of a situation is complicated, but the space and time to cover that situation is limited.

And there are additional challenges to reporting the truth of a situation. Consider the reporting on the 2018 meeting of the G7 nations, for example. That real case of photos taken at a contentious meeting at the G7 summit highlights two present realities. Many news photographs appear in global news outlets, but many more are shared via social media platforms. Today, not only are news outlets facing decisions of what images to feature in the news, but they are cognisant that *reporting* of the news often occurs outside the pages of the mainstream media.

Look at the photo shared on German Chancellor Angela Merkel's Instagram account, taken by the official Federal Government photographer, Jesco Denzel (Figure 6.1).[4] It is a photo that went viral and spawned dozens of memes, some of them adding captions as though Merkel was accusing US President Trump of destroying the global order or denying climate change.[5]

The Atlantic magazine (2018) posed the question of just how that photograph might be interpreted and the fact that that interpretation might be different. Did it depict a woman leader, in a room full of men, scolding someone who refused to co-operate? Or perhaps it was a case of a US president patriotically defying those who would stand in the way of the United States. Or it could even be seen as representing the decline of the West's unity as a political force.

FIGURE 6.1   German Chancellor Angela Merkel and US President Donald Trump at the 2018 G7 summit in Canada. The photograph was released on the German Chancellor's official Instagram account.

Most importantly, what you saw, whatever it was, is part of a larger trend: Geopolitical contention is frequently expressed through the language of online visual media. . . . The relative absence of context . . . is part of what made it so ready to become memetic.

For *The Atlantic*, this image serves as a sort of Rorschach test for today's political moment, open to interpretation by anyone, including many who might have competing agendas and narratives (ibid).

During those same 2018 G7 talks, governments other than Germany also posted their own photographs of that same "spontaneous meeting" via their official Instagram and Twitter accounts. The perspectives and precise moments captured in the photos were different in each case; each government's channel chose to feature its own leader. President Trump's social media director, Dan Scavino Jr., for example, shared a much less fraught moment on his Twitter account. Scavino posted a photo of the president at the centre of the circle of leaders, with several other world leaders clearly smiling including host Canadian Prime Minister Justin Trudeau and Japanese Prime Minister Shinzō Abe.[6] In a similar fashion, Canadian Prime Minister Trudeau's official photographer, Adam Scotti, tweeted out a multi-image tweet, including two photos from the impromptu session. In all three images Trudeau is a lead actor, underlining Canada's role as the host country.[7] Similarly, the Twitter accounts of both French President Emmanuel Macron and Italian Prime Minister Giuseppe Conte tweeted photos of the same meeting around the table. President Macron's account pictured him speaking forcefully to Trump,[8] and Prime Minister Conte's Twitter account ran a photo of Conte in the foreground, reading papers; Trump's hair is all that is visible of the US leader.[9]

What are the lessons from this accounting?

Choices of how to visually cover the news matter: the choices made by photo editors in newsrooms matter. Indeed, the notion of *the truth* is harmed, and the concept of reporting is damaged, when editors do not thoughtfully choose the images (and accompanying text) for news stories and when they fail to make transparent the reasoning for their selections, especially on stories that are known to have strong partisan perspectives.

But even if news outlets struggle to be fair, to report the facts, to at least tell *a* truth about an event, are the same decisions in play when those reporting the news are not journalists, but partisan actors (such as in the case of these G7 pictures from government officials)? The choices made by those posting on social media also matter. So, has the notion of *reporting* changed, as a result of mainstream media no longer being the default intermediaries between governments and their publics? Does the notion of *truth* in reporting need to be rethought, now that news outlets no longer own the news cycle with their images? Participants in a news story, such as the government leaders in the G7 photographs, are today capable of communicating their own picture of an event directly to their audiences via their own social media accounts. And those actors make their own decisions about what photographs to show, which is to say what *framing* of the event they prefer the public to see. The different photographs selected differently shape the meaning of an event, leading to home audiences understanding differently the meaning and import of that event.

These changes in how the news comes to the public do not augur well for the nurturing of a fully informed citizenry. It has always been the case that consumers of news need to be media literate, but it is even more the case in today's news eco-system. With such a cacophony of information coming at speed, the public needs to understand that the larger truths of events are not found in individual accounts, they are in the *aggregated* portraits of those events but, I would argue, in aggregations where deeply reported coverage by mainstream media is part of the whole.

When reporting of newsworthy events increasingly comes from social media via the actors in those events who have no professional journalism code of ethics and standards to uphold, the full import of what is occurring is harder to grasp, even if multiple voices are heard and multiple angles of vision seen. Somewhere in the fracas are truths, but so too are sins of omission and outright lies. And even if the facts as reported on social media and via government and corporate channels are accurate and images un-doctored, the tale of the whole is not well contextualised when only partisans tell the stories. Truth is diminished when news is told in ways flattering to the participants, which is what typically occurs on social media plat-forms (and admittedly, of course, also often on mainstream media platforms). Media literate publics have never been so needed.

Remembered images

According to MIT Brain and Cognitive Sciences Professor Mriganka Sur, half of the human brain is devoted directly or indirectly to vision (MIT, 1996). So it comes as little surprise then that so many of us remember our lives through images. We match our recollection of being five with the photo of our blowing out the candles on our birthday cake. When disaster threatens, we reach for the family photos to rescue from the fire or rising waters. Our own memories are not enough. We know our memories are fugitive.

When prompted to recall a past news event, even one that occurred in our life-time, we often recollect a photograph of it: a single man in the street holding off a line of tanks, the Twin Towers at the moment that a plane struck. Tiananmen Square and 9/11 were more complicated than a photo can conjure. But those sin-gular images slot neatly into our own brain's version of the game of *Concentration*. Without consciously trying, we match our mental card saying "New York plane disaster" with the photo of passengers standing on the airplane wings in the miracle on the Hudson River. We match our memory of the "Arab Spring" with the photo of Egyptians stomping on a poster of President Hosni Mubarak in Tahrir Square. Photos not only direct what we remember, they reduce the events of our lives (and the past) into slices out of time. Photographs can overwhelm our own encounters of events and insist on the importance of what has been recorded.

In his 1963 film *Le Petit Soldat*, Swiss-French filmmaker Jean-Luc Godard penned the following words for his character Bruno Forestier, a photojournalist:

"Photography is truth. The cinema is truth twenty-four times per second" (cited in Gibbons, 2011). Yet the words that Godard piped into the mouth of Forestier meant more, in that revolutionary film, than Forestier's simple lines on their face: that photography has the ability to pin the butterfly of a fleeting moment to a piece of film. Godard's point was more philosophical: that photography has the ability to see *into* what it captures on film. It sees beyond the reality; it sees to what is "true." It "remembers" what we see. In 1963, long before the digital era, a cultural-wide shift was becoming visible. As author James Roy MacBean judged in his work *Film and Revolution* (1975, p. 6):

> In Godard's films "truth" is no longer understood as immanent in things and beings; as if lying there waiting to be revealed (like God's grace): it is nothing more and nothing less than the significations and moral transformations we produce in social practice.

Ever since its invention, photography has been the world's mnemonic. But while photographs direct us on what to remember, they do not capture the totality of what we, humans, have physically seen. Our experience of sight is informed by so many things; like a synesthete, we all have a cascade of senses that collide and shape how we see the world. But photographs? Even videos? Those are still, or linear. They can be revisited, over time, again and again. That fact allows them to be engrained in our memories. That fact also allows us the time and space to judge those images, their "significations," on the visual information compressed in them – and to be informed by the "moral transformations" of our society we see encoded in those images, as MacBean had it (1975). We use (and re-use) photographs and video – those that are available in reproduction as well as those seared in our memories – to justify, undermine, or legitimate what we like or dislike about our current state of being.

Not all that happens in our world is photographed. If there are no images of an event, then most of us never know that something momentous or awful or trivial has happened, because the lack of images means all-too-often that the event is not covered in the news. Media's interest in covering the news that has been pictured is why, on one hand, distant famines in hard-to-access locations often do not make the news and why, on the other, for example, terrorists attack locations where everyday citizens are on social media and where there already is a robust mainstream media presence get considerable coverage. Terrorists want the world to see and to remember the terror they are wreaking; terrorism is about getting the public's attention.[10] Terrorists rarely have sufficient human and financial capital to defeat an enemy on the ground. That's why, said Professor Paul Wilkinson, terrorists "thrive on the oxygen of publicity" (1997). And that's why "free media in an open society are particularly vulnerable to exploitation and manipulation by ruthless terrorist organisations" (ibid).

When mainstream media cover crises in the international arena (outbursts of terror, hotly contested elections, distant natural disasters, etc.) they cover them with 24/7 reporting and on-the-scene interviews. They lead the news with dramatic images, break into regular programming with updates, and in short order post photographs or videos of the event culled in part from citizens posting on Twitter or Facebook.

After the fact, for days and weeks, and then on anniversary occasions and at times when policymakers are referencing a past terrorist attack to make a point about national security or immigration or patriotism, those news images serve as reference points. The iconic images from the September morning of 9/11, for example, are regularly deployed in the public commemoration of that event, and in so doing they also reinforce the global memory of that day in alignment with how the attacks were depicted in the photographs and TV footage of it. Such visuals are also put to the service of other events and other agendas. The 9/11 images are resurrected (sometimes with the photos themselves and sometimes just by referring to the images) in the aftermath of other terrorist attacks to draw a relationship between them – asking, for example, "Is this *this country's* 9/11?" The 9/11 images are also reprised when US politicians or even one of the two major American political parties wants to make a statement about patriotism; they are resurrected in political campaigns. The 9/11 images have become a stand-in for the American flag and the American (often argued to be *Christian*) values of strength and resilience. It is no surprise that two of the most duplicated images from that day are one of firefighters raising an American flag over the ruins of the World Trade Center and one of steel girders in the shape of a cross rising up out of the rubble. Those appropriations of *remembering* give evidence of the disruptive force of visual media and the politicisation of news photography.

It does not take a national or a global cataclysm, however, to seize the public's attention. Photos that seem rather ordinary can prompt emotional responses and engagement. Consider just a few statistics: tweets with images generate three times more engagement than basic text updates, tweets with GIFs generate six times more, and tweets with video generate nine times more (Hutchinson, 2016). Facebook posts with images get 2.3 times more engagement than posts without images (Pinantoan, 2015). And Facebook's own research found that even Facebook users who never clicked on a video on its site were affected by the still image of the video on the pages they looked at – as many as 15% of them recalled the still video later. Facebook's research also showed that those who only watched three seconds of a video ad accounted for 47% of the brand awareness and recall, and those who watched for less than ten seconds accounted for 74%. In other words, "People didn't have to watch a whole video to be affected by the ad."[11]

Why does this matter? We remember the images we see, even if we see them very briefly. In a 2014 study, MIT neuroscientists found that the brain can identify images seen for as little as 13 milliseconds (MIT News, 2014). "The fact that you can do that at these high speeds indicates to us that what vision does is find concepts. That's what the brain is doing all day long – trying to understand what we're looking at," noted Mary Potter, an MIT professor of brain and cognitive sciences and senior author of the study. That is why, arguably, the most powerful tools in today's media arsenal are photos, videos, gifs, data visualisations, etc., precisely because the images often are remembered sub rosa, below our conscious thought. In the competitive environment of digital platforms, the quartet of attraction, attention, remembering, and engagement is everything. Journalists, advertisers, and politicians have come to understand that attraction leads to attention, attention leads to remembering, and remembering leads to engagement.

Images are increasingly the start of that equation.

Invented images

It used to be thought that the power of images resided in their capturing of reality – what theorists called photo's *indexicality* – a photo's one-to-one relationship to something that exists. That is why publishers have long put photographs in the pages of the press (or why producers have put their reporters at a scene, live on camera): to affirm the present-ness of what is being covered. Photos and videos provide documentation, as it were, of what is happening. As many have observed since the invention of photography in the 1830s, photography interposes a camera's "eye" between the "taker" and what is seen and captured. The mechanical ways that photographic images are taken provide the argument that the images that result are (relatively) unaffected by human hands.

In their turn, photo commentators and critics have argued that the phenomenon of *indexicality* makes those who see photographic images eyewitnesses by proxy. Less than 30 years after the dawn of photography, Oliver Wendell Holmes, Sr., a physician, writer, and father to the US Supreme Court justice of the same name, wrote in the *Atlantic Monthly* of seeing "a series of photographs showing the field of Antietam and the surrounding country, as they appeared after the great battle of the 17th of September."[12] He described the power of those images, his evaluation informed by his own visit to the Civil War battlefield four days after the battle (American Social History Project):

> Let him who wishes to know what war is look at this series of illustrations. These wrecks of manhood thrown together in careless heaps or ranged in ghastly rows for burial were alive but yesterday. . . . It was so nearly like visiting the battlefield to look over these views.

Those images, he wrote, brought back all the emotions of the actual sight of the battlefield. Today, more than a century and a half since Mathew Brady's photographers captured those scenes of war, images are digital, not captured on huge and fragile glass plates by photographers who were as much chemists as artists. Today, we all have the functions not just of photography in our pockets, but the skills of forgers as well, with Photoshop-style apps on our phones that can tweak, remix, and completely remake images however we like.[13] Today, AR and VR technology create hyper-plausible illusions. Today, "deep fakes" are possible: AI-powered face-swapping technologies can create videos that are "reality-shattering." As *Fast Company* noted in 2018:

> The end of reality feels now truly imminent. We're on the verge of a complete reinvention of how we understand the moving image. Before, we took videotape as proof of fact – whether it showed someone committing a crime or a politician simply making a statement.

According to *Fast Company*, deep Video Portraits may be the penultimate step towards destroying the once-incontrovertible truth of video – and it could be nigh on impossible to fix this. The only answer, it argues, is to raise awareness that such technology exists (ibid).

In Mathew Brady's time, photographs could be miscaptioned and crudely altered; at times scenes to be photographed were tampered with before the fact. Today we live in an era of near-invisible falsification, when all that stands between us and the fictitious bubble of our Photoshopped, AR/VR, and Deep-Faked world is our knowledge that we will end up living in the Matrix if we are not aware of what our new tools are capable of. And awareness *is* growing: the beauty and fashion industries, for example, are walking back their reliance on airbrushed ads and on models who are lit and made up in reality-defying ways.[14] Authenticity is being sought, precisely because the tools to make the fake seemingly real are so good and so available.

It is in the midst of all this that public conversations are erupting over whether the media are trustworthy; whether certain media outlets, in the words of Trump, are "fake." Websites that verify news stories and social media posts are flourishing; some, like Snopes.com, have few evident political axes to grind, others are eager to profess that they prioritise investigating their partisan opponents' news and advertising.

Because images are treated as information, rather than simply as aesthetic filler in the information ecosystem, they are being both investigated and weaponised. Consider the 2017 story in *Politico*, reporting that Trump's "[a]ides sometimes slip him stories to press their advantage on policy." In one incident that *Politico* documented, K.T. McFarland, the president's deputy national security adviser, had given the president a printout of two *Time* magazine covers. One, supposedly from the 1970s, warned of a coming ice age; the other, from 2008, about surviving global warming, according to four White House officials familiar with the matter. Trump quickly got lathered up about the media's hypocrisy. But there was a problem. The 1970s cover was fake, part of an Internet hoax that has circulated for years. Staff chased down the truth and intervened before Trump tweeted or talked publicly about it.[15]

Following *Politico's* story, the faked *Time* cover mentioned in its article was identified. *Time* itself had exposed the cover hoax four years previously, in a story headlined: "Sorry, a TIME Magazine Cover Did Not Predict a Coming Ice Age" (2013). Those who allegedly had brought the covers into the Oval Office had hoped to convince the president that scientists had flip-flopped on climate change over the decades – implying that if scientists had once wrongly predicted global cooling, it was possible that the current prediction of global warming would also prove false.[16]

The irony in all this is that the power of fake images (and doctored captions) rests on the fact that photos remain understood to be valid evidence of a dispassionate reality – even as news almost daily exposes images fraudulently used or announces technologies capable of creating more life-like, yet fictitious, photographs. The irony is also that at times the veracity of images does not matter, and is, in fact, the point. Consider the use of self-evidently phony memes that ever-more-wildly label an image originally tethered to reality (the flurry of memes playing on the G7 photo of President Trump and Chancellor Merkel), the gleeful retweeting and *liking* of reworked videos (for example, Trump's retweeting of a video where he is portrayed wrestling and punching a figure whose head has been replaced by the logo for CNN).[17] Crudely manipulated images do not need to be seen as truthful or even plausible (for example, the viral fake photo that pictured school shooting survivor Emma González ripping up the US Constitution),[18] they just need to trigger an excuse for social media trolls to foment hate and partisanship. Even fake photographs can trigger an emotional response in those who see them, and in the meme economy, it is often the case that the more outrageously photos are captioned or otherwise distorted, the more often they are re-meme'd, prompting a sequence of reciprocal circularity.

Perhaps the greatest irony is that even fake photos, or perhaps especially fake photos, demonstrate that images matter. That "seeing" matters. Today, as Trump has repeatedly demonstrated, dominating the global conversation on social media is to wield today's power; power today is in trending on Twitter and Google. More rarely it is located in telling, or showing, the truth.

Contested images

There is nothing more powerful than a photograph. Well, except maybe a video. Although, on third thought, perhaps more powerful than either is a (partisan) mind made up.

Consider the photographs of the inauguration of US President Donald Trump in January 2017. As *The Washington Post* outlined (2017a):

> On the first full day of the Trump administration, White House press secretary Sean Spicer admonished the news media for reporting that the crowd that witnessed Trump's inauguration was smaller than other recent inauguration crowds, claiming, "This was the largest audience to ever witness an inauguration – period – both in person and around the globe."[19]

News outlets in the United States and abroad had that morning run side-by-side photographs of the crowds that came to Washington, DC's National Mall to witness Trump's inauguration and those who had attended President Barack Obama's first inauguration in 2009. Images taken from the same location (the top of the Washington Monument obelisk) at the same time (the swearing in of the presidents) showed a far larger crowd for the Obama ceremony.[20] And the ridership figures reported by the DC Metro also indicated that more than twice the number of passengers took the Metro on the morning of Obama's first inauguration than for Trump's inauguration. Yet the existence of clear photographic evidence showing the differing sizes of the crowds did not stop the new president from asserting in a speech that morning to the Central Intelligence Agency (CIA) that up to 1.5 million people had attended his inauguration. *The New York Times* reported that it was a claim that photographs disproved (2017). Trump understood that in order to control his message that his presidency was endorsed by the majority of the American public he needed to challenge other sources of the "truth." So in that same CIA speech the president called the journalists covering his presidency "among the most dishonest human beings on earth." As his first White House press secretary Sean Spicer was to observe a few months later: "The president is the most effective messenger on his agenda and I think his use of social media . . . gives him an opportunity to speak straight to the American people, which has proved to be a very, very effective tool."[21]

For the president to advance his own case, to lead the conversation, he used the platform of the presidency (and the medium of Twitter) to undermine the reporting of the media and the journalists themselves. From that platform he was able to convince his supporters to also reject the mainstream media's reporting, even to the extent of denying the evidence presented in photographs. Trump learned these lessons early in his years in reality television and took them into the Oval Office. In late April 2017, roughly three months into the Trump presidency, *The Washington Post* (2017b) quoted Kellyanne Conway, counsellor to the president, in an article exploring his "obsession with cable TV." "President Trump," Conway said, "is someone who comes to the White House with a sophisticated understanding of how to communicate, the power of television, the power of imagery, the power of message, and how message, messenger and delivery all work together."

Five days after the inauguration, a University of Massachusetts, Amherst professor and a PhD researcher in statistical methodology at a Palo Alto research firm published the results of a survey of 1,388 Americans. The survey reproduced the two photos from the Obama and the Trump inaugurations. The survey respondents were divided into half. One half was asked which photo was from which inauguration. The other half was simply asked which photo had more people in it.

As the researchers related in an article in *The Washington Post* (2017a):

> In both cases, people who said that they had voted for Trump in 2016 were significantly more likely to answer the questions wrong than those who voted for [the Democratic candidate Hillary] Clinton or those who said they did not vote at all.

When asked about which image went with which inauguration, 41% of Trump supporters gave the wrong answer – much more than the wrong answers given by 8% of Clinton voters and 21% of those who did not vote. Even more noteworthy for the researchers was the fact that 15% of people who voted for Trump said more people were in the image from Trump's inauguration than that of Obama's. That answer came from only 2% of Clinton voters and 3% of non-voters. The researchers added that some Trump supporters had decided "to use this question to express their support for Trump rather than to answer the survey question factually" (ibid).

Photography, including network and cable news, as well as images posted on social media, can be used to spread specific messages, at times with a clear political agenda. That occurred, for instance, when the governments of the G7 cherry-picked quite different photographs of the same event, each selecting a photograph that it believed would best serve its own national interest. From the side of the audience, however, as noted above, members of the public can interpret the exact same image differently to others – as occurred in the case of the crowd shots of the two inaugurations. Usually, audiences believe what news photographs and videos show, in part because most are little more than wallpaper behind news stories; most simply illustrate some basic scenario described in the news. But what researchers are learning is that if the content of a photographic image challenges an audience's assumptions, the audience will attack the authenticity of that image, no matter how neutral on its face the photo appears to be (such as a crowd scene from an inauguration). We the public are learning, political consultants are counting on, and academic researchers are finding, that when audience members encounter an image that challenges a political partisan opinion they hold – even one that the audience presumes to be a "real" image – they may dispute the truthfulness of it, or at least the truthfulness of the caption of it.

Why? Evidence suggests that attacking the validity of that image is easier, more emotionally and intellectually comfortable, than changing one's political beliefs and affiliations. Audiences can be directed or be inclined to bend the meaning of an image to their own interests. In political science this type of behaviour is termed "expressive responding" (Bullock et al., 2013). In other words: "Individuals may offer responses that are consistent with their partisanship not solely because they believe those responses, but also because doing so gives them the opportunity to support their 'team'" (ibid, p. 524).

Truth, in other words, can take a back seat to partisanship.

Conclusion: the humanity of image

Pulitzer-Prize winning *New York Times* photojournalist Damon Winter observed (2011): "We are not walking photocopiers. We are storytellers."

Telling stories through photography is a way of making sense of what is seen. "When I photograph, what I'm really doing is seeking answers to things," photographer Wynn Bullock has said (2018).

Telling stories through photography is a way of attracting the public's attention, for good. Photography "communicates a fact, touches the heart and leaves the viewer a changed person," photographer Irving Penn has noted (cited in Celii, 2012).

Telling stories through photography is not a euphemism for telling lies like one might accuse a child of "telling stories." Telling stories through photography, Sebastiao Salgado has argued, is a form of civic engagement (cited in Berger,

2001): "I believe we have a responsibility in the time in which we are living to provoke a discussion, to provoke a debate, to ask questions."

The default of reporting has always been words. Words (and numbers) are essential to report the minutiae of facts and the narratives of stories; of what happens in the halls of government, in the boardrooms of corporations, on factory floors, in schools and on the street. Both the events being described as well as the analyses of them have historically been told (at least first) via words. Images are most familiar as journalism's dessert: so appealing, but most often supplementary to the main course. Most news photos over time have been deployed simply to describe that *this* is how the neighbourhood looked in the aftermath of the devastating storm. This is how the two world leaders looked at their fraught meeting. Most news photos, in other words, have been the aforesaid wallpaper.

Yet the reporting of news has evolved. In the 21st century, news literally does not get posted if there is "just" text to publish. Often that demand for visuals results in a never-ending scroll of forgettable photos blurring across screens. But amongst that eyes-glazing-over visual din are important visuals, images that are more than illustrations goosing up text-centric stories. Because images are capturing attention in a competitive marketplace for news, because that creates an economic argument for more visuals, newsrooms are commanding images from more locations, of more kinds of peoples, on a wider range of issues. New platforms, greater access, and better UX/UI interfaces on social media, on apps, and on websites have made image-first or image-driven stories feasible and appealing and significant. In social media and mainstream news outlets, stories are centring on the information captured via photographs, video, and visualisations. In real time, news outlets and social media platforms are showing the violence playing out on the street, the tragedies of migrants, the travails of climate change, the protests of #BlackLivesMatter and #MeToo, and yes, the good that communities are coming together to do. Proverbially, images often speak louder than words of description ever can. Visuals today are communicating what words cannot.

While objectivity is understood to be a myth, while there may be no truly clean hands in newsrooms, boardrooms, and living rooms alike, today's increasing – and increasingly innovative – use of visuals is a social good. Photos of dying children in Yemen told their story more compellingly than words have been able to do. While the images that are now seen do not always report a greater truth than words can, Rashomon-like they do report more truths, many of which have been heretofore untold, and unseen, in the record.

Yet of course, it also matters that so many images are falsified and misidentified, that they are disseminating untruths, and that even so, more of those faked photos appear more authentic than at any time in the past.

What needs to happen in today's journalism? Of course, transparency needs to be fostered, nurtured, and practiced. News outlets need to attach credit and captions to *all* images on *all* platforms, making that information available in the same space or with a hover over the images. Other institutions too that prioritise their visual information economy need to follow the same standards – the rules of photographic ethics followed by such groups as the Associated Press, the National Press Photographers Association and the Society of Professional Journalism.[22]

And because there is never a "the" truth, only "a" truths, news outlets and other institutions need to be transparent about how the images they show have been taken and selected. Such information should also be presented or linked in captions or via hovers, and foregrounded in stories known to have partisan perspectives.

But such meaningful information added to the news ecosystem is only valuable if the public engages with it. That suggests that the teaching of media literacy needs to be mandated, from elementary education through professional schools. But workplaces too – from corporate offices to military barracks, from government ministries to the field offices of grass-roots nonprofits – must commit to media literacy training to their cohorts. And, of course, the easiest way to encourage good media literacy habits is to put media literacy in the defaults of the digital tools used to communicate. In mid-2018, Google Docs finally embedded a grammar checker on its platform;[23] machine learning suggests that such checkers could also alert for instances where critical thinking skills and mindfulness are lacking.

Similarly, AI can nudge those conducting searches to see that there are other venues covering the same issues, much as Google News in 2018 institutionalised a "Full Coverage" interface for its top stories. In that instance, a lead story from FoxNews, for example, is followed on the same screen (or with a swipe on a mobile platform) by news (and clearly labelled "Opinion" pieces) on the same event from a half dozen other news outlets, often from different political positions, and from sites including social media.[24]

But we cannot rely on the technology of picture taking to save us. We have learned that digital tools and education will not eradicate trolls and bad actors.

Consider, finally, what we see in our news, however it comes to us. Those photographs we see make visible what media care to show about humanity. The photographs make manifest the ways that media, and we ourselves, understand our responsibility to humanity. The photographs reflect back to us how deep and abiding is our commitment, our obligation to the founding principles of democratic governance: "We hold these principles to be self-evident, that all men are created equal," as the American Declaration of Independence asserted in 1776. General George Washington, later to become the first US president, wrote in a letter two years earlier that "truth will ultimately prevail where there is pains taken to bring it to light" (1794, cited in George Washington's Mount Vernon). What *are* we bringing to light? What are we *not* seeing? News photographs not only should be true, they should expose truths, even when those truths cause discomfort, distress, or unrest.

And we the audience? We have great responsibilities too. If we don't seek out news, if we tolerate the obfuscation of news, if we fail to challenge those who assert fallacies, then we, too, are complicit in undermining the humanity of all.

At the top of this essay, I quibbled about the use of "the" versus "a" in *The New York Times*' branding campaign. But, ultimately, I champion the *Times*' assertion. "The truth demands our attention." Yes. It does.

Notes

1 The title of this chapter is a nod to the book by the late historian Bernard Lewis. (1975). *History: Remembered, recovered, invented*. Princeton: Princeton University Press.
2 The two were freed in May 2019 after more than 500 days in jail.
3 For original tweet containing the two images. Available at: https://twitter.com/BESorenson/status/1035351499596017664.
4 See available at: www.instagram.com/p/Bjz0RKtAMFp/.
5 See global order meme. Available at: https://imgflip.com/i/2by49k; Climate change meme. Available at: https://knowyourmeme.com/photos/1381133-merkel-and-trump-g7-summit-photograph.
6 See available at: https://twitter.com/Scavino45/status/1005464870551150592/.
7 See available at: https://twitter.com/AdamScotti/status/1005512215816962048.
8 See available at: https://twitter.com/EmmanuelMacron/status/1005465065976418304.
9 See available at: https://twitter.com/GiuseppeConteIT/status/1005494531024797697.
10 Even before 2001, coverage of terrorism had been part of the international news repertoire, but what was so diabolical on 11 September, was that Al Qaeda had planned it so that the world would be watching live as the second plane hit the World Trade Center. The first plane prompted every news outlet in Manhattan to train its cameras on the Twin Towers. And the TV cameras were still running when the second plane struck – and still running when first one, then the other building imploded, with all the loss of life that their collapse implied. Terrorism live, terrorism conducted explicitly so the whole world could watch was different than an act where the intent was simply to destroy something or someone. The terror of 9/11 was not just the deaths of thousands; it was that those deaths were packaged so that the world became witnesses to those deaths, over and over again. Parts of this section are adapted from my book *Packaging Terrorism: Co-opting the News for Politics and Profit* (2009).
11 See available at: www.facebook.com/business/news/value-of-video. When considering remembering and engagement, there is at least one additional statistic that stands out: on the visually centric site Instagram, photos showing faces get 30% more "likes" than photos without faces. If images attract attention, images of people seize even more attention. Available at: www.news.gatech.edu/2014/03/20/face-it-instagram-pictures-faces-are-more-popular.
12 The Battle of Sharpsburg in Maryland, 60 miles northwest from Washington, DC, on 17 Sept. 1863, remains the bloodiest day in American history: 23,000 Union and Confederate men were killed or wounded. The battle changed the course of the American Civil War.
13 Of course, photographers who worked in the Brady studio were complicit in tinkering with the scenes that they photographed, as well as appending falsified information as captions to images. See available at: www.historynet.com/behind-barricade-identity-devils-den-sharpshooter.htm#prettyPhoto and www.amazon.com/Gettysburg-Journey-Time-William-Frassanito/dp/0939631970.
14 See available at: www.nytimes.com/2018/01/15/fashion/cvs-bans-airbrushing.html and www.npr.org/sections/thetwo-way/2017/09/30/554750939/france-aims-to-get-real-retouched-photos-of-models-now-require-label.
15 See available at: www.politico.com/story/2017/05/15/donald-trump-fake-news-238379.
16 In that *Time* article, reporter Brian Walsh noted that there actually were both *Time* and *Newsweek* stories on global cooling back in the 1970s (although not cover stories). He writes: "But as John Cook points out over at Skeptical Science, global cooling was much more an invention of the media than it was a real scientific concern. A survey of peer-reviewed scientific papers published between 1965 and 1979 shows that the large majority of research at the time predicted that the earth would warm as carbon-dioxide levels rose – as indeed it has. And some of those global-cooling projections were based on the idea that aerosol levels in the atmosphere – which are a product of air pollution

from sources like coal burning and which contribute to cooling by deflecting sunlight in the atmosphere – would keep rising. But thanks to environmental legislation like the Clean Air Acts, global air-pollution levels – not including greenhouse gases like carbon dioxide – peaked in the 1970s and began declining."

17 See available at: www.nytimes.com/2017/07/02/business/media/trump-wrestling-video-cnn-twitter.html.

18 See available at: www.snopes.com/fact-check/emma-gonzalez-ripping-up-constitution/.

19 For aerial photographs see available at: www.washingtonpost.com/news/monkey-cage/wp/2017/01/25/we-asked-people-which-inauguration-crowd-was-bigger-heres-what-they-said/?utm_term=.73b54d3c177e. See also available at: www.nytimes.com/2017/01/21/us/politics/trump-white-house-briefing-inauguration-crowd-size.html and www.washingtonpost.com/news/fact-checker/wp/2017/01/22/spicer-earns-four-pinocchios-for-a-series-of-false-claims-on-inauguration-crowd-size/?utm_term=.3fbb54035779.

20 See available at: www.pri.org/stories/2017-01-20/photos-compare-crowd-trumps-inauguration-obamas and www.bbc.com/news/world-us-canada-38698837.

21 Spicer made the comment in a press conference in early June 2017.

22 See also available at: www.asne.org/resources-ethics-nppa; *Images – telling the story | News values | AP*. Associated Press. Available at: www.ap.org/about/news-values-and-principles/telling-the-story/visuals; *SPJ code of ethics – society of professional journalists*. Available at: www.spj.org/ethicscode.asp.

23 See: New Grammar Suggestions in Google Docs Launching to Early Adopter Program. G Suite Updates Blog. Available at: https://gsuiteupdates.googleblog.com/2018/07/new-grammar-suggestions-in-google-docs.html.

24 See: The new Google news: AI meets human intelligence. *Google*, 8 May 2018. Available at www.blog.google/products/news/new-google-news-ai-meets-human-intelligence/.

References

American Social History Project. *Civil war photography on the battlefront*. Available at: https://civilwar.picturinghistory.gc.cuny.edu/presentations-about-visual-media/photography/.

The Atlantic. (2018). *That Merkel photo is more like a meme than a renaissance painting*. Available at: www.theatlantic.com/technology/archive/2018/06/that-merkel-photo-is-more-like-a-meme-than-a-renaissance-painting/562505/.

Berger, J. (2001). The globalised people. *The Guardian*, 28 May. Available at: www.theguardian.com/culture/2001/may/28/artsfeatures.globalisation1.

Bullock, J. G., Gerber, A. S., Hill, S. J. and Huber, G. A. (2013). Partisan bias in factual beliefs about politics. *Quarterly Journal of Political Science*, 10(4), pp. 519–578.

Bullock, W. (2018). *Wynn Bullock on photography and art*. Available at: www.wynnbullockphotography.com/quotes.html.

Celii, A. (2012). Irving Penn – all-time 100 fashion icons. *Time*, 2 Apr. Available at: http://content.time.com/time/specials/packages/article/0,28804,2110513_2110629_2110718,00.html.

Fast Company. (2018). *This new face swapping deep fakes AI is scarily realistic*. Available at: www.fastcompany.com/90175648/this-new-face-swapping-deep-fakes-ai-is-scarily-realistic.

George Washington's Mount Vernon. [online]. Available at: www.mountvernon.org/library/digitalhistory/quotes/article/truth-will-ultimately-prevail-where-pains-is-taken-to-bring-it-to-light/.

Gibbons, F. (2011). Jean-Luc Godard: Film is over. What to do? *The Guardian*, 12 July. Available at: www.theguardian.com/film/2011/jul/12/jean-luc-godard-film-socialisme.

Hutchinson, A. (2016). Images, GIFs or video – which generates the most response on Twitter. *Social Media Today*, 19 Sept. Available at: www.socialmediatoday.com/social-business/images-gifs-or-video-which-generates-most-response-twitter.

MacBean, R. (1975). *Film and revolution*. Bloomington, IN: Indiana University Press.

McCullin, D. (2019). *Don McCullin* [online]. Available at: https://donmccullin.com/don-mccullin/.

Meltzer, M. (2000). *Dorothea Lange: A photographer's life*. Syracuse, NY: Syracuse University Press.

MIT News. (1996). *Brain processing of visual information*. Available at: http://news.mit.edu/1996/visualprocessing.

MIT News. (2014). *In the blink of an eye*. Available at: http://news.mit.edu/2014/in-the-blink-of-an-eye-0116.

Moeller, S. D. (2009). *Packaging terrorism: Co-opting the news for politics and profit*. Chichester: John Wiley & Sons.

New York Times. (2017). *With false claims Trump attacks media on turnout and intelligence rift*. Available at: www.nytimes.com/2017/01/21/us/politics/trump-white-house-briefing-inauguration-crowd-size.html.

New York Times. (2018). Why we are publishing haunting pictures of emaciated Yemeni children. *New York Times*, 26 Oct. Available at: www.nytimes.com/2018/10/26/reader-center/yemen-photos-starvation.html.

Osnos, E. (2018). The central question behind Facebook: What does Mark Zuckerberg believe in? *NPR*, 4 Oct. Available at: www.npr.org/templates/transcript/transcript.php?storyId=654333466.

Pinantoan, A. (2015). How to massively boost your blog traffic with these five awesome image stats. *Buzzsomo*, 20 May 2015. Available at: www.socialmediatoday.com/social-business/images-gifs-or-video-which-generates-most-response-twitter.

Salgado, S. (2008). Popular photography. *Hachette Filipacchi*, March issue, p. 127.

Smith, N. (2018). Aung San Suu Kyi defends jailing of Burmese journalists. *The Telegraph*, 13 Sept. Available at: www.telegraph.co.uk/news/2018/09/13/aung-san-suu-kyi-defends-jailing-burmese-journalists/.

Sorensen, B. (2018). 30 Aug. Available at: https://twitter.com/BESorenson/status/1035351499596017664.

Time. (2013). *Sorry: A time magazine cover did not predict a coming ice age*. Available at: http://science.time.com/2013/06/06/sorry-a-time-magazine-cover-did-not-predict-a-coming-ice-age/.

The Washington Post. (2017a). *This is what Trump voters said when asked to compare his inauguration crowd with Obama's*. Available at: www.washingtonpost.com/news/monkey-cage/wp/2017/01/25/we-asked-people-which-inauguration-crowd-was-bigger-heres-what-they-said/?utm_term=.73b54d3c177e.

The Washington Post. (2017b). *Everyone tunes in: Inside Trump's obsession with cable TV*. Available at: www.washingtonpost.com/politics/everyone-tunes-in-inside-trumps-obsession-with-cable-tv/2017/04/23/3c52bd6c-25e3-11e7-a1b3-faff0034e2de_story.html?utm_term=.a53ad2d5c11c.

Winter, D. (2011). Through my eye, not hipstamatics. *New York Times*, 11 Feb. 2011. Available at: https://lens.blogs.nytimes.com/2011/02/11/through-my-eye-not-hipstamatic.

PART III
New pedagogies

7

NEW JOURNALISMS, NEW PEDAGOGIES

Karen Fowler-Watt

This chapter will consider how journalism education can contribute to a re-imagined journalism that is more connected and trusted:

> *From where I stand, now, I see certainly a media landscape that is full of pitfalls, full of dangers, but I am also . . . an optimist . . . because of the human decency that I see. . . . I really do fundamentally believe in the goodness of humanity. That's the message that I've taken away from all these years as a journalist and your role, as journalists, is to uphold that goodness, is to deepen our decency, our sense of connection across the world, across cultures.*
>
> *(Keane, 2018)*

This appeal for a journalism that is connected and, above all, humane was intended for journalism students around the world, who will become the next generation of journalists. In his keynote talk at the Media Education Summit hosted at Hong Kong Baptist University in November 2018, foreign correspondent Fergal Keane, now the BBC's Africa Editor, reminded us that journalists are first and foremost storytellers, who are trying to show audiences "what it is like to stand where I do and see the things I see."[1] In surveying the current media landscape, he considered the importance of accountability and responsibility, of freedom and diversity, the need to avoid "othering" and falling prey to stereotypes and the dangers of false narratives, or "fake news." As well as pursuing the age-old imperative to "speak truth to power," journalists need to challenge themselves, to have a "sense of self." Speaking "*From where I stand,*" Keane observed that, above all else, journalists must show empathy and humanity, when telling the stories of others. This presents journalism educators, too, with a series of challenges; whilst credible, trusted journalism has never been more important, levels of disaffection with the media run deep.

Hence the imperative to reimagine journalism education is urgently felt, even more difficult to design, and intensely challenging to gain traction.

Disaffected, disconnected, and distrusted

The primary reason it is all so difficult, is that journalism is in the dock – again – and this time it feels serious, with the focus widening from simply the press to "mainstream media," a term which "has changed into a term of abuse" (Snoddy, 2017).

In recent years, in the UK, print journalism had managed to avoid "drinking in the last chance saloon" following the phone hacking scandal and ensuing Leveson Inquiry and its report (2011–12),[2] its house in better order with tighter rules on privacy after the death of Princess Diana in 1997. The BBC had largely recovered from the searing criticism of the Hutton Report (2004) into its reporting of weapons of mass destruction (WMD) in Iraq and the sex abuse scandal surrounding BBC children's TV presenter, the late Jimmy Savile, in 2012.

Journalism educators and industry councils in the UK had responded with curriculum change that reflected the need for in-depth teaching and examination of ethics (such as the ethics test introduced by the National Council for the Training of Journalists) and critical evaluation of newsroom practices. Questions of trust, however, have remained and become entrenched: in 2012, "for the first time since YouGov started tracking public trust in British institutions, more people distrust[ed] BBC journalists (47%) than trust[ed] them (44%)" (Kellner, 2012). In 2016, a YouGov poll for IMPRESS "revealed that public trust in the press was at an all-time low. Only 11% of people in the UK trust journalists at mid-market newspapers such as the *Daily Mail* and the *Daily Express* to tell the truth." Fewer than one in ten trusted tabloid journalists, and those writing for broadsheets and local papers scored 36% (YouGov, 2016). By 2016, on the eve of its Charter renewal,[3] the BBC had recovered some ground, rated as the most trustworthy source of news by over 50% of the British public in a YouGov poll commissioned by campaign group 38 Degrees (*The Guardian*, 2016). The outlook remains gloomy: in Edelman's 2017 Trust Barometer survey of 1,500 Britons, the number of people who said they trusted British news outlets at all fell from an already low 36% in 2015 to a mere 24% by the beginning of 2017. In June of the same year, the Reuters Institute's Digital News Report (2017) found that just 41% of British people agreed that the news media did a good job in helping them distinguish fact from fiction. The figure for social media was even lower at 18%. By 2018, Edelman's annual reporting indicated that a continuing loss of trust in "traditional" media had become a global trend, with only six countries surveyed scoring over 50%. Nearly seven in 10 respondents worried about fake news and disinformation and there is also an accompanying decline in trust in social media and search engines: Edelman (2018) notes that:

> people have retreated into self-curated information bubbles, where they read only that with which they agree, as if selecting their playlist for music.

Whilst trust in journalists (and experts) saw a slight resurgence, trust in media flatlined, becoming globally the "least trusted institution for the first time in Trust Barometer history."[4]

Against this volatile backdrop, the Brexit vote in Britain in June 2016 and the advent of Trump's presidency in the US later that year were game-changers, once again throwing journalists back on themselves. The "post-truth" world shone the spotlight on where journalism had fallen short, losing connectivity with its audiences and failing to inspire trust in an increasingly crowded, information-saturated world. This challenging landscape is complicated by the recent observation of former journalist Emily Bell, now at Columbia University's Tow Center, that "the people who want to see journalism fail . . . have a bigger megaphone than ever" (Bell, 2017). Demagogic narratives occupy the foreground of political debate, with the media characterised as the "opposition," who, according to Trump's tweets are "the enemies of the people." Recent studies show that the alt-right dominates the "share of voice" in a context where facts that fail to conform to this agenda are designated as "fake news." Propaganda and lies become the new "truths" and we have only to look to Russia to see the dangers: as many critical observers believe Putin's demagogic narratives have created a state of affairs where "everything is PR" (Pomerantsev, 2015). Russian media producers and journalists are described as "both cynical and enlightened," but they and their audiences are likened to Nabokov's butterfly, constantly changing colour to avoid predators and so, it could be argued, losing a sense of self (Pomerantsev, 2015). Fergal Keane's appeal for us to find ourselves again has a profound resonance.

In a febrile context, honest rigorous political discourse has also been side-lined, and Mark Thompson at *The New York Times* discerns the inability to "debate honestly and in the round" as "a terrible weakness" (Thompson, 2016, p. 256). He argues that this was most evident in the slide towards the first Gulf War in 1990–1, but parallels can be drawn with the recent Brexit vote in the UK, where news coverage was dominated by hyperbole. Ultimately people lost faith in politics; the failure of journalists to ask the right questions, for some, was exemplified in the BBC's dogged commitment to impartiality, which arguably permitted the Leave campaign and its Project Fear to dominate public discourse. As *Guardian* journalist and seasoned political observer Sarah Helm noted, "just as British journalism faces its greatest challenge for decades it seems to be reaching a nadir" (Helm, 2017). This time, it will take more than a new set of editorial codes and closer testing of ethics in J-Schools to get journalism's house "in order," since the problem is largely external, rather than self-inflicted.

Fear narratives hold sway when people feel threatened by others – whether migrants or terrorists: terror attacks in Nice, London, Barcelona, and elsewhere have brought indigenous communities under suspicion (Packer, 2015). In the UK, the failure of local journalism was starkly evident in the aftermath of the Grenfell Tower fire – arguably a seminal moment in British media history, which, for

Channel 4 News anchor Jon Snow amongst others, provided a stark reminder of journalism's role in society:

> Our job is to give a voice to people with no voice. . . . Our job is to wake people up and tell them that this is being done in their name.
>
> *(Snow, 2018)*

In a setting dominated by fear narratives, information overload arising from a constant diet of 24/7 news fuels the "CNN effect," reinforcing a sense of fatigue in audiences. This "ennui" is perhaps because people are afraid rather than indifferent (Sontag, 2004), but it compounds the difficulties for journalists, often reliant on traditional styles of news storytelling or parachuting in to stories, only to tell them in superficial ways. This "smash and grab" journalism potentially exacerbates the problem of failing to build trust on the ground or with audiences. Add to this the constant noise of social media and the blogosphere, where everyman has a voice – in an increasingly distrustful atmosphere – but few are listening (Fowler-Watt, 2013), and the result is a heady cocktail.

This is the media landscape that Keane was surveying in his keynote and it presents major, critical challenges for journalism pedagogy: as educators we seek to send out into the world the next generation of journalists who, it is hoped, will produce new, improved forms of journalism and bring audiences back into engaging with stories. Political journalist Sarah Helm calls for honesty and clarity in the discourses of politics and media to rebuild trust:

> The bonfire of American values that Trump is building appears more dramatic than the slow-burn of Brexit. But the British people, led to believe that leaving the EU would save hospitals, clear out immigrants and bring jobs, need to know not just that they've been lied to, but what exactly the future may hold for them.
>
> *(Helm, 2017)*

In 2018, former *Guardian* editor Alan Rusbridger in his memoir and treatise on the broken state of news and news consumption declared that "there might soon be entire communities without news. Or without news they could trust," a problem compounded by the sense that "truth was fake, fake was true. And that's when the problem suddenly snapped into focus" (Rusbridger, 2018, pp. ix–x). This bleak outlook, with trust levels at rock-bottom, calls for more than corrective action.

So, time for a radical rethink: the Internet age requires vibrant, engaged journalism that builds connections, as the founder of Dutch non-profit Global Voices, Ethan Zuckerman reminds us, "If we want digital connections to increase human connections, we need to experiment" (Zuckerman, 2013, p. 131). Experimentation might involve close scrutiny of journalism's normative values to foreground notions of journalism that is "narrative, fair (with its sources and readers), participative, community oriented, and finally, giving priority to untold stories"

(Neveu, 2016). Debating whether journalism education matters, Mitchell Stephens at New York University champions the idea that experimentation could move journalism education from the "rearguard of the profession – merely defending old standards – to the *avant garde*" (Stephens, 2006, p. 153). Within the current challenging context, could reimagining journalism education, in a root and branch way, provide a starting point for a reimagined journalism practice that prioritises the human aspect of journalism as a craft, if only to offer a partial route through the mire?

The role of journalism education

> *The greatest task for us, as journalism educators, is to equip our students with a firm sense of the public trust – how it developed, what it means . . . and how it manifests itself or is betrayed by the work that individual journalists and news organisations do.*
>
> *(Woo, 2002)*

That word, trust, again, which for Woo (2002) means instilling in students the need to produce journalism that is *trustworthy*; Buckingham (2019) contends that there is a need to strike a balance, since

> Too little trust is dysfunctional, but too much can also be dangerous. As educators, we need students to be critical, rather than merely cynical. We want them to analyse and question media, but we don't want them to distrust or reject everything.
>
> *(Buckingham, 2019)*

Journalism education globally tends to mirror industry practice and is more often than not delivered by former practitioners. The idea of reimagining journalism education as a route to better practice has been the subject of debate for decades, and, as noted earlier in this chapter, the conversations are often given new energy during key moments of change: a collapsed business model, the introduction of new technologies and multiple platforms, ethical crises (Davies, 2009; Ornebring, 2010; Frost, 2007). Donica Mensing has advocated a move towards community journalism as a route to greater connectivity, arguing that, notwithstanding the impact of multimedia storytelling and convergence, "the essential flow of journalism education has changed little in response to the 'epochal transformation'[5] . . . taking place within communications" (Mensing, 2010, p. 512). Instead the educational focus has been on reinforcing what we already know, prioritising industry norms, and thereby affording little real change. In placing the reporter at the centre of a community, she sought to re-emphasise those connections by highlighting the journalist as citizen, since "the journalist is the handmaiden of the citizen" and as such required to find a route out of the "disrepair" of the political commons' (Manhoff, 2002 in Mensing, 2010, p. 517). As we have already seen, the landscape is now more complex, since the journalist is perceived to be a central part of the problem or is represented as *the* problem.

Whilst much rethinking has been done on practice and skills and calls for realignment (Deuze, 2006; Rosen, 2012; Tait, 2007; Gillmor, 2006), Mensing's (2010) assertion that it is important in times of rapid change to challenge students to understand how they can improve their own work rather than imitate what has gone before has resonance when continuation of the status quo is deemed to be untenable (ibid. p. 515). It is also attractive to consider the notion of moving away from an obsession with seeking "best practices," considering, instead, "new practices" (ibid. p. 513). With that in mind, this chapter considers how, as journalism educators, we can awaken in students an understanding of themselves and of others, the "sense of self" to which Keane attributes equal importance as challenging the powerful: "It's important . . . that you challenge yourself. What matters is that you rigorously investigate your opinions, that you take what you believe and you subject it to forensic examination." The reason for this is – he says –

> because your opinion only really matters when you have taken it out, taken it apart, when you've – critically – tried to see things from the point of view of the other person, that's why I believe empathy is hugely important in journalism.
>
> *(Keane, 2018)*

In other words, how can we "teach" emotional literacy, empathy, humanity – and crucially, humility? This question presents a challenge to journalism educators, since these are more intangible concepts than journalism's normative values and, as such, do not easily constitute concrete principles.

The notion of transformative pedagogies offers some useful insights, because in the pedagogical realm transformative practice "has the potential to engage students by encouraging them to be both participatory and active" (Donnelly, 2016). Mezirow's (1997) interpretation of transformation evidenced in shifting perspective, is relevant to this study, whereby students become critically aware about how assumptions (for journalists, these could be normative practices) constrain us. This heightened awareness enables "a more inclusive, discriminating and integrating perspective" (Mezirow, 1997, p. 167 in Donnelly, 2016). It also involves making choices to act upon these new understandings and as such, could be seen as a route to exploring "new practices," rather than focusing on "best practice." Keane urges us to look for something that comes from within, to engage with the interrogation of our own opinions and, as journalists, our understanding of journalism's normative values. In this sense, the essence of transformative, critical pedagogy is relevant to the quest for new practices, since "transformative learning involves experiencing a deep, structural shift in the basic premises of thought, feelings, and actions. It is a shift of consciousness that dramatically and irreversibly alters our way of being in the world" (O'Sullivan, 2003, p. 203 in Donnelly, 2016). This involves not only understanding ourselves, as Keane (2018) urges, but also:

our relationships with other humans and with the natural world; our under-standing of relations of power in interlocking structures of class and gender; our body awarenesses, our visions of alternative approaches to living; and our sense of possibilities for social justice and peace and personal joy.

(ibid, p. 203)

In the summer of 2018, a workshop at the Salzburg Academy on Media & Global Change provided a forum in which to explore new approaches to jour-nalism pedagogy that might lead to new practices. More detail on the shape and form of the academy, which brings together students and faculty from around the world (60 different institutions) to debate contemporary media issues, is given in the Introduction to this book.[6] The aim of the academy is to build "digital litera-cies and engagement around critical challenges in society." It runs a three-week programme annually to "connect young media innovators across a range of disci-plines to produce multimedia tools, to reframe curricula and research."[7] In addition, its recently formed collective, the Salzburg Media School (SMS), aims to capture the new approaches and critical thinking evident in the work of the faculty and students. One of the group's aims is to "build capacity for pedagogy that lies at the intersection of skills and theory, and that approaches learning from a point of criti-cal consciousness."[8] The theme of the academy in 2018, where I ran a workshop, was "Re-Imagining Journalism in an Age of Distrust." In experimenting with new journalism pedagogies, the workshop was conducted in the spirit of the Salzburg School, placing critical awareness at the centre of its approaches to learning.

Reimagining journalism education: "It's the Story that Matters!"

> *Storytelling is the most powerful thing in the world, it connects the dots of our communities.*
> *(Rensberger, 2016)*

Award-winning international journalist Scott Rensberger emphasises the power of storytelling for finding common ground and building a sense of belonging in our communities. I decided to focus my talk on storytelling and to run it as an interactive workshop, entitled "It's the Story that Matters!" The idea was to enable 80+ students from a range of media and communication-related disciplines (not all journalism) from universities in countries ranging from the US to China and Lebanon to Mexico, to subject their understanding of journalism and storytelling to deep critical analysis. They were asked to:

1 Scrutinise the core values of journalism.
2 Look at how these values are challenged in the current context.
3 Test whether the values are fit for purpose.
4 Consider whether we need any new values/Could any be jettisoned?

We then considered the role of voice and marginality in journalism, to engage with the concept of emotional literacy and to reflect on our own lived experiences, so that we could ask:

5   Where do we stand, in the midst of this, as storytellers and as human beings? Consider our own identities, our "sense of self." Should we put more of ourselves into the narrative? What is the role of empathy?
6   Look to the future: Connectivity restored? Journalism reimagined?

The starting point for the workshop was that reimagining does not have to mean throwing out the old to bring in the new. Instead, it aimed to encourage students and faculty, in striving to understand their own work rather than mimicking past practices, to think about how, what we might call "traditional" journalistic values could help in rethinking journalism practice and pedagogy. This is, however, to Mensing's (2010) point, different to seeking "best" practice. We have the digital skills, but are they working? Are they sufficient? It was an attempt to balance out the techno-utopians' focus on digital tools, by putting journalism's core values into the spotlight. In a drive to reconnect communities through storytelling, Rensberger (2016) advises against an obsession with "kit" and calls for a focus on the story instead:

> There is always going to be a need for great storytelling, but if you go out with a 4k camera and you shoot a shitty story, it's still a shitty 4k camera story.
> *(Rensberger, 2016)*

So, the first part of the workshop reminded us that we are all storytellers, with our own biography. This is what sets us apart as humans, since the birds in the trees do not have biographies, and we are defined by our storytelling ability: "lives and their experiences are represented in stories" (Denzin, 1989, p. 81). For the British political journalist Andrew Marr, stories are "hard-wired" into us (Marr, 2004) as we seek to tell the stories of others, which entails, for Fergal Keane, in bearing witness to others' experiences, "trying to tell them what it's like to stand where I do and see the things I see." On this basis, we could ask whether journalistic accounts of others' lives are more trustworthy than other accounts *because* of the normative values that we employ (Coward, 2009). This was the question at the heart of the workshop with its aim of seeking new routes to trusted journalism(s).

Based on this understanding of journalism as predominantly about narrative we engaged with the idea of journalism as craft – artistry. Here, the story is the journalist's craft object, as the potter has his pot, the weaver her tapestry (Fowler-Watt, 2013). There is always something of the craft-artist in the final individual artefact which is unique. What is the shape and form of the craft skill of journalistic storytelling? We also considered the importance of voice, and how easily the powers of selectivity afforded to journalists can be abused, to render the voiceless even more voiceless (Marsh, 2016). In this context, we introduced the notions of empathy, agency, and "getting inside people's lives" (Sigal, 2016) in order to listen carefully to others' accounts of their experiences, so remaining close to their stories. The workshop had the potential to provide steps along the route in our quest for credible, trusted, emotionally literate journalism; a journalism that seeks to empathise or resonate, produced by a journalist who has stayed around long enough to understand. To do so, we needed to interrogate current journalistic practice and values. Many journalism scholars have ruminated about the core values of journalism (Harcup, 2014; Shapiro, 2010). However, in reporting the stories of others, it is generally agreed that these core values are usually in play:

1   Fair and impartial
2   Truthful and accurate
3   Independent and ethical
4   Humane
5   Accountable

(adapted from EJN, Ethical Journalism Network)

This set of values was taken with us into the workshop environment, to be critically evaluated.

Activity I: unpacking journalism's values

In the first workshop activity, the students worked in small groups to unpack journalism's core values. Each group was given one of the core values and asked to:

a   Define it. Why is it important?
b   Provide example (s) of its application in practice.

These were discussed, written down, and shared back for further discussion with the entire group.

Fair and impartial

Fairness and Impartiality were defined in various ways, as *lack of prejudice in storytelling; telling facts the way they are* and *playing by the rules* (in relation to journalistic codes of conduct); journalists should be *fair with the audience* and *should not assume that people already know what you are talking about*. Voice was important in *delivering equality* by treating all sides equally and *giving them equal voice*, so that all of those in the story were given *an equal opportunity to share their experiences*. Fairness and impartiality were defined by one group as *having objectivity towards everything*, and this was enabled by being well informed and *conscious of personal and cultural biases*.

The importance of fairness and impartiality aligned with a universal ethical code, which supports *efforts to be less subjective, minimising biases* to *avoid prejudice*. They *encourage open-mindedness, honesty and protect free expression*. They were also seen as preventing *media outlets from being used to fulfil the agendas of individuals or a group*.

Fair reporting in terms of the selection of images, for example, was assured by these values, which it was agreed in the ensuing discussion, chime with the responsibilities associated with storytelling.

Examples used to illustrate the presence of fairness and impartiality in journalistic storytelling ranged from exposing Russia's role in the 2016 US Election, to reporting of Syrian refugees that was considerate, fair, thoughtful, and respectful. Reporting oppression raised an interesting ethical question about whether the voice of oppressors should be equally heard and what does "fair" mean in this case? Should the journalist stand with the weak and oppressed (i.e. as an advocate of fairness), or does fairness mean representing *both* sides of the story?

The overall consensus on the value of fairness and impartiality was that it enabled people to make up their own minds.

Truthful and accurate

Definitions of truthful and accurate reporting ranged from *not manipulating opinion, being honest and factually based* as well as *transparent, unbiased, credible, comprehensive, and research-driven* to an awareness that there are grey areas, whereby *different people have different truths.* One group asked: *What is journalism without truth? Without truth and facts, we don't have journalism.* Others saw truth as subjective but balanced out by accuracy, so that rumour and speculation could be avoided by staying *pertinent to the story.* It was agreed that truth and accuracy are contextual, and often dependent on location or proximity that this is problematic, for example, *if you tell a story from afar, you may be accurate but not truthful.*

Audiences' need for *neutral journalism* determined the importance of truthfulness and accuracy as values, since truth was perceived to be *under attack.* These values were overwhelmingly defined as *one of the basic needs to achieve effective journalism* since they *complement each other before complementing the other values.*

International news agencies, such as Reuters, were held up as exemplars of truthful and accurate reporting due to the use of *named, specified sources that are credible,* making it a credible news source in its own right. Maps such as the migration maps produced by the inter- governmental International Organisation for Migration (IOM) offered another example of how relating an accurate portrayal of the movement of people and first-hand coverage of the refugee crisis (first-person stories) have, to some extent, offered accurate accounts. The complexities of reporting refugees were, however, acknowledged, as it was agreed that many accounts and angles of the story have not received attention and the subjective and selective nature of first-person reporting presents its own challenges.

Independent and ethical

This was defined unanimously as *having core values and sticking to them.* Respect for privacy was also important. Ethical values were defined as:

- Acting with an awareness of the power of words and the consequences
- Writing in the interest of others, without self-interest, being responsible, and not taking advantage of shaping public opinion
- Clear cut, humanitarian, empathic, and *doing the right thing*

Independence was defined as:

- Not being influenced by political parties, peers, monetary interests, or dictated opinions
- Having your own opinions and mindset as an individual journalist
- Reporting the truth and transparency
- Remaining neutral and objective

The importance of these values was discerned in the need to *establish and build trust, to encourage and secure accountability*, and in order to be credible and objective. Interestingly, an independent approach and sound ethics were also deemed important in *creating different perspectives* and fostering diversity.

A wide range of globally aware examples were put forward to illustrate these values, from a positive (where the values were evident) and negative (where they were lacking) perspective. Some examples were:

- United States: an independence from the subjects you cover regardless of bias, e.g. Watergate
- United Kingdom: being exempt from influence and constraints and being able to report freely
- Mexico: having your own voice and speaking truth to power, even at the risk of losing your life (illegal prostitution and trafficking of women)
- The suspension of news sites in Vietnam was cited as an example of the values of independent journalism coming under threat.
- In Lebanon, the coverage of stories from a certain perspective based on sect was seen as subjective.
- Reporting in self-interest after a tragedy

Humane

Being humane was defined as *connecting with people*; bringing out the *human interest in a story regardless of race, gender, or nationality*; the *avoidance of materialism*. In terms of operating with humanity, journalists should *treat others with respect* and the mantra "*do not 'other'*" was cited. Global empathy was also considered important, *putting yourself in others' shoes,* and humane journalism was defined as *a mutual exchange that is consensual and intentional.*

Humanity is highlighted as an important value because it preserves equality, *promotes a caring culture*, and crucially, *differentiates humans from other living organisms.* In this sense, it constitutes a deontological imperative: it *promotes the natural good* and has no boundaries, since it *resonates across borders.*

One group suggested that humane reporting was evident in the coverage by the BBC and other news organisations of the Thai football team trapped in a cave in the summer of 2018. Similarly, China's coverage of its own two-child policies and laws was seen as emotionally impactful. Wider discussion designated emotional journalism as an example of humane reporting, highlighting examples that were shared in Daniela Rea's keynote at the academy in 2018. In sharing her lived experiences, she highlighted honesty, empathy, and humanity as key elements in her storytelling: "We have to create the time to know the things and the feelings and the experience that people who suffer violence have." She talked about the importance of making interviewees feel safe and comfortable when reporting on difficult issues (such as the disappearance of family members). By taking the time to create a safe and secure environment people will have "confidence and the protection to say what they feel about the violence against them."[9] This talk highlighted the pedagogic benefits of sharing lived experiences and helped to provide a framework for our assessment of what constitutes humane reporting.

Accountable

Accountability provided the fifth and final value to evaluate, and the discussion elicited a wide range of definitions. The mechanics of being accountable require *looking for what is hidden* and *searching for the information.* It requires upholding a system of values that are personal and institutional; *taking personal responsibility for the position from which you are reporting, taking personal responsibility for your actions* and upholding the *institutional responsibility to amplify the voices of the voiceless.* "Giving voice" was highlighted in a number of ways, for one group as *seeking the voices of unrecognised minority communities.* Another definition focused on duty and the imperative to answer "what," "why," "how," and "when." Accountability was also defined as the route to credibility.

There was a general consensus that if journalists are not accountable they cannot learn from their mistakes, hence its importance as a value was upheld. This value was seen as helping to build public trust – since if journalists are accountable for their work, then they are credible and more likely to be trusted. It also has value as supporting journalists in acknowledging their own biases. And, for one group, *journalistic voice is elevated so we have responsibility to be conscious of our power to affect broad groups of people.*

Examples of accountable journalism were evident in fact-checking before publishing, paying close attention to sources and to media choices. Newspaper value and mission statements were also seen as an example of transparency that showed an awareness of the need to be accountable. On a personal level, journalists who write articles that are *ideologically antithetical* to their own beliefs were held up as an example of accountable practitioners. Likewise, those who admit their mistakes and publish apologies were perceived to be more credible.

Activity II: challenging journalism's values

In the next stage of the workshop, we considered each of these values in the context of a range of challenges (as discussed at the start of this chapter) summarised, for the purpose of clarity, in a list of five key challenges:

1   Climate of fear: "the other," migration, extremism (demagogic narratives)
2   Lack of audience engagement, noisy, transient, *ennui*
3   Reputation and trust issues: news as "fake," journalists as opposition, PR
4   Collapse of the business model, stretched resources in the 24/7 news cycle
5   The Fifth Estate: citizen journalism, social, mobile, and user-generated content (UGC)

Each of the five challenges was applied in turn to each value to ask:

a   What effect/impact could it have on the journalistic value?
b   How can the value engage with the challenge to retain its integrity? Does it need to shift? Is it still fit for purpose?

This section of the workshop indicated that the core values of journalism are clearly under assault. The group discussion ascertained that *context* determines the intensity of the challenge – for example, where journalists are threatened with violence from the state, lack of audience engagement is not a significant problem; where the media is non-profit, collapse of the business model is less of an issue.

Challenges to fairness and impartiality

The "climate of fear" could challenge this value by creating an atmosphere where the "othering" of people became acceptable. It could also inspire fear of the state amongst journalists who might be imprisoned, even killed, for impartial reporting. Lack of audience engagement, whereby nobody is listening, leads to audiences lacking the ability to discern what is fair and impartial in the first place. Reputation and trust also come under threat in this atmosphere and the public may not trust or believe journalists, even if they report fairly and impartially. The collapse of the business model creates a reliance on corporate sponsorship that results in censorship and self-censorship, which undermines fairness.

Challenges to truth and accuracy

The groups debating this value found three of the five challenges were most evident:

- The 24/7 news cycle limits the depth and accuracy of stories, with advertisers holding sway and due to the intense competition between news networks to be first, stories lack empathy and become more fact based. However, facts are not always checked due to time constraints, leading to facile reporting.

- Engaging audiences is challenging when you are encouraging them to hear and accept uncomfortable truths.
- The climate of fear means that what people *"want to hear"* and what people *"should hear"* are not always the same. Fear can make people unwilling to hear the other side of the story. Fear can create spaces for conspiracy theories, and it can also *turn the truth into black or white.*

Challenges to independent and ethical journalism

The climate of fear held sway here too, with the migration issue highlighted as an example of a story that received distorted coverage (less on stories of suffering, more on impact and the fear of immigration). Sound ethics can be compromised in the context of a collapsing business model, where there is insufficient time to gather information and to look at all sides of the story. The workshop groups agreed that the post-truth era makes ethics difficult, since news sources are seen as fake and present the greatest challenge to the ethical, responsible journalist. Journalists could fix this by showing themselves to be "super-ethical": an example of this would be to *tell the event as it is* always clearly remaining above and beyond political influence, but this was acknowledged to be challenging in countries where journalism is not free and independent.

Challenges to humanity as a value

Humane journalism appeared to be under threat from the 24-hour news cycle, rewarding parachute journalism that *smashes and grabs stories* rather than *building relationships.* The climate of fear *puts a wedge between journalists and what/whom they are covering, since people are fearful of not receiving empathy back when they are empathic to others.* Reputation and trust issues make journalists *afraid to publish more vulnerable, brave work.* It can also help a journalist's reputation as they can build trust by becoming known as empathic. Human greed was seen as a challenge to humane reporting, also the imperative to chase ratings and algorithms.

Challenges to accountability

This group defined one major challenge: The Fifth Estate since:

- It is hard to verify user-generated content (UGC) and so it is difficult to establish accountability.
- Journalists can "play to the gallery" as they seek to integrate UGC into their narratives.
- UGC itself is not a problem, but *it is not journalism.*
- UGC can be easily shared, even though it is not always verifiable.
- It is *impossible to hold accountable the invisible.*
- There is no accountability for retweets.

The groups then debated whether consumers became accountable, in this context as they have to verify the authenticity of content and hold the platform and/or journalist accountable. Does the responsibility for accountability shift, even though news consumers cannot be held accountable?

An intervention

At this point, another consideration was brought into the room: since we are working within a context that is preoccupied with identity, an "autobiographical age" (Plummer, 2001), it is "hot," as journalist-academic Ros Coward (2007) reminds us:

> Interrogating subjectivity is now part of our culture. Even though it takes many different forms, across most areas of cultural life there's an underlying preoccupation with identity. Popular culture is dominated by questions about identity and subjectivity, about how to improve, alter or come to terms with ourselves.
>
> *(Coward, 2007)*

So, we are able to engage with narratives that are based on interrogating and reflecting on identity. As journalists, this can mean thinking about identity on lots of levels: our own identity as well as those living in communities that are different to our own, for example, those seeking refuge from oppression in camps or on migrant ships or trapped in basements in the Syrian enclave of Eastern Ghouta. This awareness of "self" (vaunted by Keane)[10] and having the confidence to put some of oneself into the story could – arguably – mitigate the danger of "othering." It could also potentially render journalistic storytelling more engaging and accessible and authentic, whilst staying true to the normative values (just scrutinised) that shape or have to date shaped journalism as a practice. There is an argument that posits that "experiential first person writing" is closer to "truth," allowing voices to be heard more clearly, because the journalist is not seeking detachment but sharing honestly how they comprehend the story (Coward, 2007, 2009). They are showing their workings.

Activity III: "sense of self" and identity

The final workshop activity encouraged the students to engage with the concepts presented in the intervention, following Fergal Keane's advice, to interrogate their own beliefs and assumptions and to consider how they present to the world. Whilst acknowledging that definitions of self are in flux and "not rigidly categorised" (Clarke, 1996), our identities are located in time, space, and history. In a keynote at the Salzburg Academy in 2017, focused on tackling extremism, journalist Robin Wright had urged us to "try to get out beyond our own sources of identity," since "as long as we're trapped in our own sources of identity, we're never going to find common ground."[11]

In this activity, each student was asked to use one word or short phrase to describe themselves to the person sitting next to them, who would then write this down on a Post-it note. This simple exercise encouraged them to think about who they are, not who they feel they should say they are, not who others say they are – but how do they see themselves? The recipient of the description would interrogate their own assumptions about that person – would they have described them in this way? We then sought to describe each other back to the room, based on our own sense of self and then to categorise the descriptions by sticking the notes under different headings: "physical," "social," "professional," "other," to illustrate the dangers of labelling others. This exercise also exemplified how difficult it is to capture in a word or a short phrase another's identity, encouraging us all to appreciate the levels of responsibility inherent in the activity of describing another person. A discussion about the importance of empathy followed: the need to put oneself in another's shoes and to seek to understand the complexities of others' lives. Could or should empathy be a news value in its own right? Is it a sixth value to add to the list of five core values insofar as it extends the concept of humane reporting to the level of emotional literacy that requires awareness of self, as well as awareness of others? Can we be empathic and impartial? It was useful, at this point, to examine the views of different journalists on the empathy question:

Empathy as a news value

"For": "I feel strongly that we have to include these stories of the suffering of civilians to get the point across" (Marie Colvin, 2012).

"Against": "A string of vivid adjectives, a catch in the voice, a shake of the head. It does not take long for the idea to catch on that reporting is bereft of authenticity if the reporter's heart fails to be in the story, preferably in view on the sleeve" (Kate Adie, 2002).

Two celebrated war correspondents, the late Marie Colvin of *The Sunday Times* and veteran BBC reporter Kate Adie, offer differing perspectives on the empathy question. For Channel 4's anchor Jon Snow (2018), "Empathy is it." Fergal Keane's "take" on journalism is founded on the crucial importance of empathy. Without it, his form of journalism, of showing people events "from where I stand" cannot exist. Whilst cognisant that empathy cannot be experienced in a vacuum, it needs to relate to people and their individual experiences (Sigal, 2016).[12] The integration of empathy into the values as a "sixth value" was widely supported in our discussions. In a second iteration of the workshop, delivered to students in the UK early in 2019, I allocated the discussion of empathy as a value to a group for the duration of the session, so that their intervention was made after lengthy deliberation and stripped of any involvement in discussions of the five normative values. Empathy was aligned to emotional literacy, which was defined by the group as being *socially adept*, being *able to sympathise*, being able to *explicitly describe people's emotions in writing*. It was seen as important in attracting an audience and maintaining one of the core values, accuracy. It also enabled the journalist to cope with difficult circumstances and to build a rapport. It is seen as a vulnerable value insofar as it can be tarnished by "sensationalism," replacing facts with emotion in order to have an effect on audience. A focus on self-awareness also needs to avoid the trap of narcissism. A value that needs to be in safe hands, at all times.

Looking to the future: reimagining journalism's core values

> *In this "post-truth" era, we must fight to ensure that journalism lives to speak truth to power another day. Not because we think it should, but because we know it must.*
> (Branham, 2017)

Branham's (2017) call for journalists to actively engage with the imperative of "speaking truth to power" ran like a red thread through the workshop discussions in Salzburg, which concluded that journalism's core values are seriously challenged. We engaged, inconclusively, with these questions:

- Are the values fit for purpose? The values were upheld as relevant.
- Are the values sufficiently robust when tested? The values were all challenged, significantly.
- What values can we add to make them more powerful/resilient? Empathy and emotional literacy have the potential to add value and integrity, but also present as vulnerable and subject to interpretation.
- Should any be discarded? No, but they all need bolstering and careful handling.

Could a new set of core values look like this?

1 Fair and impartial
2 Truthful and accurate
3 Independent and ethical
4 Humane
5 Accountable
6 **Emotionally literate/self-aware**

As journalism educators we need to be bold and to experiment. Whilst making no claims for emotional literacy as a news value, it is possible that a greater "focus on emotional literacy in journalism education could restore journalism practice as an essentially human activity, wherein journalists are, first and foremost, seen as (and understood to be) people, just like those in their stories" (Fowler-Watt, 2019). We need to invest more time and energy in devising curricula that enable learning beyond technical skills and industry codes to explore further.

Towards new pedagogies

> *Our social condition, our political contexts always are teaching us something, that maybe we don't realize so I think it's very important that we assume that in this profession we are always learning.*
>
> *(Daniela Rea, 2018)*

For Daniela Rea, whose passionate description of what empathic journalism looks and feels like inspired us at the 12th Salzburg Academy in 2018, transformative learning is embedded in the socio-political contexts within which we work as journalists, and which, crucially, we inhabit as human beings. Journalism is, after all, at its best, the most human activity. It also performs a crucial, civic function:

> Journalism is not just a craft or a profession, it is the linchpin of the foundation of democracy, an informed citizenry making informed judgments about how they will live together.
>
> *(Dates, 2006)*

Debating whether journalism education matters, more than a decade ago, Jannette Dates and Theodore Glasser (2006), amongst others, placed it at the intersection of the academy and practice. The crucial role of journalism in civic society naturally led to a view that journalism education and journalism practice shared similar goals. Agnes Wahl Nieman's gift to establish Harvard's Nieman Foundation in the US is an illustration: her aim "to promote and elevate the standards of journalism."[13] Arguably, it still sits at that same intersection today, through oft-repeated calls for reinvention (Mensing, 2010; Deuze, 2001; Rosen, 2012). More radical views can also be heard to question whether there is a place for "formal" journalism education at all – in terms of a pedagogy that is skills based, focused on journalism practice, and constrained by accreditation. If we really want to inspire change and new practices, should we rip down all the J-Schools?

The starting point for this chapter was a call to rethink journalism education as a route to rethinking journalism practice, to reimagine the core values of journalism in order to contemplate a different or reinvigorated or augmented set of values. The over-arching aim: to reinstate journalism as trusted, credible, and central to civic society. These exploratory discussions at the Salzburg Academy indicate that the core values are still fit for purpose, although seriously challenged. However, in order to address problems of marginality, voice, and lack of trust, and to reimagine journalism to inspire new practices, we need new pedagogies. Rethinking does not necessarily require throwing out the old values, but perhaps the new, sixth value of emotional literacy can infuse and inform all of the others to shape practice informed by pedagogies that champion reflexivity and self-awareness. The aspiration: dynamic, new journalism practices that are, globally, valued and trusted as the ticking heart of a healthy, connected civic society.

Notes

1 Fergal Keane's keynote, "From where I stand" was presented at the Media Education Summit in Hong Kong on 2 Nov. 2018 as a film and is now available as a global educational resource, available at: www.cemp.ac.uk/summit/2018/.
2 The Leveson Inquiry was a judicial public inquiry into the practices and ethics of the British press, set up by the government in 2011, after the *News of the World* phone hacking scandal.
3 The BBC Charter established the BBC and its governance, with an accompanying agreement on editorial independence. The most recent Charter took effect on 1 Jan. 2017 and will run until 31 Dec. 2027.
4 The 2018 Trust Barometer is Edelman's 18th annual trust and credibility survey. The Trust Barometer surveyed more than 33,000 respondents across 28 countries. Available at: www.edelman.com/trust-barometer.
5 Mensing quotes the Project for Excellence in Journalism. (2004). *2004 Annual Report*overview*. Available at: www. journalism.org/node/855.
6 See Chapter 1: "New Journalisms: Rethinking Practice, Theory and Pedagogy" Jukes, S.A. and Fowler-Watt, K.
7 Salzburg Academy on media and global change. Available at: www.salzburgglobal.org/multi-year-series/media-academy.
8 The mission statement of the Salzburg Media School (SMS) can be read here in full. Available at: www.salzburgglobal.org/multi-year-series/media-academy.html?pageId=8252.
9 Daniela Rea's keynote talk, *Telling the personal stories of violence with respect, honesty and empathy* at the 12th Salzburg Academy on Media and Global Change, July 2018. Available at: www.salzburgglobal.org/news/latest-news/article/daniela-rea-telling-the-personal-stories-of-violence-with-respect-honesty-and-empathy.html.
10 ibid, "From Where I Stand," 2018.
11 Robin Wright delivered the Ithiel de Sola Pool Lecture at the Salzburg Academy, 18 July 2017.
12 Ivan Sigal, executive director of Global Voices and fellow of the Salzburg Academy, recorded a short film for the virtual Media4Change 2016 conference, where he discussed empathy as a news value.
13 Agnes Wahl Nieman donated $ 1.4 million to Harvard University in 1938. Cited as an example of the shared goals of journalism and journalism education by Jannette Dates. 2006. Rethinking journalism education in Does journalism education matter? *Journalism Studies*, 7(1), pp. 144–155.

References

Adie, K. (2002). *The kindness of strangers*. London: Headline.
Bell, E. (2017). Quoted by Andrew Harrison, Can you trust the mainstream media? *The Guardian*, Saturday 6 Aug. Available at: www.theguardian.com/media/2017/aug/06/can-you-trust-mainstream-media [Accessed 8 Aug. 2017].
Branham, L. (2017). Journalism matters: How a "War on Truth" can create a triumph of truth-telling. *Huffington Post*, 22 Mar. Available at: www.huffingtonpost.com/entry/journalism-matters-war-on-truth_us_58d2e79be4b02d33b748569f?guccounter=1&guce_referrer_us=aHR0cHM6Ly93d3cuZ29vZ2xlLmNvbS8&guce_referrer_cs=mH0ygRKnVA4bmmOm3qEU2w [Accessed 22 Feb. 2019].
Buckingham, D. (2019). *How much trust in media do we need?* Available at: https://davidbuckingham.net/2019/03/12/how-much-trust-in-media-do-we-need/ [Accessed 8 Mar. 2019].
Clarke, G. M. (1996). Conforming and contesting with (a) Difference: How Lesbian students and teachers manage their identities. *International Journal of Disability, Development and Education*, 6(2), pp. 195–214.

Colvin, M. (2012). *On the front line*. London: Harper Press.

Coward, R. (2007). *Me, me, me: The rise and rise of autobiographical journalism*. Inaugural lecture at Roehampton University, 15 May.

Coward, R. (2009). Me, me, me: The rise and rise of autobiographical journalism, in news making: Rules, routines and rituals. In Allan, S., ed., *The Routledge companion to news and journalism*. London: Routledge.

Dates, J. (2006). Does journalism education matter? *Journalism Studies*, 7(1), pp. 144–156.

Davies, N. (2009). *Flat earth news*. London: Vintage.

Denzin, N. K. (1989). *Interpretive biography*. London: Sage Publications.

Deuze, M. (2001) Educating 'New' journalists: Challenges to the curriculum. *Journalism and Mass Communication Educator*, 56(1), pp. 4–17.

Deuze, M. (2006). Global journalism education. *Journalism Studies*, 7(1), pp. 19–34.

Donnelly, R. (2016). *Application of Mezirow's transformative pedagogy to blended problem - based learning*. Resource Paper, Dublin Institute of Technology.

Edelman Trust Barometer. (2018). Available at: www.edelman.com/trust-barometer [Accessed 22 Jan. 2019].

Fowler-Watt, K. (2013). *The storytellers tell their stories: The journalist as educator*, unpublished thesis. Available at: https://eprints.soton.ac.uk/360625/1/__soton.ac.uk_ude_personal files_users_al4_mydesktop_Fowler-Watt%2520thesis-%2520final%2520submission%2520 pdf%2520copy.pdf. [Accessed 9 Feb. 2019].

Fowler-Watt, K. (2019). Global voices in journalism education. In: Jebril, N., Jukes, S., Takas, M. and Iordanidou, S., eds., *Journalism, society and politics in the digital media era*. Bristol: Intellect Books.

Frost, C. (2007). *Journalism ethics and regulation*. Edinburgh: Pearson Education.

Gillmor, D. (2006). *We the media: Grassroots journalism, by the people, for the people*. 1st ed. Sebastopol, CA: O'Reilly media.

The Guardian. (2016). BBC most trusted source for more than half of people in the UK' by John Plunkett, 10 Mar. Available at: www.theguardian.com/media/2016/mar/10/ bbc-news-most-trusted-source-for-more-than-half-of-people-in-the-uk [Accessed 22 Jan. 2019].

Harcup, T. (2014). *Journalism principles and practice*. 3rd ed. London: Sage Publications.

Helm, S. (2017). Quoted by Andrew Harrison, Can you trust the mainstream media? *The Guardian*, Saturday 6 Aug. Available at: www.theguardian.com/media/2017/aug/06/ can-you-trust-mainstream-media [Accessed 8 Aug. 2017].

Hutton report. (2004). 28 Jan. Available at: https://webarchive.nationalarchives.gov.uk/ 20090128233934/www.the-hutton-inquiry.org.uk/content/report/chapter05.htm [Accessed 7 Feb. 2012].

Keane, F. (2018). *From where I stand*. Keynote lecture at Media Education Summit 2018, Hong Kong Baptist University, Hong Kong, 2 Nov. Available at: www.cemp.ac.uk/ summit/2018/.

Kellner, P. (2012). The BBC is not alone in losing public trust. *The Guardian*, Tuesday 13 Nov. Available at: www.theguardian.com/commentisfree/2012/nov/13/bbc-not-alone-losing-public-trust [Accessed 25 Feb. 2019].

Leveson Report, Culture, Practices and Ethics of the Press. (2011). 14 Nov. Available at: www.levesoninquiry.org.uk/about/the-report/ [Accessed 25 July 2013].

Marr, A. (2004). *My trade: A short history of British journalism*. London: Palgrave Macmillan.

Marsh, K. (2016). *Terror, identity and the voices of the voiceless*. Visiting talk at Bournemouth University, 29 Feb. 2016.

Manhoff, R. (2002). Democratic journalism and the republican subject: Or the real American dream and what journalism educators can do about it. In: Mensing, D. (2010). Rethinking (again) the future of journalism education. *Journalism Studies*, 11(4), pp. 511–523.

Mensing, D. (2010). Rethinking (again) the future of journalism education *Journalism Studies*, 11(4), pp. 511–523.

Mezirow, J. (1997). Transformative learning: Theory to practice. *New Directions for Adult and Continuing Education*, 74, pp. 5–12. In: Donnelly, R. (2016). *Application of Mezirow's transformative pedagogy to blended problem based learning*. Resource Paper, Dublin Institute of Technology.

Neveu, E. (2016). On not going too fast with slow journalism. *Journalism Practice*, 10(4), pp. 448–460.

Ornebring, H. (2010). Reassessing journalism as a profession. In: Allan, S., ed., *The Routledge companion to news and journalism*. London: Routledge.

O'Sullivan, E. (2003). Towards integrally informed theories of transformative learning. *Journal of Transformative Education*, 3, pp. 331–353. In: Donnelly, R. (2016). *Application of Mezirow's transformative pedagogy to blended problem based learning*. Resource Paper, Dublin Institute of Technology.

Packer, G. (2015). The other France. *New Yorker*, 31 Aug.

Plummer, K. (2001). *Documents of life 2: An invitation to a critical humanism*. Vol. 2. London: Sage Publications.

Pomerantsev, P. (2015). *Nothing is true, and everything is possible*. London: Faber and Faber.

Rea, D. (2018). *Telling the personal stories of violence with respect, honesty and empathy*, Ithiel de Sola Pool Lecture on the Impact of Communications Technology on Society and Politics at the Salzburg Academy on Media and Global Change 2018. Available at: www.salzburgglobal.org/news/latest-news/article/daniela-rea-telling-the-personal-stories-of-violence-with-respect-honesty-and-empathy.html.

Rensberger, S. (2016). *Why storytelling "is still everything", despite new journalism tools' talk to MoJoCon*, 30 Apr. Reported by journalism.co.uk, 3 May 2016. Available at: www.jour nalism.co.uk/news/why-storytelling-is-still-everything-despite-new-journalism-tools-and-technology/s2/a634299/ [Accessed 20 July 2018].

Reuters Institute Digital News Report. (2017). Available at: https://reutersinstitute.poli tics.ox.ac.uk/sites/default/files/Digital%20News%20Report%202017%20web_0.pdf [Accessed 22 Feb. 2019].

Rosen, J. (2012). *What should journalists be taught?* Lecture at City University, 21 June.

Rusbridger, A. (2018). *Breaking news. The remaking of journalism and why it matters now*. Edinburgh: Canongate Books Ltd Salzburg Academy on Media and Global Change. Available at: www.salzburgglobal.org/multi-year-series/media-academy.

The Salzburg School. Available at: www.salzburgglobal.org/multi-year-series/media-aca demy.html?pageId=8252.

Shapiro, I. (2010). Evaluating journalism. *Journalism Practice*, 4(2), pp. 143–162.

Sigal, I. (2016). *Global voices*. Recorded talk for virtual Media4Change conference. UK hub hosted by Bournemouth University, Nov.

Snoddy, R. (2017). Quoted by Andrew Harrison, Can you trust the mainstream media? in *The Guardian*, Saturday 6 Aug. Available at: www.theguardian.com/media/2017/aug/06/can-you-trust-mainstream-media [Accessed 8 Aug. 2017].

Snow, J. (2018). *In conversation with Jon Snow*. Interview by Karen Fowler-Watt at Bournemouth University, 20 Apr.

Sontag, S. (2004). *Regarding the pain of others*. London: Penguin Books.

Stephens, M. (2006). Does journalism education matter? *Journalism Studies*, 7(1), pp. 144–156.

Tait, R. (2007). Journalism is a profession and universities have a role. *Press Gazette*, 6 May.

Thompson, M. (2016). *Enough said: What's gone wrong with the language of politics?* London: The Bodley Head.

Woo, W. (2002). *The bridge between the classroom and the newsroom*. Nieman Reports, Winter. Cambridge, MA: Harvard University.

Wright, R. (2017). Keynote talk at Salzburg Academy on Media and Global Change, Salzburg, Austria, 17 July.

YouGov poll. (2016). Available at: http://impress.press/news/yougov-poll.html [Accessed 5 Feb. 2019].

Zuckerman, E. (2013–2015). *Digital cosmopolitans. Why we think the internet connects us, why it doesn't and how to rewire it.* New York: W. W. Norton & Company.

8

CIVIC INTENTIONALITY AND THE TRANSFORMATIVE POTENTIAL OF JOURNALISM PEDAGOGIES

Paul Mihailidis, Roman Gerodimos, and Megan Fromm

This chapter engages with debates in news and media literacy to ask whether, rather than focusing on concerns and looking for solutions, it is time to consider journalism education's civic mission.

An experiment in transformative media pedagogy

This chapter is a provocation for journalism and media educators to imagine pedagogies that aim to transform the mindsets of future storytellers through the frame of civic intentionality. As a network of people from institutions around the world gather in Salzburg, Austria, to experiment with transformative media pedagogies, they embark on an experience that asks them to abandon their long-held assumptions about media and journalism systems, and to suspend their personal ideologies and value systems. Participants, both students and faculty, embark on a pedagogical journey that is designed to offer an immersive pedagogical experience that builds from radical scholars like bell hooks, Paulo Freire, and W.E.B. Dubois, who understood the pursuit of radical pedagogy in higher education as "the development of power, the training of a self whose balanced assertion will mean as much as possible for the great ends of civilization" (Dubois, 1973, p. 12).

To focus on the development of power, the Salzburg Academy on Media & Global Changes asks its participants, faculty, and students to consider bold ideas for practice, process, and justice across media industries. Each summer's cohort works in residence with faculty and visiting media and civic practitioners to explore an intractable problem, using a thematic foundation to navigate an immersive and transformative media experience. Themes offer entry points to exploring the ways in which media influence and are influenced by social and civic infrastructures. Themes also take on specific meaning based on the cultures and social backgrounds of the participants, further complicating and enriching the experience.

More importantly, however, a thematic focus allows the pedagogy of the academy to integrate a specific curricular process alongside a series of interventions that ask participants and faculty to reconsider the ways in which they understand media, storytelling, and social change.

Since its inception, the Salzburg Academy on Media & Global Change has built and implemented experimental pedagogies that embrace tensions and challenges present in contemporary society to revert and subvert them through creative media interventions into civic life. While the design of this pedagogy is open and flexible, it follows a process that embraces transformation and the explicit focus of turning *knowledge into action*. This process, which we call "IDEA," (*inquiry, deliberation, expression, and advocacy*) takes learners through an immersive experience, where they embrace personal identities, diverse narratives, and an explicit focus on civic intentionality: pedagogies that focus on the development of agency and a form of critical consciousness that asks what "powers [people] to produce an effect, to have influence, to make a difference" (Freire, 1973, p. 4). Civic intentionality embraces the outcome of media pedagogy not as an action of creation but as a series of interventions focusing on meaningful engagement with others in the world through media and the recurring set of processes that guide this engagement with an explicit focus on cultivating strong civic dispositions for emerging journalists and storytellers.

In 2018, participants in the media academy gathered to explore journalism and storytelling in an age of distrust. Seventy-six student participants were invited to immerse themselves in journalistic norms across the world, the technological and algorithmic limitations of our time, and the storytelling mechanisms best situated to help the public decipher truth and meaning in an era of unprecedented suspicion over journalistic intentions, processes, outcomes, and reliability. Core questions anchored faculty and visiting scholars' pedagogy for this theme:

- What processes define journalism today, and which are merely relics of an outdated industry?
- What are the main challenges and opportunities impacting journalistic practice in digital culture?
- What journalistic systems and audience expectations are needed to maximise trust and credibility?

The 2018 media academy's directive was to *re-imagine journalism*. This focus was guided by the emergence of the fake news phenomenon that gripped (and still grips) the world around national elections and referenda in the United States, the United Kingdom, France, Brazil, Russia, and beyond. The emergence of fake news as a political weapon,[1] utilised by politicians and governments for explicit control and or political gain, has engulfed media and journalism institutions as they struggle to tell stories (Blanding, 2018), in what is largely a disruptive and ever-emerging ecosystem for information and communication flow. Key attributes to the emerging fake news phenomenon include the migration of news and information into social networks and digital media platforms (Srnicek, 2017), that largely dictate information flow through the design of algorithms.[2] These algo-rithms challenge traditional metrics for engagement with journalism content, cre-ating tension with longstanding business models for news industries, and altering how audiences receive and process news and information. Studies found that social networks increased levels of bias, and anger, in news audiences (Bell, 2018), and that fabricated or "fake" stories that focused on emotional resonance and negativ-ity travelled farther and faster than those stories that were rigorously reported and factual (Meyer, 2018).

The various technological impacts on journalism have instigated a crisis of trust in the profession. A number of factors – such as the architecture of digital media, algorithmic personalisation, the shift from journalism's civic mission to the quest for financial profit (or mere survival), and the weaponisation of social media by specific political and business interests – have created and amplified echo chambers and "filter bubbles" within and across media platforms. Rather than acting as a potent antidote to those ills, traditional models of journalism have often perpetu-ated partisanship, confusion, and the spread of fake news in this digital information ecosystem (Silverman, 2015). At the same time, institutes of journalism and media education struggle to adapt and reform their approach to preparing storytellers for rigour, credibility, and meaning in their media inquiry and creation.

In this chapter, we will use the pedagogy of the 2018 Salzburg Media Academy to outline our approach to transformation through journalism pedagogies that sup-port civic intentionality. Our goal is to advance a process and set of practices that distinguish media pedagogies as embedded in the civic, and oriented towards the capacity to act. We outline our theoretical approach, and some of the key tensions, challenges, and debates that build towards transformation, agency, and action-taking embedded within the Salzburg Media Academy pedagogy. This chapter provides insight to media and journalism educators interested in harnessing the civic poten-tial of technologies to support strong and healthy journalism infrastructures.

It is important to note the Salzburg programme is unique: it is rare that a global cohort with such diversity convenes for an immersive and intensive learning expe-rience. However, the models that have emerged from this experience highlight some pedagogical approaches that can harness the potential of journalism educa-tion to be transformative. The ideas in this chapter are set forth as a way to refo-cus journalism pedagogies towards a more inclusive future, where they eclipse the priority of skills for reporting and embrace the civic potential of storytelling and *making sense* of social phenomena and of the world around us.

Civic intentionality: a focus on value systems and the capacity to act

Longstanding approaches to journalism education incorporate the need to teach people skills in critical inquiry and critical production that help them develop a healthy scepticism and critical mindset towards the ways in which media mes-sages impact individuals and societies. Traditionally, these approaches prioritise skill attainment: a specific focus on learning deconstruction and analysis techniques alongside media production abilities. Such approaches to teaching and learning with and about media are inherently civic. The goal of teaching people how to critically engage with media messages – as storytellers or audiences – involves consistent interrogation and reflection on representation, meaning, and application. And with these forms of inquiry, the informed and empowered citizen is often the stated goal.

How the informed citizen is actualised, however, is less clear. The transmission of skills often increases the ability for people to analyse, deconstruct, and assess information, and this has largely been proven in media literacy research over the past decades.³ What has been less straightforward is the ability to connect such skill attainment to engagement and participation in civic life. Mihailidis writes that while media literacies focused on skill attainment are impactful, "contemporary approaches to media literacy have been unable to adequately respond to the realities of today's information environments and the extent to which they shape relationships between people, institutions, and democracy," (Mihailidis, 2018, pp. 33–34). Five core attributes – distance, transactionality, deficit-focus, content-orientation, and individual responsibility – contribute to the civic shortcomings of media and news literacies. This problem is not one of teaching impact or value, but rather one of failing to prioritise and actualise the civic identity of journalism education. Embracing such a priority means focusing journalism pedagogies on *civic intentionality*.

Civic intentionality signals a shift from prioritising skills and outcomes-based pedagogies to prioritising the values that support meaningful engagement in civic life with and through media. In this sense, civic intentionality is not a competency or skill set, but rather the design of journalism and media processes and practices that help people not only "exercise democratic power," but also find out where that "power lies and how to exercise it" (Mihailidis and Gerodimos, 2016, p. 386).

Journalism pedagogies that prioritise civic intentionality embrace "the technologies, designs, and practices that produce and reproduce the sense of being in the world with others toward common good" (Gordon and Mihailidis, 2016, p. 2). Common good, while subjective at its core, focuses on "actions taken that benefit a public outside of the actor's intimate sphere" (ibid, pp. 3–4). This orientation prioritises citizens as conscious members of a community, who share fundamental rights and responsibilities and whose individual and collective freedom and welfare depends on being able to understand the values, identities, and power dynamics embedded in media processes and practices, beyond just the skills needed to navigate the consumption and production of messages.

How does civic intentionality work in practice? In Salzburg, this incorporates contemporary debates on journalism practice alongside a deep exploration of the civic and cultural identities that guide the work of journalists in global and digital culture. This orientation prioritises the civic capacity of journalism, taking students through a scaffolded model that begins with deep *investigation* of current media and journalistic systems, and *deliberation* around how our personal and public identities impact these systems and processes. The Salzburg model then asks students to design *expressions* of experimental, alternative, or novel approaches to journalism and storytelling that respond to the challenges posed, and to *advocate* for how their ideas can impact the civic capacity of media around the world.

This framework allows the pedagogies of the Salzburg Academy to incorporate the personal and the public, the theoretical and the applied, the practical and the experimental. It also allows journalism education to approach some of the main challenges of our time without a need to find explicit solutions, but to embrace their complexity.

The Salzburg context: reimagining journalism pedagogies in an age of distrust

The thematic, intellectual, and pedagogical explorations for the 2018 Salzburg Academy were rooted in a deep investigation of journalism's shifting processes and outcomes. By positioning our educational approach within a historical and critical context of journalism, faculty made a deliberate choice to make questions of truth, integrity, and discourse central to students' inquiry at the academy. In previous years, academy topics focused on political and social issues or trends such as populism or migration. While thematically focused and relevant to contemporary global challenges, these issues placed methods of journalism and storytelling as somewhat peripheral to the topics themselves. The pedagogical implications of exploring truth and activism in the storytelling of migration are vastly differently from the pedagogical implications of exploring the very nature of truth and storytelling themselves. As democratic practices around the world continued to come under siege in 2018, with journalism repeatedly used as a weapon or salve, the academy's curriculum was reoriented to face this reality and to ask students to consider, first and foremost, the nature of journalism.

Shifting from a thematic, issues-based curriculum to one rooted in a specific industry and professional process allowed students to consider how journalism's promise has in many ways gone unfulfilled in their lifetime. And yet, perhaps never before has the role of journalism been so vital to the functioning of societies across the world. As nations around the world rely ever more on digital platforms for basic information and communication needs, journalism's responsibility to navigate such emerging platforms is paramount. These platforms, at the same time, have changed the ways in which politicians and public officials communicate, which in turn impacts what is considered newsworthy. As a result, journalism as an institutional check on power across all levels of society is in jeopardy. As a 21st-century profession, journalism suffers both a substantive identity crisis and a public relations problem. Those entrenched in the industry have in many ways failed to adapt to modern economic realities and have yet to supplant their aging audience with loyal, young consumers. Students at the academy in many ways embodied this failure: they were deeply interested in journalism but also questioned whether its true potential could be reached.

Framing the academy's curriculum around journalism also meant exploring journalism education – both through the practical experiences of students in the cohort and through a historical and critical lens. Journalism education itself has progressed so slowly that advances in technology far outpace curriculum and practice for emerging journalists. Even more, the innovation and dynamism in media technology that might infuse journalism with relevance for the digital age is too often relegated to the technology sector because of outdated and myopic conceptualisations of practices such as objectivity and fact, concepts that are often weaponised against a grounded and contextual understanding of truth. On the audience side, readers, listeners, and viewers are increasingly unable to decipher truth from advertising, propaganda, sensationalism, and disinformation. The increase of "noise" fortifies the boundaries of our media diet, making citizens unlikely to engage with media outside their typical exposure platforms. Many students at the academy reflected this cynicism and embraced these typical media habits even as they recognised the need for change from both the profession and consumers.

As young adults on the cusp of developing their own professional and civic identities, students recognised how these realities have created space for journalism to evolve in ways that could truly benefit citizens and consumers. In response, global coalitions of journalists[4] are looking for ways to articulate what journalism means in the 21st century, and the 2018 academy was uniquely designed to put young thinkers at the forefront of that discussion.

The IDEA framework

To approach the problem laid out above, the academy designed a curricular process around a pedagogical framework called IDEA.[5] IDEA stands for *Investigation, Deliberation, Expression, and Advocacy*, with each term anchoring a pedagogical scaffold that takes learners through a process in which they engage in active, hands-on explorations, personal reflection, and applied learning experiences. At the conclusion of this process, participants produce a creative intervention that takes the form of a multimedia publication that responds to the challenge posed at the onset of the programme.[6] International teams work through a design process in which they use the IDEA framework to identify problems, pitch ideas, ideate, and create speculative and expansive spaces for response. The final publications live online and offer a diverse set of interventions and creative multimedia outputs.

In the *investigation* phase, participants are asked to explore the norms of journalism which have enabled success and distortion in the field. In doing so, academy participants come face to face with the constraints, failures, and expectations of journalism today. Students rely on both their lived experiences with media, rooted deeply in their communities and the geopolitics of their home regions, while also exploring case studies and historical constructs of journalism around the world. In doing so, students learn how traditional norms of journalism such as neutrality or objectivity are being replaced with conceptual priorities such as "truth." The shift is more than semantics, as illustrated in discussions[7] about best practices of the craft.

The investigation phase, then, lays the groundwork for students to understand the dynamics contributing to distrust in journalism today. Despite global differences in journalistic practice, students find that many approaches to journalism share a belief that journalism's first obligation is to truth, a meaningful choice over the word "facts." This larger narrative of truth relies on an understanding of issues through evidential analysis, comment, debate, and, of course, fact-finding. Demanding that journalists pursue "truth" over "facts" obliges them to eventually help audiences understand why things happen and what they mean in the context of a consumer's social, professional, personal, or civic life. Student-led inquiry in this investigative phase reveals areas of nuance and discord in these formative ideas about journalism's role in the world, setting the stage for personalised and self-motivated deliberation about these concepts and the future of journalism.

In the *deliberation* phase, students are asked to begin synthesising their findings. While the investigation phase relies on a deep and scaffolded inquiry process to build understanding, the deliberation phase of the academy curriculum purposefully asks students to step *back from*, but not *out of*, the conceptual framework. This portion of the curriculum builds on students' broad search for understanding in phase one and asks them to begin considering both personal and collaborative proposals for addressing the challenges to journalism they uncover. In short, students are asked to propose innovations that help to solve myriad crises in journalism. Groups might tackle trust, diversity, or any other challenges identified in the investigation phase. These potential solutions take the form of iterative "pitches" in which student groups share and refine ideas based mostly on peer feedback with minimal input from faculty. This process uses a design thinking approach that allows students to ideate without conditioning their solutions on limits to feasibility or implementation. During the deliberation phase, faculty intentionally step away to allow students to own their ideas and rely on interactive and informal peer feedback. This emphasis on lateral instead of hierarchical feedback aligns with radical pedagogy that redefines the student-teacher dynamic. The group pitch process allows students to hold each other accountable for the integrity of their ideas, and vetting each other's potential solutions leads to a natural revision process that strengthens all potential outcomes. Finally, this deliberative process models the civic, collaborative, and community-oriented process that is ideal for both innovative journalism and transformative education.

The third step in the IDEA framework, the *expression* phase, empowers students to put their ideas for innovative solutions in journalism down on paper, codifying their pitches into verbal and visual expression that articulates their vision for stronger, more impactful journalism around the world. Still working collaboratively, students must determine the best way to educate, inspire, and respond to the need for new approaches to journalism in an age of digital abundance. Their final project, a digital publication, features these ideas – both practical and experimental – for a more robust, inclusive, and responsive future of journalism around the world. As in the first two phases, students are given incredible leeway for how they envision this publication. In fact, the academy curriculum specifically avoids models or templates so that each student group is empowered to incorporate a multitude of ideas for innovative actions, new approaches, and processes that are both applied and realistic, and that can be experimental and abstract. Each group's final product, a chapter in the digital publication, must tell a compelling story that illustrates the need for the group's ideas or methods, complete with an articulation of the problem statement or issue framework. More specifically, groups must articulately answer these questions: Why does this problem matter, and why are these the right ways to reimagine journalism as a response? Stories in this digital publication must also establish a call to action or a push for a creative intervention. This requirement segues students into the final phase of the IDEA framework.

The *advocacy* phase directs the work towards application and intervention in the real world. Groups must articulate clearly a theory of change and a specific set of impacts that their intervention will have on communities. Groups must also position their idea to advocate explicitly for impact on specific existing practices or processes that they are hoping to reform or change. Prioritising explicit civic impact allows the curriculum to focus on the constraints of speculative ideas as they are considered for application into the real world. Focusing on advocacy also allows for dynamic group dialogue to happen amongst diverse participants: when considering if an idea could work across borders and cultures, participants are able to share the intricacies of their own experiences and cultures with others, which enables a powerful form of exchange and peer learning. Advocacy, in this sense, is about civic intentionality becoming an explicit part of the pedagogical process.

Approaching meaningful tensions in journalism education

The IDEA framework allows the pedagogy of the Salzburg Academy to prioritise personal identity and culture nuance along with deep critical immersion and active engagement with media and news models. Through a focus on process, the academy opens meaningful spaces for addressing core tensions that face journalism and media in digital culture. Through the framework, the faculty and students are exposed to divergent views and contemporary approaches, opportunities, and challenges for journalism and storytelling in digital culture.

The incorporation of current challenges to journalism education is important, as it allows for real-world applications to support the personal and conceptual inquiries grounded in the curricular process. This integration reinforces intentionality, in that it supports the types of deep human engagement and meaningful encounters that scholars show cannot be replicated meaningfully by individual exploration alone, or by any singular technology.[8]

Four main challenges were addressed in the 2018 Salzburg Academy on Media & Global Change. The pedagogy embedded these challenges across the IDEA framework and used them to bring diverse voices and viewpoints into the experience, and to allow for meaningful engagement with pressing challenges in journalism to be confronted. These challenges were met not by any singular curricular process or approach, but through engagement across and within each phase of the IDEA framework.

Challenge 1 – shifting modes of audience engagement

Two distinct approaches to news were presented during the academy. The first one has long been associated with traditional news organisations (or so-called legacy media, although the term "legacy" implies that these already belong to the past), such as *The New York Times*. The second model is that of viral news as disseminated through emerging digital outlets, such as BuzzFeed. While there may be differences in news-gathering and agenda-setting processes, what is particularly distinct about these two approaches is the presentation of news – in terms of layout, language, emphasis, and editorial input – as well as the intended audience and their role. An implicit but crucial difference in these two models of journalism – the established and the emerging – is the role of borders and the perception of the global. If we were to schematically reduce them to two contrasting examples, the first model would be of a literary long-read produced by an authoritative and established news organisation, which attempts to make the exotic Other meaningful to a domestic audience; the boundaries between the two being implied but clear. An example of the latter would be a social media-savvy article that blends human interest and popular culture with hard news, opts for speed and shareability over gravitas, and is aimed at a younger *global* audience sharing a common digital culture, for which the boundaries between the individual lifeworld and hard news are either fuzzy or non-existent. What are the implications of this tension for journalism education and practice? These two approaches are not mutually exclusive and may come to an equilibrium of co-existence as part of a more diverse ecosystem of news provision. What is important to acknowledge here is that traditional conceptualisations of news theory and citizenship that evolved in an era of a powerful, trusted institutional press may not necessarily apply to emerging forms of news consumption and user-generated content in a messy, global, digital public sphere. The crucial question to ask is what kind of journalism pedagogies are needed so as to enable 21st-century journalists and citizens to effectively identify and hold to account agents of power, and to relay meaningful narratives about other members of the community? Furthermore, journalists play a vital role in engaging audiences with global current affairs – with stories, communities, events, and people that are geographically or culturally remote to them (Gerodimos, 2012). In today's globalised world, this function is as critical as that of engaging with our immediate local community. A journalism pedagogy for the 21st century ought to put global current affairs – the interdependence of issues, flows, networks, and communities – at the heart of the curriculum, as media literacy becomes a core tenet of global citizenship.

Challenge 2 – core values and storytelling

In her keynote address to the 2018 Salzburg Academy, award-winning filmmaker and journalist Daniela Rea[9] led a debate on empathy and truth, arguing that values such as "resonance" may prove to be better tools for the audience to arrive at an emotional truth, as opposed to more established notions of objectivity. At the core of the academy's curriculum, and of the concept of civic intentionality, is the question of facilitating empathy and engagement, by bringing down barriers to communication and understanding of the Other and of the self. This vocabulary of emotional literacy is not in conflict with core elements of journalism education – such as an emphasis on sources and fact-checking – but with contemporary phenomena such as celebrity broadcasters effectively parachuting into a community – e.g. warzone – for a limited number of days and scratching the surface of an issue. A journalism curriculum that has been designed with civic intentionality emphasises all-rounder, immersive, and immersed journalism, which approaches sources and communities with respect and an open mind, relating it to the audience with visual literacy and emotional authenticity. An example of how these values can be embedded into journalism education and practice is the methodology of the Human (or Living) Library.[10] The Human Library is a safe space for meaningful and "unplugged" conversations between individuals who either wish to share or learn about stigma, stereotypes, marginalisation, and exclusion in their various manifestations. It allows participants to open up and achieve a level of self-realisation and empathy that is emotionally significant: not only does it create transcendent moments of truth, but it also effectively trains participants in asking meaningful questions, listening respectfully, and making connections between the self and the Other; qualities in short supply in this era of polarised, tribal publics.

Challenge 3 – youth identity and culture

A curriculum of civic intentionality ought to engage with questions of individual and collective identity, power, agency, voice, and social and global change. These questions are at the core of our curriculum. Taking a conscious and critical approach to pedagogy, journalism, and citizenship means questioning what may seem to be even fundamental assumptions, such as: What does it mean to have power and voice? Why is it normatively good for citizens to be empowered in an era of massive, complex global challenges, and what are the potential limitations? What kinds of hierarchies and structures do we need in an era of globalised, multi-level governance? What kinds of role models should we look up to, and, ultimately, what kind of world do we want to live in? Our pedagogic approach involves extensive and interactive plenary debates on these questions, as well as an exercise of "Civic Imagination" in which students are given the opportunity to envisage alternative realities and futures. These foundational exercises allow us to then identify and critically dissect contemporary cultural phenomena that carry global agency – such as YouTube influencers, whose home-made vlogs are seen by millions of young people around the world. The role of journalism education is not merely to enable students to mechanically produce and reproduce successful formulas of video monetisation, but also to understand the underlying editing techniques, monetisation strategies, and cultural, political, and economic drivers; to expose the power laws and inequalities inherent to a supposedly "egalitarian" mode of communication and to understand the social needs that this caters to.

Challenge 4 – algorithms and artificial intelligence

The race to develop technology to conquer areas that were traditionally governed by humans remains largely unchecked, unregulated, and outside the realm of everyday debates. Public awareness and understanding of advanced technology are limited, and many people are happy to leave decisions of design and architecture, which have profound moral implications, to experts. But what happens when even those experts struggle to understand technology and the way it behaves? This is the case with AI, which now dominates significant parts of our life, despite our apparent inability to comprehend its inner workings. From driverless cars to credit applications, from chatbots to court decisions, AI is here to stay. Algorithms have become a key component of user journeys, search results, advertising, and news production and consumption online (Cohen, 2018). As such they directly shape the architecture and infrastructure of democracy and citizenship in the 21st century, as they affect citizens' access to news, views, and social interactions, as well as the use of their private data. Bartlett (2018) argues that through

> our unquestioning embrace of big tech, the building blocks of democracy are slowly being removed. The middle class is being eroded, sovereign authority and civil society is weakened, and we citizens are losing our critical faculties, maybe even our free will.

Whereas journalism's civic mission in the past was to act as a Fourth Estate to national executives, legislatures, and judiciaries, it now may be the case that – for journalism to continue to act as a pillar of civic engagement – it has to turn its attention to those same agents of technological change that sustain it. A civically minded journalism education is therefore a tool that may prove to be critical to the survival of democracy as it can afford a critical awareness of the power, function, and architecture of technology.

A pedagogic imperative: civic intentionality in journalism education

This chapter asks us to consider the ways in which journalism and media educators can design and implement pedagogies to inspire a future for storytelling that embraces civic intentionality. Such a task is ambitious in scope and breadth. Transformation requires that educators and learners both concede their long-held personal and professional views. It also means they will have their core values and beliefs challenged. In Salzburg, the IDEA framework guides this process of disruption, but it is not the steadfast adherence to a framework that leads the path of transformation. Rather, in Salzburg it is the combination of pedagogical structures with the fluidity of the environment and the tone of project that allows for transformation to emerge. Immersion, intimacy, and experimentation around the three weeks are necessary for the IDEA framework to succeed at challenging participants and faculty in new and unique ways. And while Salzburg is unique in setting and the diversity of its participants, out of this experience emerges core considerations that can harness the potential of journalism education to be transformative. We provide these considerations as an attempt to refocus journalism pedagogies towards a more inclusive future, where they eclipse the priority of skills for reporting, and embrace the civic potential of storytelling and *making sense* of social phenomena and of the world around us.

The first consideration asks us to focus on the processes and practices that encapsulate civic intentionality. In their work on learning and human connection, Sloman and Fernbach (2017) highlight the potential of technologies to expand our productive capacity but last caution their readers to not over-rely on technologies to advance our core civic structures. They write:

> Machines are intelligent enough that we rely on them as a central part of our community of knowledge. Yet no machine has that singular ability so central to human activity: no machine can share intentionality.
>
> *(Sloman and Fernbach, 2017, p. 141)*

Journalism education often prioritises the technological knowledge to report effectively over the human knowledge needed to tell stories with intentionality. This is something that happens from *learning with others*. The participants in Salzburg find the value of human activity together to empower their ability to tell stories far more than any singular technology or platform can ever do.

The second consideration asks us to prioritise the transformative potential of journalism work. Story, as we know, is core to the human experience.[11] In their work on changemaking, Danielle Allen and her team put together a set of guiding questions to help activate the civic power of young people interested in reform, change, and progress.[12] Their framework asks people to situate themselves in the larger context of the issues and ideas they are working to change. Questions range from "How much should I share?" and "Where do we start?" to "Are we pursuing voice or influence or both?" and "How do we get from voice to change?" Journalists are traditionally asked to step away from their civic identities. Questions as such are to be left to the audiences only after the facts have been shared. This model is antiquated in practice, and more so in pedagogy. In Salzburg, our approach is to harness the transformative potential of storytelling and inspire journalists to be what *Washington Post* national reporter Wesley Lowery calls activists for truth. "Any good journalist," writes Lowery, "is an activist for truth, in favor of transparency, on the behalf of accountability."[13]

The third consideration asks us to embrace pedagogies that embed journalism in contemporary political, social, and cultural issues and structures. This means not abstracting the work of a journalist from the contexts that journalism exists within. Many of the participants in Salzburg find voice and power in the notion that they have explicit civic efficacy through their work. Ethan Zuckerman argues that voice is the first step on a path to civic efficacy. Voice, he writes, "is how people signal their affiliations, their priorities, and the issues they care sufficiently about that they share them with friends in the hope of influencing their actions" (Zuckerman in Gordon and Mihailidis, 2016, p. 69). In Salzburg, the mission is to navigate dialogue around complex contemporary issues that face our world. Only through this hard and meaningful engagement can we find a way to embed journalism more squarely in today's digital culture. Through examining contemporary issues, participants are able to reflect more honestly and critically on how their own personal identities, ideologies, and biases impact the types of stories they tell, and those who receive them.

These three considerations help the pedagogic process of Salzburg move from that of disseminating skills, tools, and ideas, to inspiring practices and processes that inspire transformation. The IDEA framework is the process that guides our work, but those involved in the design of the Salzburg Academy project have seen the transformative power of an experience that leads with the civic and is supported by the content and ideas needed to build the capacity for journalism to serve as a tool for powerful and positive civic change.

It's somewhat irresponsible to prescribe a normative pedagogic output from a particular experience like the one in Salzburg. However, a specific call to action emerges from our provocation. One that asks journalism and media educators to reimagine their pedagogy from a set of skills and dispositions as the primary output of a learning experience, to a focus on transformation of the storyteller herself. This reimagining can inspire a pedagogical process – like IDEA – to not solely focus on a new set of skills to be learned, but to a focus on the agency of the storyteller to see their work as an act of self-transformation, and continually challenging the civic, social, political, and technological norms that tend to define and guide journalistic norms and the pedagogies that support them.

Notes

1 See: Evgeny Morozov. (2018). Moral panic over fake news hides the real enemy – the digital giants. *The Guardian*, US Edition. 7 January. Available at: www.theguardian.com/commentisfree/2017/jan/08/blaming-fake-news-not-the-answer-democracy-crisis.

2 See: Carlson, Matt. (2018). Automating judgment? Algorithmic judgment, news knowledge, and journalistic professionalism. *New Media & Society*, 20(5), pp. 1755–1772; Natascha Just and Michael Latzer. (2016). Governance by algorithms: Reality construction by algorithmic selection on the Internet. *Media, Culture & Society*, 39(2), pp. 238–258.

3 See: Joseph Kahne and Benjamin Bowyer. (2017). Educating for democracy in a partisan age: Confronting the challenges of motivated reasoning and misinformation. *American Educational Research Journal*, 54(1), pp. 3–34; Adam Maksl, Seth Ashley and Stephanie Craft. (2015). Measuring news media literacy. *Journal of Media Literacy Education*, 6(3), pp. 29–45; Hans Martens and Renee Hobbs. (2015). How media literacy supports civic engagement in a digital age. *Atlantic Journal of Communication*, 23(2), pp. 120–137.

4 For more information, see the *International Coalition of Investigative Journalists'* manifesto on Safeguarding the Truth. Available at: www.icij.org/about/icijs-manifesto/.

5 The IDEA framework was developed in 2018 by Paul Mihailidis and Eric Gordon for a Civic Media Literacy project focused on youth and storytelling capacity. The framework has since been applied in subsequent projects with youth and digital literacies in India

and in the Salzburg Academy on Media & Global Change. See and read more about the project available at: www.civicidea.org/.

6 See final project work for the Salzburg Academy on Media & Global Change. Available at: www.salzburgglobal.org/multi-year-series/media-academy.html?pageId=6853.

7 See: *Elements of Journalism*. American Press Institute. Available at: www.americanpress institute.org/journalism-essentials/what-is-journalism/elements-journalism/.

8 For more on the intentionality of human connection, see: Steven Sloman and Philip Fernbach. (2018). *The knowledge illusion: Why we never think alone*. London: Penguin; Douglas Rushkoff. (2010). *Program or be programmed: Ten commands for a digital age*. New York: Or Books.

9 See: *Telling the personal stories of violence with respect, honesty and empathy*. Salzburg Global Seminar. Available at: www.salzburgglobal.org/news/latest-news/article/daniela-reatelling-the-personal-stories-of-violence-with-respect-honesty-and-empathy.html.

10 See: Human Library. Available at: http://humanlibrary.org/.

11 To read more about the potential of storytelling, see; Jonathan Gottschall. (2012). *The storytelling animal: How stories make us human*. New York: Houghton Mifflin Harcourt.

12 Youth and Participatory Politics Research Network. *Why the 10 questions?* Harvard University. Available at: https://yppactionframe.fas.harvard.edu/action-fra.

13 See: Michael Blanding. (2018). *Where does journalism end and activism begin?* Nieman Reports. 21 Aug. Available at: https://niemanreports.org/articles/where-does-journalism-end-and-activism-begin/.

References

Bartlett, J. (2018). *The people vs tech: How the internet is killing democracy (and how we save it)*. London: Ebury Press.

Bell, E. (2018). Platforms, publishers, and the uneasy alliance at the heart of journalism. *Columbia Journalism Review*, 14 June. Available at: www.cjr.org/tow_center/platforms-publishers-api-survey.php.

Blanding, M. (2018). *Where does journalism end and activism begin?* Nieman Reports, 21 Aug. Available at: https://niemanreports.org/articles/where-does-journalism-end-and-activism-begin/.

Cohen, J. N. (2018). Exploring echo-systems: How algorithms shape immersive media environments. *Journal of Media Literacy Education*, 10(2), pp. 139–151.

Dubois, W. E. B. (1973). *The education of black people: Ten critiques, 1906-1960*. Edited by Herbert Aptheker. Amherst: University of Massachusetts Press.

Freire, P. (1973). *Education for critical consciousness*. London: Bloomsbury Publishing.

Gerodimos, R. (2012). Journalism students as global citizens and mediators: Incorporating global current affairs into the journalism curriculum. *Journalism Education*, 1(1), pp. 70–86.

Gordon, E. and Mihailidis, P. (2016). *Civic media: Technology, design, practice*. Cambridge, MA: MIT Press.

Meyer, R. (2018). The grim conclusions of the largest-ever study of fake news. *The Atlantic*, 8 Mar. Available at: www.theatlantic.com/technology/archive/2018/03/largest-study-ever-fake-news-mit-twitter/555104/.

Mihailidis, P. (2018). *Civic media literacies: Re-imagining human connection in an age of digital abundance*. London: Routledge.

Mihailidis, P. and Gerodimos, R. (2016). Connecting pedagogies of civic media: The literacies, connected civics, and engagement in daily life. In: Gordon, E. and Mihailidis, P., eds., *Civic media: Technology, design, practice*. Cambridge, MA: MIT Press.

Silverman, C. (2015). Lies, damn lies, and viral content. *Columbia Journalism Review*, 10 Feb. Available at www.cjr.org/tow_center_reports/craig_silverman_lies_damn_lies_viral_content.php/.

Sloman, S. and Fernbach, P. (2017). *The knowledge illusion: Why we never think alone*. London: Penguin Books.

Srnicek, N. (2017). *Platform capitalism*. Hoboken, NJ: John Wiley & Sons.

Zuckerman, E. (2016). Effective civics. In: Gordon, E. and Mihailidis, P., eds., *Civic media: Technology, design, practice*. Cambridge, MA: MIT Press.

9

EMERGENT NARRATIVES FOR TIMES OF CRISIS – IDEAS ON DOCUMENTARY ART AND CRITICAL PEDAGOGY

Pablo Martínez-Zárate

This chapter draws on the author's career as a documentarian and artist to propose a new form of critical journalism pedagogy.

Introduction: a world beset by crisis

Sometimes, it appears that humanity is on the verge of collapse. In this world, which we have configured to meet both our strongest desires and darkest fears, it seems that we are plummeting towards self-driven extinction. Even if for some people this might be a rather extreme view of the current state of affairs, the sense of crisis is undoubtedly latent beyond regional borders. Human rights crisis, economic crisis, and ecological crisis are realities that as media makers, academics, and, of course, citizens, we need to address in order to imagine (and start building) an alternative future for ourselves and our successors. It is this potency for future imagining and future building, or what Franco Berardi has called Futurability (2017), which I want to maintain as a gravitational force throughout this chapter. How can we, as media academics and practitioners, become an active force in the development of narrative strategies that can respond to this critical world?

When we think of media in general, and specifically of journalism, we tend to attribute a certain protagonism to its function of narrating present events. Certainly, journalists and artists are witnesses of the contemporary world, those responsible for the chronicles that, in due course, will become one of the main sources of reality and, furthermore, history. Nevertheless, narratives of the world are not only a mirror or a repository of events, but also a window from which we can reimagine the future. This is especially true for the sort of media making I want to refer to here – a media making that I have called critical and that includes journalistic practices but might be better defined as documentary in nature. When I say documentary, I refer not to a genre but more to a methodological stance for content and narrative creation. This must not be confused with the *documentary mode*, which has influenced content production across platforms and has become a sort of standardised language of practice (Steyerl, 2009). One of the particularities of this *documentary mode* is that it gives people a sense of reality, mainly for its narrative functions and its aesthetic qualities. In this chapter I try to provide the basic understanding for what I am naming "*documentary art*," a set of strategies to defy some of the practices of the *standardised mode* of expressing and representing reality, to push, through experimentation, the possibilities of human thought and expression. To expand the limits of perception and imagination – an imperative for storytellers and educators alike – might well be defined as the focus of documentary art.

My proposal is based on the idea that, among the multiple crises, there is one that demands even more urgently our involvement as media makers and media scholars. It is the one crisis that is more intrinsically related to our capacity to imagine a possible future for human life. If the world is in crisis, it is also because our capacity to interpret such critical scenarios (and project our action) is crumbling. Perception and imagination, dislocated. This is what we can refer to as a representational crisis, detectable in tendencies such as "fake news," the hyper-saturation of the media landscape, the hardship that investigative journalism is experiencing throughout the world in terms of funding and outreach, or the permanent discredit – almost war – against journalism and journalists performed by politicians and conglomerates. This representational crisis translates into a narrative and pedagogical emergency that, I propose throughout this chapter, can be confronted by strategies such as documentary art and critical pedagogy. Behind the proposal of documentary art as a formative path for journalists lies the fact that the frontiers of journalism have expanded in recent years, making it necessary to introduce methodological insights for approaching incredibly complex contexts, and for producing technically consistent products that may survive the data chaos we live in. The ideas shared in this chapter could be read as alternative (or more precisely, subversive) strategies that question the boundaries of journalism and the arts of chronicle, from the field or the archive, in any format. Etymologically, subversive means to turn around. I believe that journalism has always been linked to subversive practices since its origin – journalism is a turning around in the sense that it either brings light where events are invisible or complements, if not contradicts, official versions of events. At the same time, journalism has an intricate relationship with art, first and quite obviously, because it always depends on a technical medium, be it writing, illustration, photography, audio, multimedia. Furthermore, art and journalism have shown more explicit points of encounter throughout the decades, as examples we could recall the popularity of narrative journalism in the '60s–'70s as proof of a sort of complicity between literature and journalism (with writers such as Tom Wolfe, Norman Mailer, Joan Didion, Oriana Fallaci as some of its main exponents) or the evolution of photojournalism and documentary films as two trends in visual arts since the mid-20th century; or, more recently, the use of media arts for investigative journalism, with cases such as Forensic Architecture, whose work brilliantly combines investigative journalism, media art, and technological innovation.

In this chapter I use the term *crisis* with the intention of connecting the idea of a critical environment with the necessity of a critical stance that, in this case, needs to be assumed by journalists, academics, and media makers working in the sphere of journalism. Our stance must be critical both on a discursive level:

- How do we respond to these signifying forces and power systems that engulf our educational, journalistic, and artistic practices?

and on an aesthetical one:

- How are we appropriating technical solutions that result in a specific form for our narratives?

At the same time, this critical nature of the context and of our responses to that context are linked with the notion of emergency. Crises emerge, and they usually demand a response from those who experience the crisis. At the same time, our expression is a sort of emergence on its own. It is through expression that our subjectivity emerges onto the world, and when expression is rooted in a journalistic and artistic context, then this emergence is also a sign of a professional responsibility.

As an artist and professor from Mexico, my approach is rooted in a specific Latin American tradition of radical filmmaking. I am convinced that some of the thinkers-creators of the second half of the 20th century have a lot to offer to those challenges we face today.[1] Among them is Cuban filmmaker Santiago Álvarez, who was the founder of the Cuban newsreel of the Cuban Institute of Cinematographic Art and Industry (ICAIC), established after the victory of the Cuban Revolution in 1959. Álvarez is known for his political short films – such as *L.B.J.* (1968) or *Now!* (1965), this last one considered the precursor of the modern music video – and also for being the main cameraman to Fidel Castro during most of the Communist leader's career. From Álvarez' scarce writings, I would like to extract central ideas that will allow me to establish a solid starting point for developing the notion of critical media that I want to expound here. In his text *Art and Compromise*, he wrote:

> A man or child that's dying from hunger or disease cannot be a spectacle that expects us to wait that either tomorrow or the day after, hunger and disease will disappear by gravitation. In this case, inertia is complicity, conformity is incidence with crime.
>
> *(Álvarez, 1988, p. 35)*

Álvarez was a militant, an almost blind supporter of Castro's regime. Even if this is a constitutive feature of his work, a feature which is impossible to overlook, I invite the reader to set aside this ideological filiation in order to analyse his words within both a contemporary media landscape and the critical scenario that I took as a starting point for these reflections.

Álvarez appeals to a compromise held by artists and journalists that implies resisting a spectacular approach to critical situations, such as the hunger and disease he evokes, but which can, without effort, be applied to other crises we are currently facing throughout the globe. This "spectacularity," latent across platforms, is defined by what could be synthesised as a vertical approach to reality. This approach is defined by the denial of historical processes and their complexities. In that sense, it is a colonial perspective, for it imposes versions of reality that are alien and even untrue to those who experience events. In this line of thought, the film *Reassemblage* (1983) by Vietnamese filmmaker and thinker Trinh Minh-ha is eye opening for her famous voice-over that is a declaration which manifests her ethical stance as a witness and narrator of events: "I do not intend to speak about, just speak nearby." This approach is a clear confrontation to the vertical treatment of events characteristic of a colonialist approach. It is also a calling to journalists and artists to take an ethical stance not only with the subjects they portray in their stories, but with storytelling itself.

When we narrate difficult situations, we are facing a challenge in the way we approach these realities, on the position we ourselves assume in relation to the concrete panorama we are portraying: How and where do we place our camera? How do we relate to those we are documenting? How do we behave ourselves when writing, reviewing, and editing the material we have gathered? What adjectives do I choose when I am writing a text? What are my final decisions on the music when it comes to producing a video documentary? *Speaking nearby* is speaking next to the problem and those who are affected; it is, in a way, becoming a part of the problem itself, fusing with its historical conditions; it is ultimately becoming a truly historical subject, what often implies diving into critical circumstances, almost as an act of self-sacrifice. Speaking nearby, then, rejects passivity, transgresses the comfort zone; speaking nearby means taking a leap into uncertainty, recognising the "other" in our best capacity. Speaking nearby is to sustain an intercourse within history, and so, it is an archival practice – it not only registers but produces history, and so, moves historical narratives towards openness and diversity. On the contrary, spectacularity, or what is the same, presenting events from the distance of the spectacle – what Minh-ha calls *speaking about* – is usually a closed and limited experience of history.

The colonial spectacle is so deeply imbued in our livestream of information, almost as a repetitive glitch of the colonial system we live in, that it is sometimes impossible to detect. Being a vertical approach that supposes closing the doors on alternative versions of reality, it widens the space between the producer and the consumer of those narratives. This is what I can refer to as a colonial glance, a conditioning of our perspective that needs to be challenged in order to achieve a more humane – horizontal – understanding of human suffering. Contrary to spectacle that sets us in an illusory privileged position in relation to what we are witnessing, this critical understanding forces us into the stage of events, partners us with those who are suffering, and in the best art and journalistic pieces, it even obliges us to recognise our complicity with their suffering. When we defy spectacle, we see ourselves as co-responsible for the situations that threaten life both in our neighbourhood and on the side of the world, appealing to at least a reflection if not a plan of action that alters our positioning in the world we experience.

In the film with the English title *The Vampires of Poverty* (*Agarrando Pueblo*, 1977), Colombian filmmakers Luis Ospina and Carlos Mayolo make a powerful critique of this spectacular treatment of human hardship by pushing the limits of genre and enacting themselves what they defined as *porno-misery*, that is, the exploitation of misery for commercial purposes, the mercantilisation of humans and their suffering. In what's considered a sort of mockumentary, we see a film director (Mayolo) and his crew exploit scenes of poverty in Santiago de Cali (this in 16mm black and white film) intercut with the rawness of poverty (in super 16mm colour). Several moments of the film are illustrative of the colonial glance I have referred to already. For example, there is one moment where the fake director is in his hotel room, and a minute after receiving the family of actors that will play the role of poor people in his documentary and giving them instructions, he proceeds to the bathroom and consumes a couple of lines of cocaine before going out to the streets to film. At a different moment, for example, they are riding a taxi and the cab driver asks what kind of film it is, to which they respond that it is a foreign production that seeks to portray the misery of Third World Countries. In one of the most obnoxious moments, we see Mayolo as the fake director throwing coins into a public fountain in order for street children to jump into the water to fetch the money. In a presentation of this film in Europe, Ospina and Mayolo refer to the genre they are trying to critique with the concept of "porno-misery," that is, the exploitation of poverty and the objectification of those who suffer it for the purpose of entertainment.

The gesture of Ospina and Mayolo proposes a critique of the colonial glance, but it also suggests that as creators of narratives that face the portrayal of difficult situations, radical formal strategies must be implemented so that we may convey the intended messages. On the other hand, *The Vampires of Poverty* is evident in what I implied as a "self-sacrifice," which seems indispensable in any investigative work, be it journalistic or artistic – the filmmakers need to put themselves in the narrative in order to explain a sort of filmmaking that is alien to their own ethical stance. This self-sacrifice resounds with the ideas of Álvarez, who intended to link art and journalism in what he called cinematographic journalism: "In a convulsed reality such as ours, like the one experienced in Third World, the artist must inflict violence to oneself, he must be taken, consciously, to a creative tension with his profession" (Álvarez, 1988, p. 35). When Álvarez speaks about a "creative tension" with our profession, he is inviting us to push the limits of our work as media makers. The limits of form, the limits of technique, the limits of narrative, and the limits of discourse must be reinvented in order to confront the representational crisis that afflicts contemporary journalism and documentary art. In this sense, critical media must be experimental based, which implies the questioning of tools and the renovation of their use in order to meet our narrative challenges.

The spectacle as a principle of colonial narration poses what I define as a narrative emergency associated with the crisis of representation evoked at the beginning of this chapter. This narrative emergency can be faced with what I suggest is a shift from storytelling to history-telling. My argument does not imply the sacrifice of story itself, but its relocation based on the fact that the culture of spectacle uses story models to annihilate human diversity and its historical experience. Álvarez, as a communist militant, said: "To the deformed and colonized version that our enemy wants to perpetuate as historical truth, we need to vigorously oppose our work" (Álvarez, 1978, p. 19). As established above, we stand before a radical member of the Cuban Revolution. Again, I propose that we transcend the specificity of Álvarez' partisanship and ideology in order to apply such militant attitude to our current media landscape and the role that media makers can assume as critical agents in truth history and future building. For example, in 2016, the word of the year elected by the *Oxford Dictionaries* was "post-truth," "an adjective defined as relating to or denoting circumstances in which objective facts are less influential in shaping public opinion than appeals to emotion and personal belief."[2] This tendency is, in an almost caricaturesque incarnation, obvious in many political leaders of our world – the US President Donald Trump and his Mexican counterpart, Enrique Peña Nieto (2012–8), are two good examples. This systemic negation of events or fabrication of alternative realities is a true challenge for journalists and documentary artists throughout the world. I find a rather natural connection between this post-truth world and what Álvarez designates as "historical truth."

Exploring "historical truths" – a personal project

Taking the notion of "historical truth" as a connector, I would like to share an example of my own artistic work to illustrate how we can critically approach current events by designing alternative methodologies and amplifying the spectrum of what traditionally is understood as documentary. The term "historical truth" was actually an expression used by a former attorney general of Mexico during a press conference to explain the case of the 43 disappeared students from the Ayotzinapa rural school.[3] The precise sentence was the following, expressed after presenting what afterwards would be denounced as an impossible and therefore spurious version of the kidnappings: "This is the historical truth, based on the data provided by science."[4] This sentence resonates directly with Álvarez' quote.

I undertook this project from 2015 to 2018. It consisted in the documentation of cases such as the press conference of the Ayotzinapa case in order to register and denounce this denial of events as a constant in the Mexican government of Enrique Peña Nieto (2012–8). The project consisted of archiving the public speeches of the members of the government at the moment of their cynical non-acceptance of reality. These were the stages of the project:

1   I downloaded the speeches from the official channels (hosted on YouTube).
2   Once they were "in my possession," I selected a precise moment, such as the proclamation of the "historical truth," mentioned above, regarding the

abduction of 43 students, and I digitally slowed down what was barely five to ten seconds of the video containing one specific moment of the declaration, a gesture of each of the selected characters from Peña Nieto's circle, including his wife.[5]

3 I took each of these single instants of a fake discourse and then put them all together in a single video.

4 The actual work started when I projected this video of the instances of deceit for their capture in analogue film formats of 8, 16, 35, and 120 millimetres. This sort of counter-gesture, in the first place, aimed to give a physical location in the world to this governmental mythomania. Transform their lies into concrete, palpable matter, a sort of photochemical version of deceit. In the second place, the analogue material suffers iterations (digital and analogue) in order to multiply the faces of this public dishonour. The most representative of them all is the manipulation of three super 8 rolls in the dark room and editing table. The super 8 material I worked with is black and white reversal film, which means that under normal circumstances, it needs to be developed and exposed in two steps with intermediate bleach and second exposure to light, to end up with a positive film after the process – a film strip that can be projected in positive, not negative.

- One of the 50-foot rolls was processed in this way, in order to have an ordinary version of the faces of dishonesty.
- Another of the rolls was processed in a similar way with two variations; *solarisation* – exposing it to light while the film is in the first developer – and *over-exposing* during second exposition that takes place before final development. The resulting roll reflects a disappearance of the faces of deceit themselves – the images fade away and reappear whimsically, as a mirror of the political practice that this project wants to critique.
- Finally, the third roll was processed only as a negative (one step of the development process and then I intervened to tint it frame by frame with cochineal,[6] which when properly diluted resembles the colour of blood.

The intention of this piece is not only a critique of the violence implied in the policy of shutting off history by imposing "historical truths" and, henceforth, the closure of the horizons of possibility. It is also a call to action for the public to recognise the complicity and responsibility that we all have in the intervention of that reality and the configuration of history, which is in every case constructed collectively.

5 The resulting materialities (negatives, silver and digital prints, film rolls, digital versions in USB) are all placed inside a small container that travels from place to place for its exhibition.[7] The idea is that the archive itself becomes an opportunity to intervene with the historic, to reimagine the relationships that as citizens we can establish with these facts and our role in building a fairer future.

The title of the project is *These Images are Truth. A Microarchive of Ignominy* (Figure 9.1). It allows me, in the context of this chapter, to establish several aspects that I consider pivotal in the shift from storytelling to history-telling, and when we think of educational practices, it has proved to be incredibly liberating and stimulating for students to explore alternative techniques for documenting their stories. First of all, with this project I emphasise the historic as part of a material and technological dimension that demands the viewal and reviewal (that is, the identification first of these images, and then the analysis and relocation of them), and then the registering and sometimes intervention of data sets. Instead of understanding facts as a defined series of events, as a fixed and hermetic set of accidents, series of dates, chains of names, this project evokes the potency of reinventing the relationships that make these events significant to us as individuals and to the communities we belong to. This example helps us imagine how experimental approaches to media broaden the horizons of storytelling into the realm of what I call history-telling. In the context of journalistic practice, examples such as this serve only as references from the art-world that enable alternative readings and analysis of the events journalist face in their daily coverage of news. It is also an invitation, then, to build methodological bridges between strictly artistic and journalistic practices.

The storytelling/history-telling techniques employed in this project are in some way inspired by the conceptualisation of history presented by Lebanese artist Walid Raad and his approach to the Lebanese Civil War. From 1989 to 2004, Raad undertook the project "The Atlas Group," an exploration of alternative ways of

FIGURE 9.1 Jesús Murillo Karam, Mexico's former attorney general, during the Ayotzinapa students' press conference. Scan of 35 mm b/w negative. Part of the project *These Images are Truth. A Microarchive of Ignominy.*

representing the Lebanese Civil War. His definition of facts is incredibly revealing when trying to establish the horizons of history-telling:

> We are not concerned with facts if facts are considered to be self-evident objects always already present in the world. Furthermore, we hold that this common-sense definition of facts, this theoretical primacy of facts, must be challenged. Facts have to be treated as processes. One of the questions we find ourselves asking is: How do we approach facts not in their crude facticity but through the complicated mediation by which facts acquire their immediacy?
>
> *(Atlas Group, 2003, p. 179)*

The processes of mediation evoked by Raad are the essence of history-telling as an act of resistance to our culture of spectacle, which even in the digital world and social networks has not diluted yet. This implies finding methodologies to identify and portray invisible connections that constitute events as historical processes; it demands from the journalist and the artist the capacity to analyse, dissect, and reconstruct political, economic, and social relationships behind the events s/he is reporting. Even though this methodological requirement might be more suitable for investigative journalism than for daily news coverage, it could also reside in practical methodologies for the newsroom. These implications invite us to question how we mediate our relationship with events. And also, how are our own narrations introducing themselves in the ongoing stream of "circulationism," as Steyerl (2015) has defined the current state of information flows?

Raad, in his explanation of the Lebanese Civil War, upholds this complex notion of facts as something more than a data set subject to archival petrification:

> We do not consider 'The Lebanese Civil War' to be a settled chronology of events, dates, personalities, massacres, invasions, but rather we also want to consider it as an abstraction constituted by various discourses and, more importantly, by various modes of assimilating the data of the world.
>
> *(Atlas Group, 2003, p. 179)*

The Lebanese artist is telling us that our understanding of history affords a group of perspectives of the world that coexist in perpetual tension, versions of events upon which we base our understanding not only of those past events, but also of our presence (present) in relation to those events and those other presences around us. Even more, this perspective on history-telling reveals our capacity to make decisions and project an analysis of events into the future. In this set of enunciations, we unequivocally refer to the archive as the main territory where we negotiate our place in the world.

Intervening to produce meaning

In the same line of thought proposed by Raad, my project *These Images are Truth. A Microarchive of Ignominy.* assumes the archive not as a closed universe of existing documents, but rather as a territory that we need to explore and moreover, inter-vene with, in order to produce meaning from the documents that constitute it. This activity consists basically of tracing emergent relationships between these constitu-tive materials and also introducing new materials (producing new documents) that reshape the universe of the archive. The intervention of the archive understood in this way is key to (re)opening the signifying processes of events (both historical and current). According to Ariella Azoulay, Israeli thinker and artist who has delved into alternative ways of visualising the violent process experienced by Palestinians since their exodus in 1948, there is a constituent violence that is comparable to the pro-cess of imposing a "historical truth." In order to defy such institutionalised versions of events (and to subvert them) archival practices are one of the key fields of action where artists and journalists can explore emergent narrative patterns.

> What has been institutionalized as the order of things is not only disgraceful but reversible, and archival work is one of the keys for such reversal. Inter-vention, imagination and transmission are the main practices through which researchers and artists exercise their right to (and of) the archive; that is, the right to share it, to make use of it in ways that is not taken merely as a deposit of the past, that stores materials which document what has been finished and what has been done.
>
> *(Azoulay, 2014, p. 17)*

Journalists and artists, then, have the right to reshape history through the interven-tion of the archive: to defy and propose modes of representation. One of the several ways Azoulay has managed to do this is by working with photographic archives of the Palestinian exodus. For example, she accessed a closed Red Cross archive that held photographs that were not allowed to leave the archive, and in order to make them visible to the public, she copied them by hand and organised an exhibition with the "illustrated photographs." Similar strategies may be used in different cases, as for example more journalistic projects that turn to animation in order to repre-sent realities that are almost impossible to portray, in order to achieve those neces-sary *images in spite of all* (Didi-Huberman, 2004).

Two examples serve to illustrate this approach:

1　A short film that I produced and co-directed with a team of students,[8] on the topic of sexual torture perpetrated by Mexican officials belonging to the police and the army. The research process involved talking to the victims and then writing a script that integrated three different testimonies into one single female voice-over that, apart from sharing the testimonies, offered a profound critique to the human rights conditions in Mexico. The narration is then animated in a simple yet powerful style. This strategy, used both for protection of the victims and due to the impossibility of generating images of the events, is common in documentary film and, increasingly now, in journal-istic practices.

2 A project done by three Mexican journalists is enlightening in this sense; *Chain of command* (*Cadena de mando*, 2016), created by Daniela Rea, Mónica González and Pablo Ferri with the support of the Mike O'Connor grant of the International Center for Journalists (ICFJ). The project, hosted on the site cadenademando.org, includes narrative journalism (text), and a comic style animation both in strips and videos, that shape the testimonies and case files of soldiers who were accused of killings following their superiors' orders.

These examples approach the archive and create new documents for the archive with testimonial material, a reason why we can understand the intimate relationship between the archive and the testimony, two complementary forms of memory.[9] The archive, in this sense, is an ever-evolving territory that investigative journalists and artists intervene with by creating new relationships between documents and introducing new documents to the archival realm, reshaping its horizons. And the archive is also a territory of daily journalism, since most of the reportage feeds the archive itself, a complicity that is also a sort of intervention.

In summary, the intervention of the archive opens windows that amplify the existing relationships supporting our understanding of the world. Moreover, the process of intervening the archive is a humbling process; it forces our perspective out of its established relationships, shedding light upon alternative ways of being human (both existent or potential). It is an opportunity both to reimagine our history (to build "potential history" in terms of Azoulay, 2014) and to reshape our future.

Integrating different media

Finally, a crucial insight provided by the project *These Images are Truth. A Microarchive of Ignominy.* is the technological question. Journalism and media arts suffer the direct impact of technological development. In this context, it is imperative to acknowledge a transmedia paradigm as a way of operating both professionally and within our journalism schools. When I say transmedia paradigm, I refer to a process of appropriating technology that integrates different media according to our narrative needs, and not the other way around. This is not only a narrative necessity, but also a professional one. This transmedia approach demands from the journalist and artist the confidence of navigating in different media (text, photography, video, audio), as part of a new sensibility and also a market demand. Of course, a crucial consideration is that of resources and access to technology. In this line of thought, narrative design – especially for the critical media I am imagining – needs to start from doing what is best with what is available. An unavoidable tension with the market will emerge from this critical appropriation of technology. It is the responsibility of journalists, editors, and artists to (re)shape the market constantly, put it to the "creative tension" proposed by Álvarez. This condition is especially true when speaking about educational spaces and practices, where even if students must be familiarised with the work conditions for journalists and media makers, they should be encouraged to imagine ways of challenging possible limitations, and even imagining new narrative standards. For this precise reason educational spaces must be prominently experimental; they are the place where minds should reshape disciplinary boundaries.

Towards a critical pedagogy

I also take Latin American inspiration as a point of departure for the articulation of a critical pedagogy that attends the demands of this "documentary art" as a methodological approach for journalistic practice. As it can be inferred at this stage, my proposal of a documentary art responds to the urgency of designing alternative methodologies for exploring the labyrinths of our contemporary crises and their representation. Documentary art must be understood as one of the multiple terrains where journalism and art can find opportunities for expanding their impact on the world and their capacity to reshape the horizons of possibility.

Brazilian educator and philosopher Paulo Freire has had a profound influence in the pedagogical practice and research that I have implemented in the last decade or so, both independently and as part of the Iberoamericana University in Mexico City, where in 2016 I founded the Iberoamerican Documentary Lab (iberodocslab. org). As early as the '70s, Freire enunciated a critique against "the banking model of education" (Freire, 1970). This model is erected over the understanding of education as a process of transference between the knowledge of the professor and the ignorance of the student, product of an economic and political system. In the most recent stages of my research, I have correlated Freire's banking discourse with a language critique, contained in authors such as Franco Berardi and Michel Butor, who establish that our current use of language is dominated by the monetary and financial systems, making it urgent for writers and artists to defy such machinic conditioning, since they are the ones who can take expression to its limits. Moreover, if "every type of education corresponds with a determined conception and practice of communication" (Kaplun, 1985), then education itself is, as an art, a decisive field where language is questioned in itself and taken to its limits. Therefore, journalistic and media education is perhaps the ideal terrain to question the expressive conditionings that define the representational crisis we experience today.

I have spoken in this chapter of the need for experimental practices as one of the central characteristics of educational spaces. When speaking about art, language, and education, the experimental refers to the liminality of expression itself. Liminality read (and lived) as the potency of transforming, if not transgressing, the meaning production practices of contemporary society – of taking human expression to its limits using all the media resources that are available to a creative subject in a determined moment of history. Considering journalism as a form of art, one that is somewhat related with justice, then journalism is most certainly one of the main targets of a critical pedagogy as presented here. The reason is twofold:

1   Because documentary, as understood in this discussion, is a core component of the methodological tradition behind investigative journalism, and

2 Journalism has played, since its origins, the role of the watchdog within modern and contemporary societies.

    This confers a special power to journalism in relation to the horizons of perceptibility of whatever we call reality: i) and ii) mean that documentary art can be considered as an art of a critical emergence of perception, precisely because it plays with the horizons of visibility or perceptibility of a given phenomenon.

We need to experiment with alternative ways (peripheric perspectives) of portraying (and so imagining) reality (and all its elusive ways). Educational spaces are ideal for experimentation, since they present their communities with a flexibility that is usually not present. or rarely found, in most professional environments. It is a matter of form, or more precisely, of information: Generating information, creating relationships, communicating. My emphasis on an experimental critical pedagogy responds to the belief that experimentation is a space of emergence for alternative relationships; the field from which we can articulate new relationships between the plethora of dynamic forms that shape our world. Experimentation can therefore be interpreted as a terrain of emergence (and emergency) from where, through the deployment of strategies for researching *the real*, previously unknown forms and meanings can be brought to light by the researcher. This could be through the conjunction of distinct forms – the weaving of meaning – that result in new configurations of the world or through the artist-researcher's collaboration with the colossal archive of humanity through the creation of new aesthetic manifestations; In both cases, the researcher provides something emergent to reality, new world orders that are, at least, imaginable. The crisis of representation (of meaning production) must be assumed as one of the key impulses of the sort of dialogic education I want to establish. Nevertheless, it must be said that if the title of this chapter appeals to "emergent narratives," it is because apart from the narrative emergency that is evident at times of crises, art and education tend to be spaces of creative emergence of their own accord.

    I believe that Freire's proposal of a problematising education (1970, 1996) is based on a communication model of sorts, a reading that is useful for understanding the role played by journalists and artists in the world. The purpose of a problematising education is, in a few words, the inquiry of reality and, I would add, the design of possible solutions – and even, its implementation. For the critical pedagogy for a documentary art that I propose, one needs to execute experiments (observation, intervention, systematisation of media and media archives – as I did with my project) in order to identify the topics confirming the inquired universe we are working with. There are multiple ways of designing these experiments, as they are to execute a problematising education. For example, Diaz Bordenave proposed the arc method: first, from self-observation to the analysis of society, then from identification of topics to the naming of problems, and finally, to the reflexive return over oneself and one's capacity to act within the observed society. It is quite important to note that Freire's education is a universal model in the sense that it does not target a specific audience or group of the population. I think this has something to do with the context from where he is imagining this type of education, environments that differ considerably from the conditions of the educational debate in developed nations.

Trying to achieve some design insights from where we can imagine a pedagogical framework for the exercise of a documentary art in the context of journalistic education, I find two main considerations that are related to the ways we as humans inhabit our world: the technical and the narrative (discursive). The first refers to the production and use of tools, the processes of learning and understanding the configuration of the technical universe in a determined moment in history. This process of technological appropriation derives from what we understand as human perception; its potential limits are associated with our coding and decoding artefacts. In a way, this technological level of inquiry and exercise is represented by the material realm of our shared experience (bodies, forces, processes). The technical potency for an individual or a group depends on the sort of resources and ideas that are available in a particular moment in history. From here the political and economic debates arise. Conjointly, the technical domain is in direct correlation with the horizons of our perception and our capacity to action (potency) in the sense that, through the invention and use of technologies, we are able to discover new aspects of the world, things that were previously hidden are made visible (perceptible and, therefore, subject to meaning). Consequently, the narrative or discursive aspect refers to the position that results from the act of manipulation of tools for expanding our perception and stance before those problems that are identified by the documentary artist. Our discourse is a byproduct of perception, the conscious or unconscious positioning of a subject in a specific time and space of perception. We narrate ourselves through acts of technical appropriation. Documentary art is, then, an art that explores the function of the narrative (the narratable reality) in the exercise of technique – in other words, the ways we become aware and share what is experienced (in any time-space order that we can imagine). This is why documentary art is profusely historic and its historical horizons are ever changing. It is an art of navigating memory, both by the study of pre-existent documents and the production of new documents. An art of memory itself; it activates memory, exercises it, manipulates its effects within a given context. Therefore, apart from the learnings of documentary film and photography, it is an art that depends deeply on the studies of media archaeology and media arts, as well as those of journalism and anthropology. Journalism has nurtured its methodologies from other disciplines, and this might become one of the main forces that could be experienced in educational proposals for journalism, as documentary art offers a platform for journalism and media educators to draw on new approaches and techniques for investigating reality.

Furthermore, in a way, we can affirm that documentary art is an art of testimony, or more precisely, the art where testimony is constantly transformed into memory. This means public memory, since documentary art consists of transferring testimonies from one medium – usually the subject's internal world or the world of the archive – to other media – be it text, audio, video, etc. In addition, documentary art is a kind of machine of testimony, an art where testimony emerges persistently (as a product of the researcher-artist's incursion, of the way we use the pen, camera, microphone – whatever our weapon of choice may be – but also of the audience's reaction to the work that is presented). Documentary art is deeply implied with the cycling, recycling, and revolutionising of human history through the documentation, interrelation, generation, and intervention of testimonies from the most diverse origin. The idea of something that is witnessed, registered, and somehow communicated (accessible and usable), is the core of documentary art as the basis of journalism and media education. For what has been established, I can affirm that documentary art holds an intimate relationship with Freire's proposal, since documentary art is deeply rooted in the decodification of the world, the exploration of themes, and the identification (and expression) of problems concerning human destiny, which are three axes of Freire's problematising education. I defend documentary art, as an art concerned with the limits of perception and the narration of history, which has a profound impact on the construction of what we ordinarily call reality.

Imaginable worlds: balancing perception, narration, and justice

If I said that documentary art is a matter of use and access to technical resources, it is also a matter of exploitation in multiple ways – exploitation of natural resources, of economic (dis)advantages, of cultural traits and symbols. Documentary art, this site where anthropological curiosity and scientific experimentation meet, where document creation and archival practices collide, is also concerned directly with a matter of justice (how we perceive and represent the horizons of justice, of what can be done in a determined society). One common trait between perception, narration, and justice is the sense of proportion. How do we balance our perception of events? Are we agents of balance or of unbalance in the established relationships that configure what we call *The World*? Every artform – every manifestation of human expression with its own technical appropriations and aesthetic principles – supposes both an ethical and a political dimension. Again: it is a matter of information, of agency, and so, of responsibility. All agencies have a degree of impact on the world's course of events; this is why art and journalism hold a rather strong set of responsibilities. We can see that their agency has a direct impact on the mechanisms that support our imaginaries, of what is represented of the world (and therefore on the way the world is imagined).

Documentary art points towards a new understanding of objectivity in journalism. Even if objectivity as an aspiration has been redefined in the last few decades, it is still one of the main values of journalistic practice. Documentary art, on the one hand, supports the consolidation of a media making that is more compromised with reality. In this sense, even if it does not appeal to objectivity as such, it does pose several research standards that suppose a profound study of the subjects and contexts explored by journalists and artists alike. Additionally, even if I have called for the imperative of "taking a stance," this implies avoiding the imposition of our own unjustified opinion on events and the way we present them to the audience. Conversely, documentary art involves the questioning not only of the context we are exploring, but also of the ways we are exploring it. By this I mean that documentary art is first and foremost a self-critical methodology. This perspective invites the reader to understand documentary art not only as a set of methodologies that allow us to investigate the world, but also that demand the researcher-journalist-artist to question the effectiveness of such techniques, the implications of their approach, and the consequences of the versions of history they are promoting through their stories. This approach is rooted in the fact that journalism, as a subversive practice, is one of the main forces of historical construction. In this sense, if we reimagine the ways we approach and narrate events, then we are also reimagining the world itself (the building blocks of our collective narratives, those that articulate our being in the world).

In my understanding, when we speak of journalism and media making in general, and its spaces and modes of education in particular – the way journalism and media making are taught in universities worldwide – I believe there is a decisive role played by the incessant collusion between the two dimensions of human activity established above – technique and narrative:

a   The design and usage of tools that, through extending the effects and affections of human action, facilitate the addressing of problems;

and

b   The means (the intentions and manifestations) that support such ever mediated interaction with the world.

These two dimensions of practice that constitute media making are the fundamental components of expression.

Expression is one of the most distinguished forms of *occupation* of the world. Here I speak of occupation both as a provocation but also as an opportunity to question the ways we inhabit the habitat, the ways we reclaim space, place, and time for us to breathe, move, and speak. I echo Steyerl (2016) when she pushed forward her *demands for autonomy of life* by reflecting on *art as occupation*. Occupation implies the notion of labour and specialisation; it also refers to ways we are spending time and moving in space, or the character of our acts of expression. We live not solely in the habitat, but form part of its organic evolution (whether we are alive or not). Naming and expressing are both core components of art and journalism; they constitute some of the most intensively active forces that we humans have for building and imagining the world. What comes out of our habitation? What are the effects and affections of this informing agency of ours? How are we reshaping the world with our stories? To end up with a final thought on art education (and let us remember journalism is a form of art), I follow Maxine Greene's belief that art stimulates and nurtures our imagination and, therefore, our capacity to build a more liveable future. If multiple crises signal above the landscape, could we articulate alternative versions of reality that trace routes for confronting such crises? Art and journalism are not only mirrors of what happens in a specific time in history, they are also beacons of future possibilities. Journalism as a form of art, therefore, can help us build the blueprints of our future world.

Notes

1 I refer to Latin American filmmaker-thinkers such as Fernando Birri (Argentina), Julio Garcia Espinosa (Cuba), Tomás Gutiérrez Alea (Cuba), Octavio Getino y Fernando Solanas (Argentina), Glauber Rocha (Brazil), and Rubén Gámez (México).
2 Word of the Year 2016. Oxford Dictionary. Extracted from the Internet on 2 June 2018, available at: https://en.oxforddictionaries.com/word-of-the-year/word-of-the-year-2016.
3 To find out more about the specifics of the case, which are not the objective of this chapter go to https://en.wikipedia.org/wiki/2014_Iguala_mass_kidnapping.
4 An extraordinary article on the subject, written in English by Mexican writer Francisco Goldman, may be found on *The New Yorker*'s website. Available at: www.newyorker.com/news/news-desk/the-missing-forty-three-the-mexican-government-sabotages-its-own-independent-investigation.
5 One historical parenthesis: only a few weeks after Ayotzinapa's crime, there was a scandal disclosed through a journalistic research that evidenced the unlawful use of public funds, including the purchase of *La casa blanca* (The White House), a mansion registered under the name of Angélica Rivera (Mexico's first lady). Immediately after the research was published, she came out in a video transmitted via Internet and TV, where she explained, in the corner of what could have easily be a *telenovela* set, just like when she was a famous actress, giving more than a version of events, an earful explanation and demonstration of her indignation after such public humiliation.
6 An insect that grows on cactus that is used as a tint in Mexico since ancient times.
7 Documentation of the project is available at pablomz.info/eisv.
8 Cuando me di cuenta que estaba viva (When I realized I was alive). Co-directed by Inés Argueta and animated by Santiago Moyao. Watch online available at: https://vimeo.com/234673991.
9 In this subject, the proposal of Italian thinker Giorgio Agamben is of interest: "In opposition to the archive, which designates the system of relations between the unsaid and the said, we give the name testimony to the system of relations between the inside and the outside of langue, between the sayable and its existence, between a possibility and an impossibility of speech. To think potentiality in act as potentiality, to think enunciation on the plane of langue is to inscribe a caesura in possibility, a caesura that divides it into a possibility and impossibility, into a potentiality and an impotentiality; and it is to situate a subject in this very caesura" (Agamben, 1989, p. 39).

References

Agamben, G. (1989). The archive and the testimony. In: Merewether, C., ed. (2006). *The archive. Documents of contemporary art.* EUA-Reino Unido: Whitechapel Gallery and MIT Press.
Álvarez, S. (1978). El periodismo cinematográfico. In: *Cine Cubano.* Cuba: ICAIC, no. 140, pp. 18–19.
Álvarez, S. (1988). Arte y compromiso. In: *Hojas de cine, testimonios y documentos del nuevo cine latinoaméricano.* Mexico: UAM, Fundación Mexicana de Cineastas, vol. 3, pp. 35–37.

The Atlas Group. (2003). Let's be honest, the Rain Helped. In: Merewether, C., ed. (2006). *The archive. Documents of contemporary art*. EUA-Reino Unido: Whitechapel Gallery and MIT Press.

Azoulay, A. (2014). *Historia potencial y otros ensayos*. México: t-e-eoría y Conaculta.

Berardi, F. (2017). *Futurability: The age of impotence and the horizon of possibility*. New York: Verso.

Didi-Huberman, G. (2004). *Imágenes pese a todo. Memoria visual del Holocausto*. España: Paidós.

Freire, P. (1970). *Pedagogía de la oprimido*. México: Siglo XXI.

Freire, P. (1996). *Pedagogía de la autonomía*. México: Siglo XXI.

Kaplun, M. (1985). *El comunicador popular*. Argentina: Editorial Humanitas.

Steyerl, H. (2009). A language of practice. In: Stallbrass, J., ed. (2013). *Documentary. Documents of contemporary art*. EUA-Reino Unido: Whitechapel Gallery and MIT Press.

Steyerl, H. (2015). Too much world: Is the internet dead? *E-flux Journal* [online]. Available at: www.e-flux.com/journal/49/60004/too-much-world-is-the-internet-dead/.

Steyerl, H. (2016). *Los condenados de la pantalla*. Argentina: Caja Negra.

10

GENOCIDE AND THE MEDIATION OF HUMAN RIGHTS

Pedagogies for difficult stories

Stephen Reese and Jad Melki

This chapter explores ways in which media literacy approaches to journalism pedagogy can lead to more responsible reporting of human rights abuses across national and cultural divides.

> *The Lord said, "What have you done? Listen! Your brother's blood cries out to me from the ground"* (Genesis 4:10, NIV).
> — *From memorial marker, Mauthausen-Gusen*
> *Concentration Camp, Austria*

New forms of emerging journalism not only have transformed the networks of production and distribution but have put new demands on those who tell the stories of journalism across traditional lines of demarcation: whether national, political, cultural, or ethnic. In the new media ecosystem, centrifugal forces are pulling in many directions, toward increasing polarisation and xenophobia. Radical and anti-institutional media have their own story to tell – often not one of global harmony, including anti-immigrant, populist, and illiberal voices. Even traditional mainstream media have been guilty of furthering stereotypes and failing to document cases of oppression in the developing world. Such global stories of human rights present a special case for journalism, both traditional and emerging, challenging the way we talk about these issues and teach deeper understanding to those who will fill these roles in the future. We need a globally reflective, yet historically rooted form of understanding.

We have been involved in exploring issues of genocide, as part of a larger media literacy initiative for college students from around the world. We have sought to exploit the annual project's local setting in Salzburg, Austria, to humanise global issues, understand how media are implicated in genocidal dynamics, and encourage taking personal responsibility for change. In this chapter we consider the special pedagogical challenges – social, intellectual, and emotional – of presenting this material to a diverse body of students, with a focus on one infamous case of geno-cide, the Nazi-led Holocaust during World War II, to those who do not share the same cultural, political, and religious context. We revisit the participants in this educational experience to better understand how the programme affected them. Results show that although it is difficult to communicate genocide across national lines, students can be pushed out of their comfort zone into a more global per-spective and common human rights narrative. This gives us hope for journalists themselves, which many of these students aspire to be or to engage with, as they are called by a moral responsibility to bear global witness.

Bearing witness

There are many examples of citizens taking ownership of injustices in their own country – for example, Argentinians using forensic archaeology to uncover and document remains of those "disappeared" under military government. Often, how-ever, this witness involves holding governments to account other than one's own, such as the Serbian strongman Slobodan Milosevic, brought to trial under inter-national law at The Hague. These rights cases can be extremely sensitive, arousing national defence mechanisms long after the events in question and blending the functions of journalists and historians. Poland, for example, has passed a contro-versial law criminalising any linking of Poland to Nazi atrocities. As a global issue, human rights abuses cut across boundaries, extending beyond one's national and tribal affiliations. One must resist relative morality, chronic voyeurism, passivity, and inaction, particularly when witnessing mediated pain and suffering on a global scale (Sontag, 2003).

Media systems, however, are often not well equipped to tackle these issues, with at best an under-resourced, short attention span co-opted by contested political frames (Wolfsfeld, 1997), yielding to compassion fatigue (Moeller, 1999), lacking historical context (Seib, 2004), and providing an abundance of stereotypes and xen-ophobic narratives (Said, 1997). Media in authoritarian systems are more directly proscribed from dealing with stories reflecting negatively on the regime and national pride (e.g., Turkey's Armenian genocide and Poland's historical cleansing, above). And, from a more general ideological perspective, not all media are com-mitted to bearing witness, with a parallel structure of nationalist media promoting revisionism, conspiracy theories, and outright denial of historical events, such as the Holocaust,[1] or (re)inventing historical events to serve present policies and state interests (Lewis, 1987).

Human rights as global issue

Peter Berglez (2013) has advocated that journalists take a global outlook, a new epistemological perspective necessitated by globalisation, where issues and crises take on meaning transcending national borders. He argues that traditional for-eign news reporting deals with separate events and processes, oriented around a particular geographical context. Global journalism, on the other hand, deals with relations among people and the places where they act. This distinction reminds us that even in a globalised world, everything happens somewhere local, and journalists need a deep understanding of the context of those happenings, while at the same time placing them in a larger web of relationships (e.g., Reese, 2010). Human rights, environmental protection, and terrorism are among the issues that have become identified as global concerns, with their own stakeholders, institutionalised structures, and regimes (e.g., Stohl and Stohl, 2005). Other implications for media are more dysfunctional, in the dynamics of dehumanisation and propaganda that lay the groundwork for state-sponsored violence. Journalists can be caught up in these dynamics, but they can also be an important bridge to a more humane outlook. That is where educating future news professionals, NGO advocates, and citizens more broadly becomes important.

The pedagogy

In this section we review our experience with teaching within a media literacy context, built into a larger international study academy. Founded in the wake of World War II, the Salzburg Global Seminar brings together emerging and established leaders from every region of the world to broaden thinking, challenge perspectives, encourage collaboration, and build networks that support future cooperation.[2] Launched in 2007, the three-week Salzburg Academy for Media and Global Change provides students with a global perspective – beyond any one country. Partners of the academy include on the American side Emerson and the Universities of Maryland, Texas, Southern California, and Miami, and select other non-US universities from the UK, China, Africa, and Latin America. A significant number of students from the Middle East come from Lebanese American University and, prior to that, the American University of Beirut (both of which attract students from throughout the Arab region, especially the Levant). Students engage with other participants, visiting media experts, NGO professionals, and equally international faculty (see Reese, 2012). In approaching the challenging subject of genocide, the academy provides a unique intersection of local geography, history, media, and current global political trends, with a special emphasis on empowering young people for social change. The authors have been involved with it until the present and bring their own different cultural and national backgrounds to bear in the analysis that follows.[3]

The programme

Most of the academy involves teaching around global issues, which in the past has included immigration, terrorism, and the rise of populism. From the beginning, the schedule has included an evening devoted to issues of genocide, a session placed at the end of the second week, after students have bonded as groups, trust each other and the faculty leadership, and learned basic principles of media literacy. In part, this is a typical study-abroad strategy, to exploit the local setting to bring insights more vividly to life, but this programme has proved particularly taxing for both students and faculty, as we wrestle with the difficult issues and connect them to family histories and perceptions of regional injustice.

Because genocide is a societal project we need to understand the larger systems that yield these cases and work to dehumanise the victim group. In more recent years, we have placed the discussion within the current political framework. In 2017, for example, the academy's master theme was global populism, which is closely related to dynamics of xenophobia and fear of the other. Taken to extremes and left unchecked by journalists, this kind of polarising political rhetoric may activate deep-seated prejudices (Mazzoleni, 2003), promote the dehumanisation of certain minorities, and subsequently pave the way for a warped justification of mass murder.

With this background established we focus next on the specific historical case. The Holocaust in which 6 million Jews and other groups were systematically exterminated during World War II is well known but unevenly taught, even in US school systems. Given the history of the Seminar's location at Schloss Leopoldskron (formerly owned by the Jewish founder of the Salzburg Music Festival, Max Reinhardt, but confiscated by the Nazis) and proximity to Hitler's Bavarian headquarters in Berchtesgaden, the case has great local resonance. We ask how an industrialised, cultured society could descend into such evil in such a short time? The German experience, in particular, shows how – using the means of total cultural leadership (including media) – anti-Semitism can be used to justify injustice and naturalise relationships of oppression, leading to systematic violence on a mass scale. Drawing from Hannah Arendt's memorable insight on the "banality of evil," we show that evil does not necessarily come in the form of a monster.

The choice of film has been *Night and Fog*. This short (32 minutes) documentary from 1955 was directed by Alain Resnais and features the abandoned grounds of Auschwitz and Majdanek, along with other graphic images of prisoners in those camps. Other possibilities have been considered but declined for either being too long or introducing too many other issues. The most difficult part of the evening for faculty leaders has involved leading a discussion about the issues raised by the film and introduction. In the early years, the discussion session was relatively informal, where one faculty moderator would carry the microphone from one student to another, allowing several students to make multiple comments. The whole discussion would last one hour or so, with only one or two faculty members present. In later years, the authors were assigned to conduct a more structured moderation with the following stipulations:

- This is an open, safe space, open to different voices.
- There is to be no direct response to comments by others.
- Share ideas but do not be critical of others.
- This is not a debate.
- One must speak from his or her own experience.
- And, perhaps the most difficult to enforce, no one is allowed to have a second turn to speak.

The following day students travel to a nearby concentration camp. In previous years, the chosen destination was Dachau, near Munich, but since 2013 we have visited Mauthausen (a couple of hours' drive from Salzburg). The trip includes a guided tour of the grounds, buildings, nearby memorials to the victims from their countries, and a museum. Like Dachau, the Mauthausen camp lies within sight of a nearby town, helping make the point that genocide happens with the awareness and participation of ordinary people.

To examine the impact of our pedagogical efforts we invited participants to reflect on their experience with the entire programme. We wanted to know how the impact may have changed over the 11 years of the academy and how regional context affected their responses. We explore the extent to which the programme was successful in encouraging critical thinking, taking a global perspective, applying historical lessons, and taking personal responsibility for change.

Methods

We used a cross-sectional, self-administered online survey[4] using SurveyMonkey and sent via e-mail to all former participants of the Salzburg Academy since its inception in 2007 until its most recent session in 2017, using the most up-to-date addresses acquired from the Salzburg Global Seminar's alumni list. After receiving Institutional Review Board approval, a total of 688 students were sent e-mail invitations to complete the questionnaire along with six reminders over a period of two months (14 May–16 July 2018). A total of 165 participants (24% response rate) completed the online questionnaire, which required on average 22 minutes, contained 14 closed-ended and eight open-ended questions, and generated 45 variables and 37,030 words of textual data.

Overall, three quarters of respondents were female, and most were undergraduate students (73%) at the time they attended the academy, while around a quarter (23%) were enrolled as master's students, and 4% as doctoral students. These demographics roughly reflect the actual distribution of participants over the years. As for the geographic regions represented, 11% (18) were from Europe, 17% (28) from Latin America, 31% (51) from the US, and 32% (53) from the Middle East, which also roughly reflects the distribution of all academy participants. Fifteen participants came from other parts of the world, including East Asia, Africa, and Australia, but their numbers were not sufficient for meaningful comparisons across regions. The Europeans were also few, so we do not draw any strong comparisons regarding that group. Respondents were unevenly distributed across the past ten years (Table 10.1). Most respondents (58%) came from the last four years of the academy (2014–17), while fewer (20%) came from the first four years (2007–10).

Results

Because we rely heavily on self-reflection we first wanted to determine how memorable different aspects of the programme were. According to students' responses

TABLE 10.1 Distribution by year participants attended the academy

Year	Participants
	% (n)
2007	6 (10)
2008	5 (8)
2009	2 (4)
2010	7 (11)
2011	8 (14)
2012	5 (9)
2013	8 (13)
2014	10 (16)
2015	13 (22)
2016	13 (22)
2017	22 (36)
Total	**(165)★**

★ *Numbers do not total exactly to 100 due to rounding.*

(what they "still remembered"), the most memorable component of the programme was the concentration camp visit (95%), followed by the student discussion (76%) and the film screening (62%). The faculty introductions were the least memorable, but still 45% of students said they remembered them. We had expected the student open discussion to be the most memorable given its emotional intensity. The faculty-guided introduction was less well remembered, but this was the programme element that was less consistent and more formalised only in recent years. To better understand these results, we compared the survey data across three periods to reflect the major changes that took place in the programme, especially the faculty presentations (first period: 2007–9, second period: 2010–14, and third period: 2015–17). Throughout these three periods, the two elements of the programme that remained constant were the film and the concentration camp visit. Although the post-film student discussion was conducted every year, the moderation changed over time, and so did the number of students (and faculty) engaged, which started at roughly 40 students in 2007 and increased to around 85 in 2017.

In the first period, the faculty-led introduction was brief (recalled by 36%). In the second period (recalled by 38%), it sometimes extended to over an hour, and included one year a guest speaker from the US Holocaust Museum. That year, the programme started at 8 pm and extended beyond midnight. Ever since, we became more cognisant about time limitations. The changes in the third period, featuring a more substantive faculty-led introduction, produced improved recall for this element to 51%. Nevertheless, the recall for the concentration camp visit remained almost constant over the three periods (100%, 94%, and 93%), while recall for the film was higher over time (43%, 53%, and 68%), as was recall for the discussion (48%, 73%, and 87%).

In addition to analysing recall over time, we compared the findings across the four major geographic areas from which our students came: Middle East, Europe, US, and Latin America.[5] Although the overall trends were similar, some interesting differences emerged. Again, all four groups recalled the concentration camp visit almost equally (ranging from 93% for Middle Eastern students to 96% for US students). However, more European students (94%) than any other group recalled the student discussion session, followed by US (86%), Middle Eastern (72%), and Latin American students (61%). The same order emerged for the film (89%, 71%, 58%, and 39%) and the faculty introductions (67%, 47%, 40%, and 39%).

These differences remind us that the Holocaust is not equally salient or sensitive around the world. Latin American students are the farthest away geographically and perhaps the least implicated in Holocaust memory, but European students were geographically most proximate to these sites of genocide, and their education systems emphasise the memory of the Holocaust. Despite the geographical distance, the same applies to US students (some of whom have been Jewish) who study the Holocaust in school, visited Holocaust museums, and watched films about it, making it culturally salient. While Middle Eastern students are geographically closer than US students to Europe, most education systems in that region don't cover the Holocaust and cultural productions ignore it, partly because it has little to do with Arab history, which is rife with other more relevant past and present genocides. This omission also has much to do with the Arab-Israeli conflict, following the establishment of the State of Israel, which has used the Holocaust and European anti-Semitism as a justification for a Jewish state in Palestine.

The social dimension

We were interested in assessing whether such an emotionally and intellectually charged experience affected the interpersonal dynamics of the group – whether it encouraged or discouraged students from discussing sensitive and serious issues, or from building relationships with others from different backgrounds and beliefs. So, when asked if the genocide programme affected their relationship with other students, one third selected "it brought them closer to some students and pushed them away from some," and a third chose "it brought them closer to some academy participants." Only 8% chose that the programme "pushed them away from some academy participants," and about a quarter indicated it had no effect on their relationship with others (Table 10.2).

On balance then, students said they felt closer to at least some of the participants, as reflected in their responses.

> I think everyone grew closer during that discussion. It was amazing to me that a lot of people could be yelling at each other from other sides of the room and leave hugging. It gave me hope for the future.
>
> *(2013, US female)*[6]

Though I remember few details of the actual discussion this many years later, I remember feeling more like a community with the other participants after and the strong emotions that were evoked during the discussion.

(2012, US male)

It is important to note here that the effect of the programme, in spite of what many participants perceived, was not uniformly positive in bringing about greater harmony. Combining responses for either "had no effect" or the polarising outcome of "pushed me away/brought me closer" showed it to capture the majority response across regions (Table 10.2), as reflected in their open-ended responses:

Some of the fellow Jewish participants were not very happy by us (Arabs) raising the issue of Palestine during the discussion that followed the screening.

(2017, Lebanese male)

This proved to be an accurate perception, as seen in the polarised responses of the US students (42% in Table 10.2), and a number of them were disappointed in their Middle Eastern fellow students.

I grew somewhat closer to students from the US, as we had a less controversial reaction to the genocide of focus.

(2015, US female)

But this perception was not confined to the US students.

During our Camp visit, the guide showed a photograph of one of the Jewish prisoners who was being photographed right before being sent to the

TABLE 10.2 Effects of programme on relationships with other students

The genocide programme	Middle East	Latin America	USA	Europe	Overall*
	% (n)	% (n)	% (n)	% (n)	% (n)
Brought me closer to some	26 (14)	40 (10)	27 (13)	29 (5)	31 (49)
Pushed me away from some	9 (5)	4 (1)	6 (3)	18 (3)	8 (12)
Pushed me away from some, and brought me closer to some	37 (19)	32 (8)	42 (20)	29 (5)	34 (53)
Had no effect	28 (15)	24 (6)	25 (12)	24 (4)	27 (43)
Total % (n)	100 (53)	100 (25)	100 (48)	100 (17)	100 (157)

* *Note: some participants missed responses, which resulted in slightly different totals for some cases. In addition, some participants from outside the four regions are included in the Overall.*

gas chamber. The guide showed the exact wall where the photo had been taken, and one of the students posed in front of the wall and clicked photos. It seemed so horribly weird and insensitive. So yes, it pushed me closer to many, but a little distant from some indeed.

(2014, South Asian female)

I was angry that people were competing with each other about pain and also that some were trying to focus on their own country's history.

(2017, European female)

Similarly, the programme did not in every case make conversations easier afterwards (Table 10.3): 43% agreed that the programme did make it easier, while it made discussing other subjects harder, and 36% said the programme made discussing some sensitive subjects easier; 11% said it made discussing sensitive subjects only harder, and 10% said it had no effect. When comparing these statements by region, Table 10.3 shows that European students were almost twice as likely as any other group to say the programme made it easier to discuss some subjects, while Middle Eastern students were almost twice as likely as any other group to say the opposite. Students from the US and Latin America were much more likely than students from the Middle East and Europe to say the programme made discussing some subjects easier whilst making other subjects harder. We may conclude that although a relatively small percentage (19%) of the Middle Eastern students said it made discussing subjects harder, that was still higher than the other regions, pointing to how conflicted this group was on the issue relative to the others.

A few students reached the regrettable conclusion that the solution to conflicting views is to not bring up sensitive historical issues. Rather than treat it as a learning opportunity, the programme seemed to disrupt the surface-level conviviality they had been enjoying.

TABLE 10.3 Effects of programme on discussing sensitive topics

The genocide programme	Middle East	Latin America	USA	Europe	Overall*
	% (n)	% (n)	% (n)	% (n)	% (n)
Made discussing some subjects easier	34 (18)	36 (10)	27 (14)	61 (11)	36 (60)
Made discussing some subjects harder	19 (10)	7 (2)	8 (4)	11 (2)	11 (18)
Made discussing some subjects easier, other subjects harder	34 (18)	50 (14)	57 (29)	22 (4)	43 (71)
Had no effect	13 (7)	7 (2)	8 (4)	6 (1)	10 (16)
Total % (n)	**100 (53)**	**100 (28)**	**100 (51)**	**100 (18)**	**100 (165)**

* *Note: some participants missed responses, which resulted in slightly different totals for some cases. In addition, some participants from outside the four regions are included in the Overall.*

It didn't affect my relationship with others because I do believe people should move on! What happened in the past stays in the past! I don't like the fact that many people still mention the same subject which provokes hate and keeps people away from each other.

(2017, Lebanese female)

The pedagogical challenge

We turn next to the most difficult pedagogical challenge presented by the programme, how to balance the specificity of the particular case study we presented – the Holocaust – with the desire to understand broader genocidal dynamics. We found that overall the programme was effective in reaching our objectives. An overwhelming majority of students agreed (or somewhat agreed) that the programme helped them empathise more with peoples' suffering throughout the world (92%), better understand the suffering of genocide victims (92%), the importance of bearing witness and historical memory (92%), how the Holocaust can be exploited for political reasons (90%), become more aware of the difficulty in understanding suffering from the perspective of other national cultures (88%), become more critical about the role of media in genocide (87%), better understand racism (82%), become more aware of taking personal responsibility for change (82%) and other genocides (81%), better understand the roots of war/conflict (81%), and other current or recent conflict, including other genocides (61%). In addition, 81% of students agreed (or somewhat agreed) with the statement "I am grateful that the programme made me aware of the Holocaust."

The choice, however, of the Holocaust case study cut both ways. Some thought it, by definition, diminished other genocides and revealed an instructional bias, while others concluded the reverse was true – that introducing other genocides served to "relativise" the importance of the Holocaust in its own right, as one student argued:

> The whole programme … appeared to operate from the perspective of diminishing the Holocaust and opening up genocide as nature of measure and debate. … It turned a group of supposed intellectuals into a twitter brawl, with the overall goal of the session seeming to be diminishing the scale of the Holocaust.
>
> *(2013, UK male)*

We found that 62% agreed or somewhat agreed that the programme should have focused on more recent genocides and conflicts, and 41% "felt that focusing on the Holocaust diminished the suffering experienced in other genocides and conflicts."

> Why are we *focusing on only this genocide* while there are lots of others that happened throughout history that people are barely made aware of. Like the Armenian genocide, Rwanda, Bosnia … etc.
>
> *(2013, Lebanese female)*

TABLE 10.4 Overall perceived effects of the genocide programme

Students who agree or somewhat agree with the following:	Middle East % (n)	Latin America % (n)	USA % (n)	Europe % (n)	Overall* % (n)
The programme helped me empathise more with peoples' suffering throughout the world.	83 (44)	100 (28)	92 (47)	94 (17)	92 (151)
The programme helped me become more aware of the difficulty in understanding suffering from the perspective of other national cultures.	78 (40)	96 (27)	88 (45)	89 (16)	88 (143)
The programme helped me become more aware of taking personal responsibility for change.	75 (40)	93 (26)	78 (40)	89 (16)	82 (135)
The programme helped me become more aware of other genocides.	74 (39)	82 (23)	82 (42)	94 (17)	81 (133)
I was grateful that more people were made aware of the Holocaust.	62 (33)	89 (25)	90 (46)	89 (16)	81 (134)
I thought that focusing on such an emotional and potentially divisive topic was counterproductive.	53 (28)	18 (5)	12 (6)	11 (2)	27 (45)
I felt that focusing on the Holocaust diminished the suffering experienced in other genocides and conflicts.	75 (40)	36 (10)	24 (12)	17 (3)	41 (68)
I felt that we should have focused on more recent genocides and conflicts.	92 (49)	61 (17)	39 (20)	50 (9)	27 (102)
Total (n) per group	**(51–53)***	**(28)**	**(51)**	**(18)**	**(163–165)***

* Note: some participants missed responses, which resulted in slightly different totals for some cases. In addition, some participants from outside the four regions are included in the Overall.

But this view was not confined to the Middle Eastern students.

> It made me angry that we were going over such a cliched conflict which I had constantly studied throughout my life, while ignoring other current conflicts and genocides.
>
> *(2013, Latin American female)*

> I would have liked a *more global perspective* including Russian pogroms, colonial violence, Rwanda, Bosnia, Palestine, etc.
>
> *(2007, US female)*

Some (27%) even agreed or somewhat agreed that focusing on such an emotional and potentially divisive topic was counterproductive.

When comparing the responses over the three time periods, most statements evaluating the programme garnered roughly the same level of agreement with the exception of four statements that showed significant increase over time: "I thought that focusing on such an emotional and potentially divisive topic was counterproductive" increased from 4% in the first period to 32% in the second period and 28% in the third period. The following statements showed similar change over time: "I felt that focusing on the Holocaust diminished the suffering experienced in other genocides and conflicts" (16%, 44%, 46%), "I felt that we should have focused on more recent genocides and conflicts" (42%, 65%, 63%), and "The programme helped me become aware of other genocides" (71%, 78%, 85%). Here we observe a paradoxical trend that, as they were made more aware of other genocides, they thought we should emphasise them more!

When comparing across regions, Table 10.4 shows that the primary rift was between Middle Eastern students and others. On one hand, Middle Eastern students were less likely than students from other regions to agree that the programme helped with empathising with people's suffering throughout the world, understanding suffering from other national perspectives, becoming more aware of taking personal responsibility for change, and being grateful that more people became aware of the Holocaust (although these differences were not dramatic). On the other hand, Middle Eastern students were much more likely than the others to agree that the programme's focus on such divisive topics was counterproductive, that focusing on the Holocaust diminished the suffering of other genocide victims, and that the programme should have focused on more recent genocides and conflicts.

The third rail of Israel

Obviously, as mentioned earlier, the Holocaust is understood differently by different cultural groups. US students are familiar with the Holocaust as a historical example of genocide, and of course the Jewish students (most from the US) had their own deep connection with the Holocaust as a core moment in their cultural and religious identity. Responses indicate that the Israeli-Palestinian conflict can in some cases overwhelm more detached critical thinking about the Holocaust, even for these well-educated students. Students from the Middle East found it particularly difficult to separate the Holocaust from the Israel issue and the conflict that continues to the present, one that particularly the Palestinian students are intimately familiar with.[7] One Palestinian student (2014) even referred to other (presumably Jewish) participants as "Israelis," but other students from the region were just as sensitised to it.

> It is (un)acceptable to present one side of the story only. This is what screening the Holocaust movie did. It justified the Israeli war crimes on the Palestinians . . . I hope . . . at least the case of Palestine is presented when talking about the Holocaust.
>
> *(2017, Lebanese female)*

Other students, particularly from the US, found this conflation to be frustrating, hampering the discussion of other issues:

> The discussion distanced me a little from a select few people who seemed unwilling to separate their feelings towards the current Israel/Palestine conflict from the Holocaust.
>
> *(2016, US female)*

> I will never forget the sheer anger and borderline hatred that was expressed during the student discussion. Immediately, the Holocaust was conflated with the Israeli–Palestinian conflict.
>
> *(2015, US female)*

> I feel that making the Holocaust the main focus is counterproductive, . . . it made it almost a taboo afterwards to be more critical of the Israeli government and its actions.
>
> *(2016, Mexican male)*

In expressing this frustration one of them did his own conflation, of religion with the ethnic origin of the diverse Middle Eastern students, many of whom were Christian.

> We CANNOT have *Islamic* students band together to blame the handful of non-Israeli Jews in the room for the current situation in the Middle East. We CANNOT deny the Holocaust existed.
>
> *(2013, US male)*

Ultimately, most students were able to see the value of using the Holocaust as a case unto itself, and yet articulate the importance of balancing it with broader contemporary lessons.

The Holocaust is a valuable experience on it is own, but what made it more valuable was the discussion afterwards that connected to suffering of victims of various other conflicts.

(2011, Middle Eastern male)

I could not imagine anyone NOT being willing to see the film and NOT being willing to contemplate the plight of those who suffered so horribly during the Holocaust. To look ahead, one MUST look back so we don't make the same mistakes twice.

(2010, US female)

Overall assessment

Overall, the vast majority of students reported a positive impact, agreeing that it was a very (65%) or somewhat (26%) valuable learning experience, while only a small group (8%) said it wasn't. The responses to this question fluctuated over time but remained very high, with 100% in the first period saying the programme was very or somewhat valuable, 85% in the second period, and 94% in the third period. And when comparing across regions, both Latin American and US students offered the highest positive response (96%), followed closely by European students (94%) and more distantly by Middle Eastern students (81%).

Beyond their overall perceptions, we asked them to rate the effectiveness of specific programme components in deepening their understanding of the "genocides, past and present." Again, the concentration camp visit garnered the highest positive responses, with 95% saying it was "somewhat" or "very" effective. This was followed by the student discussion (82%), the film (78%), and the faculty introductions (71%). When comparing these results over the three periods, the visit to the concentration camp remained relatively constant, where almost all students considered it to be somewhat or very effective (100%, 93%, 95%). However, in the third period (2015–2017) the effectiveness of the film was rated higher (73%, 65%, 87%). A gradual increase over time registered for the student discussions (65%, 82%, 87%), but only a slight increase in the last period registered for the faculty introductions (67%, 67%, 75%).

When comparing these findings across the four geographic groups, a consistent trend emerged. Table 10.5 shows that for the faculty introductions, the *Night and Fog* film and the concentration camp visit, Middle Eastern students were the least likely to say that these elements were effective in deepening their understanding of genocides past and present, although still a majority of them did. European students were the most likely to say so, followed by US students and then Latin American students. This trend was almost reversed, however, when it came to the student discussion component, where Middle Eastern students were the *most likely* to say it was effective, and the US students the least likely to say so. Reflecting back on the student discussions, we recall many Middle Eastern students eager to engage in the discussion and raise the issue of the Palestinian-Israeli conflict. Because this was

TABLE 10.5 Effectiveness of four programme components in deepening understanding of genocides past and present

This genocide programme component was very or somewhat effective	Middle East	Latin America	USA	Europe	Overall*
	% (n)	% (n)	% (n)	% (n)	% (n)
Faculty introductions	66 (35)	71 (20)	74 (35)	72 (13)	71 (114)
Film	71 (36)	77 (20)	82 (40)	83 (15)	78 (123)
Student discussion	88 (46)	79 (22)	78 (38)	83 (15)	82 (132)
Concentration camp visit	89 (47)	96 (27)	98 (49)	100 (17)	95 (155)
Total (n) per group	(51–53)*	(26–28)*	(47–50)*	(17–18)*	(165)

* Note: some participants missed responses, which resulted in slightly different totals for some cases. In addition, some participants from outside the four regions are included in the Overall.

their moment to be heard it is understandable they rated it more highly. Simultaneously, many US and Latin American students would complain that the discussion was monopolised by this conflict. Nevertheless, it is important to highlight that overall an overwhelming majority of students from all geographic groups ranked all the components of the programme as effective, and the differences even in the most extreme cases were less than 15%.

The affective and cognitive paths

Finally, we recognise that the programme packs a powerful emotional punch, so that a major part of the impact is on an affective level. But we also wanted to consider the intellectual process, of specifically how the students' thinking and perspective had changed. The responses suggest the role emotions played. It is certainly understandable that a Jewish student, especially someone whose relatives were victims of the Holocaust, or an Arab student whose relatives were victims of the Israeli occupation would be affected by it on a much more emotional level. But overall, students reported a greater sense of empathy, as the emotional energy of the programme propelled them to experience the pain of others and identify with the victims. These comments touched on a connection to a deeper human dimension rather than particular political differences.

> The discussion we had that night, the emotions that we all felt, was perhaps one of the hardest yet rewarding discussions I have engaged in, in my entire life.
>
> *(2015, Middle Eastern female)*

> It was a very powerful moment, in a good way. It is one of those few times where I was actually able to feel a different vibe in the room. It went silent, then it turned into a powerful and emotional discussion, then it ended.

Though it was very intense, it left me with a good moral in the end. It allowed me to understand the Holocaust through different eyes, and for that I'm very thankful.

(2016, Mexican female)

It was real. A number of students disagreed with the programme, but it was necessary and it started an important dialogue. After the heated debate, we all danced and drank together at the bierstube [bar], and that was the beauty of the Salzburg Academy.

(2015, US male)

I was very emotional and distressed but having people from all over the world feel the same outrage is soothing.

(2016, Mexican female)

In addition to feeling closer to each other, they expressed identification with a broader human community, a response shared across groups.

Because I saw a lot of people in tears, I stood with all of them, all sides, because no one deserves to suffer. We are all victims of politics eventually, whether we want it or not.

(2015, Lebanese female)

I guess, for me, the programme evoked a deep sense of loyalty to the concept of common humanity. I hate the notion of "us vs. them" and/or any effort to "dehumanise" some group of people.

(2012, US female)

The feelings towards each other will become less relevant as time goes by, but we hoped that there would be changes in their ability to think more critically. In that respect, the programme succeeded, as summed up by a US student: "It completely altered the way I think. For the better" (2011, US female). We saw evidence of more critical thinking, with some particularly telling insights from the Middle Eastern students.

A few years later, a friend of mine attended the Salzburg academy and we discussed the Holocaust programme when she got back. That discussion made me realise the impact the programme had on me; I no longer felt the anger I had felt before and saw the matter in a completely different perspective. The programme and most importantly the discussions that followed, allowed me to see a point of view that the media I'm exposed to did not allow me to see. It made me more critical and helped me see the matter more objectively.

(2012, Lebanese female)

As a part of critical thinking, we found the matter of perspective being repeatedly mentioned. In part this was brought about from simply being exposed to a point of view not previously encountered, including the Middle Eastern students who overall presented themselves as the more aggrieved party.

> It was the first time I get in touch with people who have the opposite opinion about Palestine, especially after we got so close to each other.
>
> *(2015, Middle Eastern male)*

> At first, I was so judgmental but then . . . I got to hear my classmate's opinion.
>
> *(2017, Middle Eastern female)*

> Growing up in Lebanon, I had only been aware of local genocides. I also grew up listening to my Armenian grandmother's genocide stories. The programme allowed me to hear stories that I wouldn't have heard elsewhere. It definitely enabled me to perceive yet another perspective.
>
> *(2015, Middle Eastern female)*

But this broadened perspective went for students from other regions as well.

> I had always studied genocides with people who shared my same point of view and context. This was different, and the cultural contrast gave me a sense of perspective that I hadn't encountered before.
>
> *(2016, Mexican female)*

> I remember the discussion being particularly powerful and hearing different points of view I never would have considered. I remember feeling ashamed of my ignorance and curious to learn more.
>
> *(2012, US male)*

> My (Middle Eastern) colleagues . . . had a diametrically opposed opinion to mine on the Arab-Israeli conflict, but what surprised me the most was that they seemed shocked that someone with my opinions even existed. That was an eye-opener for me, but I'm glad I was able to experience it and get to know them nonetheless.
>
> *(2015, US female)*

For others, this matter of perspective included the awareness that different points of view can coexist peacefully.

> I will always say the academy helped me to broaden my understanding of global perspectives and offered me further proof that though you may not always agree with someone you can live alongside and get on with them, finding common ground as you go.
>
> *(2016, UK female)*

I remember watching students from different sides of a conflict having emotional discussions. It left a strong impact on me about how there are always two or more sides to a story and no side is completely right.

(2011, Chinese female)

Finally, from the standpoint of this chapter, some students were able to articulate a specifically *global* dimension of this broader perspective, what Berglez calls the "global outlook."

As much of a nationalistic Jordanian I was/considered myself to be, I started labelling myself as a global citizen since [attending] the programme [I] distance myself from direct political issues in my own country because I came to realise that the WHOLE WORLD needs fixing.

(2010, Middle Eastern female)

Yes, I am thinking more globally. I care about other countries more. Before I cared but I didn't think about that much I didn't share my thoughts about it with people in my country. Now I do, and I share. I hope I bring other people in [my country] to change and to think more globally.

(2016, European female)

Conclusion

Our assessment of this programme shows that it had a number of positive impacts, teaching students how to think outside their own national and cultural limitations. At the same time, it raised one of the most difficult challenges of "cross-national" education: How can a case associated with one particular group, such as the Holocaust, work with a group that comes to the experience with dramatically different cultural understandings? For some, any emphasis on the Holocaust without an equal or greater discussion of their own "Holocaust" is unacceptable. For others, this attempt to extrapolate from the Holocaust to broader lessons in other parts of the world worked to diminish the unique Jewish character of the Holocaust – to de-Judaize the historical meaning of the event. This is the global challenge: paying attention to one case without negating the importance of others.

In addition to the *horizontal* dimension, generalising from one genocide to others, there is another more subtle challenge, a *vertical*, chronological dimension, that we faced regarding the value of any historical case for understanding the present. One student quoted above flatly preferred to "move on," to put the painful past behind, while others offered up a more problematic notion – not that we don't need to know about the Holocaust, but that there are more "actionable," current, and pressing problems that need attention. For example, one recent US academy alumnus posted an angry message on Facebook earlier this year that illustrates both dimensions. He said he was tired of the Holocaust being over-emphasised when children in the Middle East were being bombed in the present. When the first author queried him about his comments, he explained that he objected to the attention paid to the Holocaust *while ignoring* current atrocities. Furthermore, he regarded the Holocaust as *historical*, while other current injustices were more *actionable* – not just the Israel-Palestinian issue but suffering in Venezuela, Puerto Rico, and Syria. This attitude toward history carries a special irony and concern, in light of a survey recently released on Holocaust Remembrance Day noting that it is not that people deny the Holocaust but that it is fading in memory among millennials.[8] We, of course, do not think the lessons of history preclude social action in the present – just the opposite.

The "third rail" of the programme proved to be the Israeli-Palestinian conflict, especially as it involved students from the Middle East. Although most were able to accept the Holocaust as an educational lesson in its own right, they had a hard time accepting that its use (even with emphasis on other genocides) did not diminish modern injustice close to home. Although contentious from the founding of Israel, we have observed in our own recent experience that the Palestinian issue now looms larger in these discussions. In the last several years, actions of a right-wing Israeli government, along with its close ties with the sympathetic current US administration, make it ever more difficult for many to differentiate between the human rights catastrophe of the Nazi Holocaust and the policies of the modern Israeli state (e.g., Weisman, 2018). In the eyes of the Arab world, the victim has become the oppressor – a terrible irony that makes it more challenging to use the Holocaust as a case study with students from the region.

This highlights the fact that past injustices continue to carry heavy present political relevance. We can imagine similar contentious discussions for other 20th-century injustices, such as the Armenian genocide and Turkish official denialism. Some countries have even adopted historical amnesia as a state policy to avoid dealing with past atrocities. For example, the Lebanese government avoids any official historical account of the 1975–90 civil war that killed tens of thousands of innocent civilians, many massacred by their own neighbours because of their religion or ethnicity. In fact, any discussion of the civil war among a diverse group of Lebanese is guaranteed to stir up deep hatred and belligerent quarrels, as demonstrated by the reaction to a recent movie about that period.[9] But this contentious political dimension, when structured carefully, offers an added pedagogical value. It not only educates participants about human rights and past atrocities but also offers a complex narrative about the conditions that led to them, the grave possibility of their reoccurrence, the importance of witnessing and remembering, the dangers of forgetting or denying, and the politics of abusing them as justifications for present and future injustices. These are principles with direct relevance to the practice of journalism.

Although we continue to experiment with the ideal combination,[10] we see value in each of the programme elements as conducted so far, which seem to have an effective synergistic impact. The faculty introductions contextualised and justified the programme and its importance, keeping the programme from becoming a primarily emotional experience. The graphic documentary film, acting as a stimulus, triggered important emotions and memories that elevated the gravity of the topic. The discussion afterwards offered a venue to express perspectives and hear those of others – allowing individuals from disparate backgrounds to discuss extremely diffi-cult topics under high emotional pressure – yet with civility and open-mindedness. Finally, the concentration camp visit offered a dimension of material reality, beyond, but benefiting from, the abstractions of film, lectures, and discussion.

We realise that our study design did not provide the kind of social scientific rigour we might desire. Although the basic structure and guiding philosophy of the academy has remained constant since 2007, the overall enrolment, mix of nation-alities, and approach to the genocide education programme itself have varied. In addition, some students now arrive already sensitised, with an expectation of the programme based on what their peers from previous years have told them. There-fore, we interpret our findings with caution, using them to provide impressionistic insights that guide the interpretations of the authors, based on our own experience from having been present throughout most of the entire life of the academy. We also realise that we are relying on the memories of the participants, and as time goes by these memories are less reliable. But the responses show that this programme experience is still relatively fresh in their minds, even after 11 years. Nevertheless, we do not draw strong conclusions based on these over-time trends but, again, use them to triangulate our understanding. We ourselves are known to the participants, and although we promised anonymity in our e-mails, there is a social-desirability response given our objectives for the programme. These, for the most part, are students who are relatively privileged, already internationally inclined, and grateful to have been a part of the Salzburg Academy. Still, the honest and at times critical responses suggest that they were not inclined to hold back if they had something on their mind. As we have learned, being privileged and well- travelled unfortunately does not necessarily translate into being open-minded, and these students can be just as oblivious to the world outside their own social bubble as anyone else.

Overall, students reported the programme was effective and a valuable learning experience. The Holocaust provides what is arguably the most heavily researched, compelling, and emblematic case of genocide in the 20th century, but presenting something shocking by itself without laying the proper groundwork only activates filters and pre-existing barriers to deeper thinking.[11] We realise that no matter how the programme is presented, we will not be completely successful communicating the message we intend. Our study shows, however, that it is possible to construct an intellectual experience with great emotional power, a combination that can sharpen critical thinking and bring about a more global self-identification.

We started this study with the goal of exploring how to best communicate the dynamics of genocide, especially across national fault-lines. These are lessons with direct relevance for media, which not only can serve to perpetrate xenophobia through sensationalised coverage but can also be part of the solution. Media literacy education has emphasised teaching citizens to be more discerning about these mes-sages and deconstructing their implicit meanings, but some stories affect deeply felt tribal affiliations and emotional commitments. Of course, we hope that participants have carried these lessons into media practice, and we think they have. Although we did not specifically ask about this, one volunteered that "this experience has helped me to shape my current career in the defense of human rights" (2009, Latin American female). Although it is tempting to regard journalists as unwitting participants in larger media systems, we should not lose sight of their agency and capacity to be instruments of social change. This requires a new outlook, which will not happen automatically.

As we stated at the beginning of this chapter, effectively telling global stories of human rights requires being both historically rooted and globally reflective about deeply rooted filters and cultural boundaries. That is where programmes that help train both diverse media literate students and journalists in international settings are so valuable, whether at the Salzburg Global Seminar or other centres like the Reuters Institute for the Study of Journalism (Oxford) where a collaborative spirit of trust and comparative frameworks are available. As the participants we studied reported in our case study experience, it was a hard conversation but an important one to have – and one that needs to be held more often in the "new journalisms."

Notes

1 We realise that the term "Holocaust" is itself contested, and although closely linked to the 6 million Jewish victims, other groups suffered as well. For our purposes here, we refer simply to the Holocaust.
2 The ethos of the Seminar is summed up in the quote from the great anthropologist and one of the first faculty members, Margaret Mead: "Never doubt that a small group of thoughtful, committed citizens can change the world. Indeed, it is the only thing that ever has."
3 The bi-national, co-authoring process for this chapter has been a stimulating task. As with the students themselves, we have contemplated the meaning, impact, and cross-national sensitivities of a programme like this in conversation with each other and with our Salzburg colleagues. Our experience over several years in trying to lead a balanced discussion, which often becomes emotional and contentious, has intrigued us to explore the dynamics further in this research. We would like to express our appreciation to founding director Susan Moeller, current academy director Paul Mihailidis, and our many other faculty colleagues for their friendship and support.
4 The project was approved with exempt status by the Lebanese American University Institutional Review Board, Apr. 2018.
5 The Middle East included students from Egypt, Iraq, Jordan, Lebanon, Palestine, Syria, as well as Iran and Pakistan. Latin America included students from Argentina, Chile, Mexico, and Columbia. Europe included students from Austria, Finland, Russia, Slovakia, and the UK.
6 We identify the students by year they participated and region, rather than by country of primary affiliation, to preserve their anonymity.
7 The deep suspicion surrounding this issue was illustrated by one of our student comments. When we chose the word "programme" as a useful way to refer to the combination of elements constituting our teaching, a Palestinian student replied, "I just realized through this survey that part of the academy there is something called Genocide/Holocaust programme . . . not an 'activity' or an optional field visit to a historical site . . . it's a whole Programme!" The Lebanese co-author of this chapter also was questioned in this student's comment about where his true loyalties lay.
8 Available at: www.nytimes.com/2018/04/12/us/holocaust-education.html.
9 This Oscar-nominated film, *The Insult*, includes a line pertinent to our reflections here: "No one has a monopoly on suffering."

10 Our 2018 experience provided somewhat of a contrast with past programs. A scheduling conflict prevented being able to show the film and conduct an academy-wide discussion prior to going to Mauthausen. That plan was not as emotionally charged and taxing for the faculty, but we still thought something was missing. We will continue to revise the programme, including trying to identify a film that accomplishes the same result without being too lengthy.

11 The Salzburg Global Seminar itself has a programme on Holocaust Education and Genocide Prevention, begun in 2010 in connection with UNESCO and the US Holocaust Museum. Unlike ours, local relevance was baked into the programme, which proposed to use the "lessons and tools" of Holocaust education, in which participants from different regions shared expertise and developed pilot projects, specifically designed for their own national context. Its report speaks to the same sensitivity we encountered, stating that "it may be necessary to discuss the Nazis' systemic repression more broadly before focusing on Jews as the victims of the Holocaust." (See *Combating Extremism and Promoting Pluralism*, report from the Salzburg Global Holocaust Education and Genocide Prevention Program 2016–2018. holocaust.SalzburgGlobal.org.)

References

Berglez, P. (2013). *Global journalism: Theory and practice*. New York: Peter Lang.

Lewis, B. (1987). *History remember, recovered, invented*. New York: Simon & Schuster.

Mazzoleni, G. (2003). The media and the growth of neo-populism in contemporary democracies. In: Mazzoleni, G., Stewart, J. and Horsfield, B., eds., *The media and neo-populism: A contemporary comparative analysis*. Westport, CT: Praeger, pp. 1–20.

Moeller, S. D. (1999). *Compassion fatigue: How the media sell disease, famine, war and death*. New York: Routledge.

Reese, S. D. (2010). Journalism and globalization. *Sociology Compass*, 4(6), pp. 344–353.

Reese, S. D. (2012). Global news literacy: The educator. In: Mihailidis, P., ed., *News literacy: Global perspectives for the newsroom and the classroom*. New York: Peter Lang.

Said, E. (1997). *Covering Islam: How the media and the experts determine how we see the rest of the world*. New York: Random House.

Seib, P. (2004). *Beyond the front lines: How the news media cover a world shaped by war*. New York: Palgrave Macmillan.

Sontag, S. (2003). *Regarding the pain of others*. New York: Picador.

Stohl, M. and Stohl, C. (2005). Human rights, nation states, and NGOs: Structural holes and the emergence of global regimes. *Communication Monographs*, 72(4), pp. 442–467.

Weisman, J. (2018). *(((SEMITISM))): Being Jewish in America in the age of Trump*. New York: St. Martin's Press.

Wolfsfeld, G. (1997). *Media and political conflict: News from the Middle East*. Cambridge: Cambridge University Press.

INDEX